Winegrowing in
Eastern America

Winegrowing in Eastern America

An Illustrated Guide to Viniculture East of the Rockies

by LUCIE T. MORTON

Illustrations by Dawn L. McDowell

Foreword by Leon D. Adams

CORNELL UNIVERSITY PRESS · ITHACA AND LONDON

First published 1985 by Cornell University Press.

International Standard Book Number 0-8014-1290-0

Library of Congress Catalog Card Number 85-47696

Printed in the United States of America

Librarians: Library of Congress cataloging information appears on the last page of the book.

*The paper in this book is acid-free and meets the guidelines for
permanence and durability of the Committee on Production Guidelines
for Book Longevity of the Council on Library Resources.*

To my parents, Louisa and Brown Morton—
  the Potomac is not the Gironde,
  but the vines didn't seem to care.

CONTENTS

FOREWORD

During the past decade hundreds of new vineyards and wineries have sprung up between the Atlantic Coast and the Rocky Mountains—the eastern two-thirds of the United States. Moreover, eastern and midwestern winegrowing districts that flourished a century ago but were smothered by national Prohibition are reawakening to their past greatness and are now looking to potential future eminence. Some are already producing world-class wines.

Lucie T. Morton, the first modern viticulturist to explore and study this entire vast region, has written an authoritative, sparkling, richly illustrated book, which reveals the reviving eastern vineyard regions as American viniculture's new frontier.

District by district, grape variety by grape variety, Morton compares our climatic regions to those of Europe, identifies eastern districts suitable for the Old World's noble Vinifera grapes, and weighs the future of eastern wines compared with California and northwestern wines.

Her sections on the vinicultural histories of three dozen states and eastern Canada, on their natural and political climates for winegrowing, on vineyard site selection and cultural practices, and on the economics of modern wine production in the East are the first and most complete to be published anywhere. Many people who live east of the Rockies, still unaware of the past and of the current revival of winegrowing in their own backyards, will be surprised by what they can discover in her book.

Morton, a leading U.S. grape and wine authority, European-trained and widely traveled, and an avocational winemaker who in the past twelve years has operated her own vineyard and directed those of clients, is uniquely qualified to write on these subjects.

Everyone who considers investing in any aspect of winegrowing in the eastern two-thirds of North America—in fact all those who enjoy visiting eastern vineyards—will welcome this important book.

LEON D. ADAMS

Sausalito, California

9

PREFACE

The fact that recently there has been a dramatic revival of eastern viniculture is still something of a national secret. The little-known truth is that the East has come to life with new wine-grape varieties, new technology, new wine styles, and new social attitudes toward wine. Gourmet restaurants are serving local wines, wine tastings are a focus of social gatherings, and families are experimenting with winemaking from their own grapes. Visiting vineyards is becoming a favorite weekend pastime. Most of the new eastern wineries are small, family operations whose combined production has little impact on the quantity of world wine production (now approximately ten billion gallons annually) but whose presence adds significantly to the quality and diversity of wine production in North America. Although California is still the source of most American table wine today, the region east of the Rockies is an exciting source for tomorrow.

When Alexandre Dumas said, "Wine is the intellectual part of a meal, meats are merely the material part," he was speaking strictly from a consumer's standpoint. For winegrowers, wine is the final reward for years of struggling with weeds, climatic and economic vicissitudes, bureaucracy, and a host of both beneficial and maleficent microorganisms.

One purpose of this book is to expand the reader's perspective on the true nature of the world's number-one fruit—the grape—and its foremost use—wine—and thereby to enhance ensuing wine tastings and vineyard visits. I have tried to introduce this special, multifarious region in a comprehensive yet entertaining way, and to bring the reader up to date on its dynamic future. It is intended to satisfy the curiosity of those who say: "What! They grow grapes in ———?" (Fill in any of the thirty-seven states and two Canadian provinces east of the Rockies.)

I thank John McGrew, Philip Wagner, Leon Adams, Dawn McDowell, John Boslough, my editors, Carol Betsch and Robb Reavill, and the book's designer, George Whipple, for their many helpful suggestions and insights. Nearly everyone in the eastern winegrowing community has contributed in some way to this book and I am grateful for their cooperation and encouragement. For their patience and support, special personal thanks are due to Kenneth Garrett, Vaughn P. McDowell, and Dan Snodderly.

Lucie T. Morton

Broad Run, Virginia

Winegrowing in
Eastern America

INTRODUCTION:
A NEW FRONTIER

Wine is the most inspiring and mysterious agricultural commodity on earth. Such a religious and romantic aura surrounds wine that it has always occupied a place apart from other farm products. Indeed, tractors and hoes rarely come to mind when we think of wine. Rather, we have visions of good food, friends, and happy times. Most of us associate wine with candlelight and foreign accents. Yet as table wine becomes increasingly a part of American life and local wine becomes as common here as it is in Europe, wine will come to be a less exotic, more familiar part of our life.

Every wine reflects the vineyard and surrounding flora where it is grown. One purpose of this book is to expand our perception of wine: wine as the transformation of locally grown grapes. This transformation need not take place on some faraway hillside or valley to achieve the character and magic that inspire poets. An important function of the farm winery today is to correct the misconception of wine as one of the manufactured beverages of the world. Anyone who has witnessed the growing cycle in a vineyard and the fermentation process in a winery, especially in one's home territory, develops an appreciation of wine as an organic transformation, the product of a fascinating interplay of climate, grape variety, and vinification techniques.

The eastern United States, with its largely untapped potential for wine production, is a new frontier for American wine much as the West once was for American pioneers. Establishing a vineyard and winery east of the Rockies has many parallels with homesteading in the Old West: developing a modus operandi in a new environment, aiming to transform dreams into realities.

Our forebears had a profound interest in producing their own wine, but their attempts to cultivate grapes along the Atlantic Coast were frustrated by indigenous pests and diseases. Today, after nearly a century of research and development in North America and abroad, great progress has been made in winegrowing (viniculture), which includes the sciences of grape growing (viticulture) and winemaking (enology). For the first time in history, European grape varieties (*Vitis vinifera*) are producing wine in nearly every state east of the Rockies. This alone is cause for celebration by wine aficionados. In addition, new grape varieties, bred for specific environments, are producing exciting new wines.

The challenge in the East is to provide wines to meet the demands of the Wine Revolution that began in the 1960s, in which Americans have discovered the pleasure of drinking wine with meals. The East and Midwest have long produced fine champagnes, ports, and sherries. These regions' table wines, however, have been dominated by strong *Vitis Labrusca* (commonly referred to as "foxy") and other native flavors, which do not complement food. Now made from different grapes, eastern table wines are becoming more international in character. Even veteran native varieties are tasting different thanks to improved vinification methods.

An advantage of winegrowing in the East is that the climate produces fresh-tasting wines, with higher acidity and lower alcoholic content than most from California, the largest wine-producing state. The recent white wine boom in the United States has brought new attention to such northeastern native grapes as Catawba, Dutchess, and Delaware. Traditionally used in champagne production and blended sweet white wines, these varieties, which do not grow well in California, are now being used to produce light, flowery varietals.

Eastern wines in the nineteenth century received praise at home and abroad. Then Prohibition killed the impetus to grow wine grapes and brought about almost exclusive cultivation of the Concord for juice and jelly. Progress in vinicultural development after Prohibition was inhibited by dry influence on government agencies. Every use of grapes was studied except the most important—for wine. Research did yield innovative vine-training techniques and mechanical harvesting, but the task of rebuilding an eastern wine industry was left to amateurs and to the few large wineries that survived the Noble Experiment.

For many years after Repeal, individual eastern grape growers supplied a few large wineries with grapes. Very few growers made and sold their own wine. Since the Wine Revolution, however, the situation has changed. Equipment

necessary for producing fine wine is now available in small sizes. An increasing number of states are offering training in grape growing and winemaking. Today the majority of the East's over four hundred wineries are small estates producing wine largely from their own or neighboring vineyards. Each vineyard and winery is a mini–research station generating information—ecological, economic, and enological data adding up to the present and pointing to the future.

Comparisons and value judgments are an integral part of the wine experience. Absolute standards have traditionally been set by a few European role models: Bordeaux, Burgundy, Champagne, Rhine, Sauternes, and so on. Wine writers use these classics to help classify and describe new wines. Winemakers often aim to emulate these models. To the connoisseur, the color, smell, and taste of the first sip not only suggest a wine's geographic origin but also rank it in the hierarchy of one's memory—good, bad, indif-

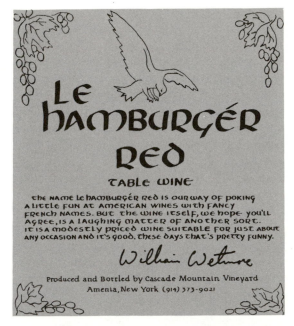

Le HAMBURGÉR RED
TABLE WINE

THE NAME LE HAMBURGÉR RED IS OUR WAY OF POKING A LITTLE FUN AT AMERICAN WINES WITH FANCY FRENCH NAMES. BUT THE WINE ITSELF, WE HOPE YOU'LL AGREE, IS A LAUGHING MATTER OF ANOTHER SORT. IT IS A MODESTLY PRICED WINE SUITABLE FOR JUST ABOUT ANY OCCASION AND IT'S GOOD. THESE DAYS THAT'S PRETTY FUNNY.

William Wetmore

Produced and Bottled by Cascade Mountain Vineyard
Amenia, New York (914) 373-9021

According to the label, "Le Hamburger Red" from Cascade Mountain Vineyard is "our way of poking a little fun at American wines with fancy French names. But the wine itself is a laughing matter of another sort. It is a modestly priced wine suitable for just about any occasion and it's good. These days that's pretty funny." Red wine can make even the simplest meal taste better.

ferent, or superb. Some traditionalists are no more able to accept new wines than new styles in art or music.

Duels between California and French Chardonnays have been well publicized. To these contenders we can now add Chardonnays from many eastern states and those of the Pacific Northwest. Old absolute values are beginning to evolve, now that Chardonnay need no longer emulate Montrachet to be considered "great."

Picture Humpty Dumpty as King Chardonnay in the form of a great white Burgundy. Once he has fallen off the wall, all the king's horsemen would be well advised to ride off, stopping in Virginia and Ohio on their way to Napa while waiting for a new shipment from the Côte d'Or. If some of them decide to settle in the East and become acquainted with their own Seyval, Vidal, or Chardonnay, their allegiance to the old king will soon become largely ceremonial.

It has long been thought that we in the New World could never even approach the revered wines of the Old. "Made in Japan" and "California wine" once were synonymous with poor quality. Now the opposite is true. Who thirty years ago would have believed the international acclaim and open comparisons accorded American versus French wines today? Who today would believe a gourmet restaurant that served only New York wine could survive, much less thrive? The wine list at Turback's of Ithaca had (at last count) 199 wines from forty-six New York wineries—no imports, not even from New Jersey!

The renaissance of local food and wines—for example Virginia ham/Virginia Chambourcin, Long Island duck/Long Island Sauvignon blanc, Minnesota wild rice/Minnesota Millot, Georgia peaches/Georgia Chenin blanc—is a healthy antidote to the homogenization of American culture—hamburger/cola. If variety is the spice of life, the most flavorful wine region of all lies east of the Rockies. The East's many climates and cornucopia of grape varieties provide an exciting challenge for wine adventurers—whether the adventure is producing one's own wine or enjoying new experiences in wine tasting.

Part One

A Brief History of Eastern Viniculture

I  COLONIAL TIMES

Nearly a millennium ago Norse explorers named the eastern North American shores "Wineland the Good." From the time of Lucky Leif Ericson, circa A.D. 1,000, to the time of Sir Walter Raleigh's scouts in 1584, there are reports of temptingly laden vines. Early explorers, settlers, and even presidents made wine by harvesting directly from nature. Their early observations are confirmed by modern botanists, who have found a greater variety and number of *Vitis* species here than anywhere else in the world.

During the entire colonial period, settlers tried to bring Old World viniculture to the New in order to establish a domestic wine industry. *Vitis vinifera* vines were brought across the ocean by French, British, Spanish, Portuguese, Italian, Swedish, Swiss, and Dutch immigrants. The European vines did not succeed, however, and their failure was blamed on everything from Indians to incompetence. The true culprits—indigenous insects, fungi, and bacteria—were not discovered until the nineteenth century.

From about the year 1000 to the late 1700s American wine was derived only from nature's bounty—wild vines. Today anyone who becomes familiar with vines growing in local for-

ests, often visible from car or canoe, can re-create colonial-style wine. To experience the vinous beverage of the earliest settlers, follow this old-fashioned recipe, drawn from John Adlum's *Memoir on the Cultivation of the Vine in America:*

Harvest wild grapes only when they appear to be fully ripe. Reject unsound berries. Crush grapes, but not the seeds. Place in wooden vat. Add one to two pounds of sugar for every gallon of must (juice and skins). Stir several times during first 24 to 36 hours. Let stand for two to six days.

Selected Grapevine (*Vitis*) Species

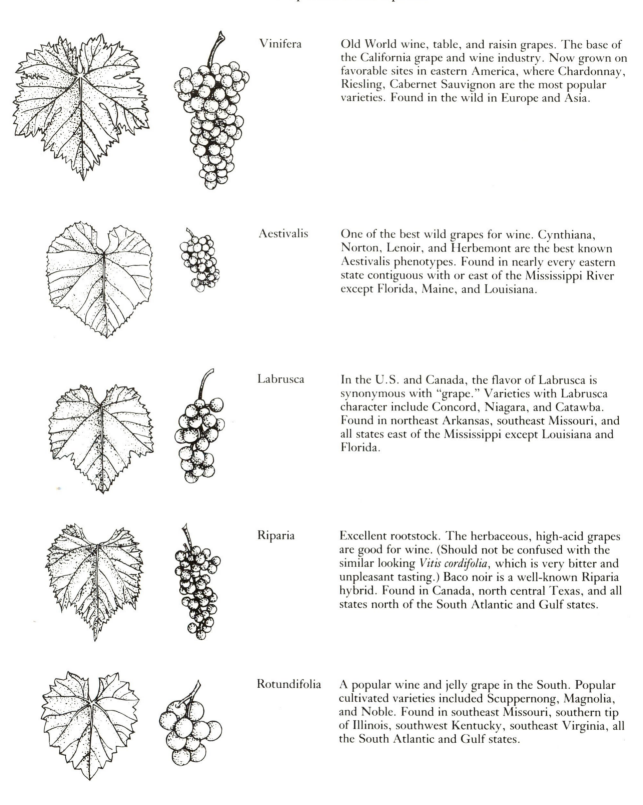

Vinifera

Old World wine, table, and raisin grapes. The base of the California grape and wine industry. Now grown on favorable sites in eastern America, where Chardonnay, Riesling, Cabernet Sauvignon are the most popular varieties. Found in the wild in Europe and Asia.

Aestivalis

One of the best wild grapes for wine. Cynthiana, Norton, Lenoir, and Herbemont are the best known Aestivalis phenotypes. Found in nearly every eastern state contiguous with or east of the Mississippi River except Florida, Maine, and Louisiana.

Labrusca

In the U.S. and Canada, the flavor of Labrusca is synonymous with "grape." Varieties with Labrusca character include Concord, Niagara, and Catawba. Found in northeast Arkansas, southeast Missouri, and all states east of the Mississippi except Louisiana and Florida.

Riparia

Excellent rootstock. The herbaceous, high-acid grapes are good for wine. (Should not be confused with the similar looking *Vitis cordifolia*, which is very bitter and unpleasant tasting.) Baco noir is a well-known Riparia hybrid. Found in Canada, north central Texas, and all states north of the South Atlantic and Gulf states.

Rotundifolia

A popular wine and jelly grape in the South. Popular cultivated varieties included Scuppernong, Magnolia, and Noble. Found in southeast Missouri, southern tip of Illinois, southwest Kentucky, southeast Virginia, all the South Atlantic and Gulf states.

When skins have floated to top and much of their color appears dissolved, but before the skins begin to sink, draw wine from a hole in the side at base of vat. Be prompt or the wine will become musty, or worse, vinegar.

Run the new wine through a sieve into a wooden cask in which sulfur has been burned. Fill full (if necessary add a sugar-water solution to fill up the cask: 3 pounds sugar per 1 gallon water). Place bung tightly in hole. Since fermentation is not complete, bore a small gimlet hole near the bung and plug it with a wooden peg. Every few days for the first month, remove the peg to allow gas to escape.

In December, on a clear cool day, rack (siphon) the wine into a clean, sulfured cask. Rack it again into clean sulfured barrels in March and May (when it may begin a secondary fermentation). By July, it should be clear, bright and ready to bottle. If the bottled wines are still sweet, keep in a cool cellar or they are likely to blow their corks.

Amateur vineyardists and home winemakers have made significant contributions to eastern winegrowing progress. Had he not been so busy, George Washington would have become one of our most illustrious amateur vignerons, as the following letter attests. Washington was responding to an offer by the French minister of state, Chrétien Guillaume de Lamoignon de Malesherbes to send him Vinifera cuttings.

Headquarters, Newburgh, July 9, 1783
To cultivate Exotics for the purpose of making Wine, or for my amusement was never contemplated by me. The spontaneous growth of the Vine in all parts of this Country; the different qualities of them and periods for maturation,

led me to conclude that by a happy choice of the species I might succeed better than those who had attempted the foreign vine; accordingly, a year or two before hostilities commenced I selected about two thousand cuttings of a kind which does not ripen with us (in Virginia) 'till repeated frosts in the Autumn meliorate the Grape and deprive the Vines of their leaves. It is then, and not before, the grape (which is never very pallitable [sic] can be Eaten.

Several little Essay's [sic] have been made by Gentlemen of my acquaintance to cultivate the foreign grape, for Wine but none had well succeeded; owing either to an improper kind or the want of skill in the management; for the most part their Wine soon contracted an acidity, which rendered it unfit for use; one cause of which I ascribed to the ripening of their grape in our Summer Autumnal heats and to the too great fermentation occasioned thereby. This consideration led me to try the wild grape of the Country; and to fix upon the species which I have already described, and which in the Eight years I have been absent from my Estate has been little attended to. Had I remained at home, I should 'ere this, have perfected the experiment which was all I had in view.

Thomas Jefferson tried to establish a wine industry in Virginia. He gave a two-thousand-acre estate next to Monticello to Tuscan horticulturist Philip Mazzei. In 1773 Mazzei brought thousands of Vinifera cuttings with him to Charlottesville as well as men trained to care for them. Land was cleared and vines planted, but events of the Revolution overpowered the project. Jefferson's viticultural endeavors never again exceeded garden size. Mazzei did make a couple of barrels of "colonial-style" wine with wild grapes collected by his men from vines in the treetops. Apparently the results were satisfactory because Mazzei consumed his wine and his men sold theirs for a shilling a bottle.

Jefferson's interest in winegrowing, however, did not die with the Mazzei vineyard. In a letter to John Adlum on October 7, 1809, Jefferson not only acknowledged the need to cultivate native varieties but indicated his approval of a wine made with the first commercially cultivated native American grape.

> Sir: While I lived in Washington, a member of Congress from your state (I do not recollect which) presented me with two bottles of wine made by you, one of which, of Madeira colour he said was entirely factitious; the other, a dark red wine was made from a wild or native grape, called in Maryland the Fox grape, but was very different from what is called by that name in Virginia. This was a very fine wine, and so exactly resembling the red Burgundy of Chambertin (one of the best crops) that on fair comparison with that, of which I had very good on the same table imported by myself from the place where made, the company could not distinguish the one from the other. I think it would be well to push the culture of that grape without losing our time and efforts in search of foreign vines, which it will take centuries to adapt to our soil and climate.

Adlum responded to Jefferson that the "factitious" wine had been made with currants and the burgundy facsimile was produced from a Vinifera-Labrusca cross later known as the Alexander, a grape that brought American vines out of the trees and onto trellises.

The origins of the Alexander go back to the viticultural interests of another colonial leader, Governor William Penn. Penn established a Vinifera vineyard in 1684 on the east bank of the Schuylkill River on a tract now enveloped by Greater Philadelphia. Pollen from this vineyard probably blew onto a wild Labrusca vine and created the vine discovered in the area by James Alexander, gardener to Penn's son Thomas, circa 1740.

When he established the Pennsylvania Wine Company at his Spring Mill vineyard in 1793,

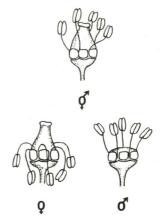

Perfect flower (top), female, and male

Pierre Legaux became the first commercial American winegrower. His winery venture was short-lived, and Legaux is better known for falsely promoting the Alexander grape as a Vinifera variety he had obtained from the Cape of Good Hope named "Cape of Constantia." Legaux profitably disseminated cuttings of the "Cape" grape throughout the Northeast and west to Ohio.

In 1798, a Swiss named Jean Jacques Dufour founded the Kentucky Vineyard Society and planted what he thought was an all Vinifera vineyard. All the vines soon died except the Cape/Alexander. The Dufour family attributed their viticultural woes to climate and moved to Vevay, Indiana, where from 1802 to 1835 they expended a great deal of energy and capital trying to establish European varieties, with the same result as before: only the Alexander bore them fruit and wine.

In his book *American Vine-Dresser's Guide*, published in Cincinnati in 1826, Dufour gives a detailed account of his own trials as well as those of other vineyards he visited during his travels. Dufour's prejudice that only European vines were worthy of culture was so strong that he refused to believe the Cape (Alexander) was not Vinifera despite the similarities of its foliage to the native "fox" grape. In the preface of his book, he said he would "try to save the character of our Cape grapes from being made merely wild grapes, because some are now found in the woods."

Defending his position, Dufour pointed out that wild vines have either male or female flowers while the Cape was self-fertile or perfect-flowered like Vinifera. His observation ignores the reality of hybridization between species in which perfect flowers are dominant. Whereas other winegrowers could accept American blood in wine grapes as the wave of the future, foreign-born Dufour was filled with disdain at the idea, and he may have been the world's first grape-variety "racist." He was not the last.

As the first cultivated vine to survive while others perished, the Alexander served to establish commercial winegrowing in several states. It was quickly eclipsed by other varieties destined for more enduring careers, such as Isabella, introduced in 1816, and Catawba, introduced in 1823. Literally thousands of new native American varieties were developed in the nineteenth century.

The numerous and widespread, albeit fruitless, attempts to transplant European viticulture to the colonies illustrate the importance of wine to our forebears from Maine to Florida. The fact that winegrowing was not a commercially successful agricultural endeavor left a void in home and tavern which was filled by such beverages as rum, whiskey, and imported dessert wines. Cider, beer, and peach mobby were popular libations on the farm.

2  BIRTH OF AMERICAN VINICULTURE

One of the earliest American winegrowers was John Adlum, a native of Pennsylvania, who grew grapes in Havre de Grace, Maryland, and on property in the District of Columbia called The Vineyard. His book *A Memoir on the Cultivation of the Vine in America*, published in 1823, is the first devoted exclusively to American viticulture. Unlike his contemporary Dufour, Adlum embraced the new native varieties and is credited with recognizing the merits of and distributing the Catawba grape.

Besides doing his viticultural work, Adlum made wine. Imprinted on the back cover of the 1828 edition of his book is the following advertisement:

"Various kinds of domestic Wines for Sale" Tokay and Champaign [*sic*] from $10–12 per dozen bottles; Catawba, Bland Madeira, Columbia at $6/doz. And it will be delivered at any place in the City of Washington or Georgetown, free of any expense for cartage, when not less than one dozen bottles are taken, and for twenty-five cents additional, it will be carefully packed in a neat box, in such a manner that it may be transported in safety to any distance, either by land or water.

By 1849 a United States Department of Agriculture (USDA) survey reported: "The total produce [217,000 gallons of wine from 32 states], although not large, gave expression to the beginning about the year 1830, of a new era in grape history, namely the culture, use, and improvement of American euvitis." Small vineyards and wineries proliferated, as did grapevine nurserymen, hybridizers, and vinicultural authors.

National and international acclaim first came to a U.S. wine through the Catawba grape in Ohio. Cincinnati lawyer Nicholas Longworth began winegrowing with cuttings purchased from Adlum in 1825. Thirty years after Longworth's first taste of Catawba wine, Ohio was the number one wine-producing state in the Union. Thousands of acres of vines, mostly Catawba, grew up around Cincinnati and along the Ohio River in Kentucky and Indiana. Longworth's sparkling Catawba was America's first champagne. The Ohio became "America's Rhine," and Catawba wines were compared with the Hocks and Champagnes of Europe.

By 1859 there were 1,627,000 gallons of wine from thirty-nine states with 35 percent coming from Ohio and 15 percent from California. Nine-tenths of the vineyards east of the Rockies were planted to Catawba, except in the South where Scuppernong was the favorite. It was in the 1850s that commercial winegrowing was born in the United States.

Henry Wadsworth Longfellow's "Ode to Catawba Wine," written in 1854, is not the finest example of his talent. His verses do, however, give an accurate portrayal of the American vinicultural scene of his day, including the use of native American grapes and the favorable comparisons of American wines to those of Europe, which American wine writers often accused of fraudulence and adulteration. The ode was inspired by a gift of Catawba wine sent to Longfellow by Nicholas Longworth:

. . .

It is not a song
Of the Scuppernong
From warm Carolina valleys,
Nor the Isabel
And the Muscadel
That bask in our garden alleys.

Nor the red Mustang
Whose clusters hang
O'er the waves of the Colorado,
And the fiery flood
Of whose purple blood
Has a dash of Spanish bravado.

. . .

Very good in its way
Is the Verzenay,
Or the Sillory soft and creamy;
But Catawba wine
Has a taste more divine
More dulcet, delicious, and dreamy.

There grows no vine
By the haunted Rhine,
By Danube or Guadalquivir,
Nor an island or cape,
That bears such a grape
As grows by the Beautiful River.

Drugged is their juice
For foreign use,
When shipped o'er the reeling Atlantic,
To rack our brains
With the fever pains,
That have driven the Old World frantic.

To the sewers and sinks
With all such drinks.
And after them tumble the mixers;
For a poison malign
Is such Borgia wine,
Or at best but a Devil's Elixir.

While pure as a spring
Is the wine I sing,
And to praise it, one needs but name it;
For Catawba wine
Has need of no sign,
No tavern-bush to proclaim it.

. . .

For the first time in the long history of viniculture, international interest was focused on a wine made with other than Vinifera grapes. Responsible for this interest was the fruity Catawba grape flavor captured in the wine. In California, grape culture was being established with European Vinifera varieties, but the popularity of eastern Catawba wines resulted in the planting of Catawba there as well. Catawba is the only native American variety described in an 1877 ampelography, *Grapes and Grapevines of California*. Catawba was also planted in Europe.

Growth of the eastern wine industry was extraordinary in spite of serious problems in the vineyards. Indigenous fungus diseases (black rot, oïdium/powdery mildew, and downy mildew) along with the destructive root aphid phylloxera had been frustrating attempts at Vinifera culture in the East since the early 1600s. The true nature of these vine pests was not discovered until the mid-1800s, when they took passage across the Atlantic on some native vine cuttings sent to curious European botanists and caused one of the most catastrophic horticultural disasters of all time. In Europe, phylloxera and the American fungi found perfect climatic conditions and millions of Vinifera vines with no natural defenses against them.

Vineyards centuries-old began to wither and die for no apparent reason. Because wine was its country's most economically important agricultural commodity, the French government quickly invested in scientific research to discover what was threatening their six million acres of vineyards. French scientists discovered that by

Grapevines Spread Across the United States (1859–1879)

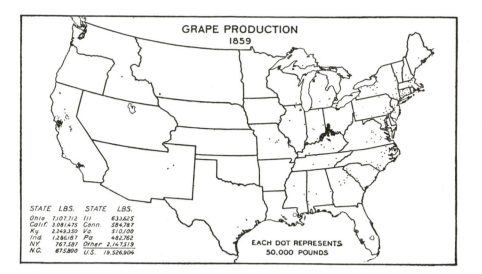

GRAPE PRODUCTION
1859

STATE	LBS.	STATE	LBS.
Ohio	7,107,712	Ill	633,625
Calif.	3,081,475	Conn.	584,787
Ky.	2,249,350	Va.	510,100
Ind.	1,286,187	Pa.	482,762
N.Y.	767,587	Other	2,147,519
N.C.	675,800	U.S.	19,526,904

EACH DOT REPRESENTS
50,000 POUNDS

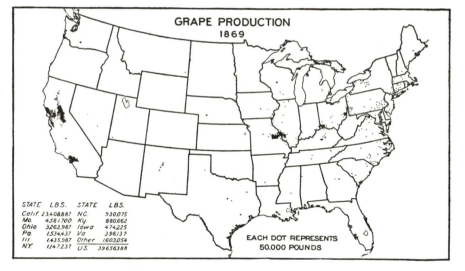

GRAPE PRODUCTION
1869

STATE	LBS.	STATE	LBS.
Calif.	23,408,887	N.C.	930,075
Mo.	4,581,700	Ky.	880,662
Ohio	3,263,987	Iowa	474,225
Pa.	1,534,437	Va.	396,137
Ill	1,435,987	Other	1,603,054
N.Y.	1,147,237	U.S.	39,656,388

EACH DOT REPRESENTS
50,000 POUNDS

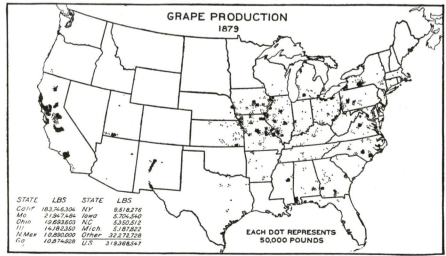

GRAPE PRODUCTION
1879

STATE	LBS	STATE	LBS
Calif	183,746,304	NY	9,518,276
Mo	21,947,484	Iowa	5,704,540
Ohio	19,693,603	N.C.	5,350,512
Ill	14,182,350	Mich.	5,187,822
N.Mex	10,890,000	Other	32,272,728
Ga.	10,874,928	U.S	319,368,547

EACH DOT REPRESENTS
50,000 POUNDS

Grapevines Spread Across the United States (1899–1919)

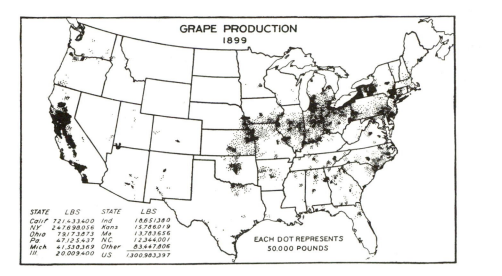

GRAPE PRODUCTION 1899

STATE	LBS	STATE	LBS
Calif	721,433,400	Ind	18,651,380
N.Y	247,698,056	Kans	15,786,019
Ohio	79,173,873	Mo	13,783,656
Pa.	47,125,437	N.C.	12,344,001
Mich	41,530,369	Other	83,447,806
Ill.	20,009,400	US.	1,300,983,397

EACH DOT REPRESENTS 50,000 POUNDS

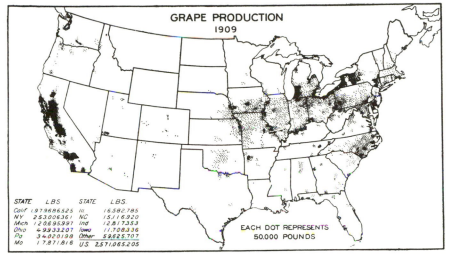

GRAPE PRODUCTION 1909

STATE	LBS	STATE	LBS
Calif	1,979,686,525	Ill.	16,582,785
N.Y	253,006,361	N.C.	15,116,920
Mich	120,695,997	Ind	12,817,353
Ohio	49,933,207	Iowa	11,708,336
Pa	34,020,198	Other	59,625,707
Mo	17,871,816	U.S.	2,571,065,205

EACH DOT REPRESENTS 50,000 POUNDS

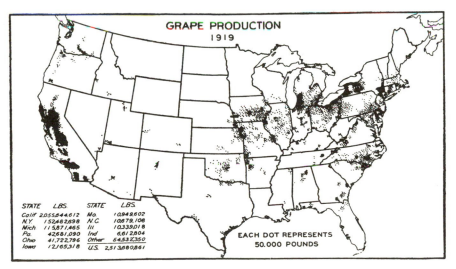

GRAPE PRODUCTION 1919

STATE	LBS	STATE	LBS
Calif.	2,055,844,612	Mo.	10,949,602
N.Y.	152,482,698	N.C.	10,679,108
Mich.	115,871,465	Ill.	10,339,018
Pa.	42,681,090	Ind	6,612,804
Ohio	41,722,796	Other	64,537,350
Iowa	12,165,318	U.S.	2,513,680,861

EACH DOT REPRESENTS 50,000 POUNDS

Black rot (*Guignardia Bidwellii*) is the East's most dreaded fungus disease, especially in the warmer, humid climates. Applications of Bordeaux mixture (copper sulfate, lime, and water) is the time-tested preventative treatment, although today the mixture has largely been replaced by modern organic fungicides.

Downy mildew (*Plasmopara viticola*), which thrives in cool, moist conditions, has been less destructive than black rot in the East, while in Europe the reverse is true. Bordeaux mixture and a variety of other materials will control this disease.

grafting Vinifera buds on resistant American rootstocks the European varieties could coexist with phylloxera. Through trial and error they discovered that only a handful of the native American species made suitable rootstocks (see p. 73). Hybridization was necessary to combine the most beneficial characteristics of the various species into one vine. Rootstocks developed by the French during the phylloxera crisis in the late nineteenth century are still used today in vineyards around the world.

Vinifera culture was saved in Europe, but grape growing, which had changed little since Roman times, would never be the same. Although grafting in no way affects the flavor of the grapes, it does add significantly to the cost of

establishing and maintaining a vineyard. Protecting leaves and fruit from the imported fungus diseases also proved costly in labor, equipment, and materials. In France the present vineyard acreage, circa three million, is only half of what it was a little over a century ago.

The benefits of grafting foreign vines on native American rootstocks had, in fact, already been observed in the East, and the practice is recommended by Adlum in his 1823 *Memoir*. On June

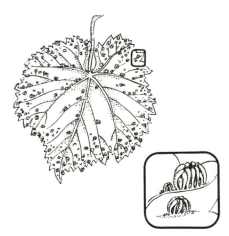

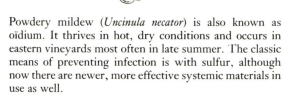

Powdery mildew (*Uncinula necator*) is also known as oïdium. It thrives in hot, dry conditions and occurs in eastern vineyards most often in late summer. The classic means of preventing infection is with sulfur, although now there are newer, more effective systemic materials in use as well.

Phylloxera vastatrix is the aphid that forever changed the world's viticulture, for the worse. Although the insect does the most serious damage by feeding on the roots, it also produces leaf galls when egg-producing stem-mothers feed on the foliage. While phylloxera leaf galls are a common sight in the East, they do not exist in California, where the insect's life cycle is limited to root feeding.

5, 1829, these comments about grafting appeared in the *American Farmer*, in a letter from Robert Withers of Green County, Alabama:

> At New Orleans, I saw a very fine muscadel vine in the garden of a horticulturist in the upper Fauxbourg; but was grafted, as he told me, on a native, while one which stood immediately contiguous, but which had not been grafted was unthrifty and insignificant in its appearance and bore comparatively no fruit at all. They were both planted at the same time, and were then sixteen years old, so that the experiment in that instance was completely decisive, that unless grafted on native stocks they will not succeed.

Grafting provides Vinifera vines with a healthy, long-lived root system, but it has no effect on a plant's rot or mildew resistance. In July 1829, Long Island viticulturist William Prince wrote to *American Farmer* of the usefulness of sulfur sprays against mildew. Sulfur is effective against oïdium, but it will not prevent devastation from downy mildew or black rot. A preventive for these fungus diseases, a combination of copper sulfate and lime known as the Bordeaux mixture, was discovered in 1885—too late to save the Catawba industry along the Ohio from dying even more quickly than it had become established.

Black rot and the mildews destroyed Longworth's sparkling empire. Had he been a younger man, Longworth himself might have led the move of Ohio's Catawba industry to the cooler northeastern regions where fungus diseases are less severe; but he died in 1863. The thousands of acres of vines along the Ohio responsible for the East's first taste of vinous glory had to be abandoned. Sandusky replaced Cincinnati as Ohio's winegrowing center, and Missouri took over as the leading grape-producing state in the East.

During the decade of the Civil War, California surpassed the East in grape acreage once and for all. The state's rainless summers and mild winters are ideal for Vinifera grapes. When Missouri viticulturist George Husmann enthusiastically predicted that America would be "one smiling and happy Wineland" from ocean to ocean, he had not yet witnessed the invasion of black rot in Missouri. When it did come, Husmann moved to the Napa Valley. Not so flexible was grape breeder Hermann Jaeger, to whom black rot and local dry laws brought financial ruin and personal despair. Jaeger left his home in Neosho, Missouri, one day and disappeared; no trace of him or his team of horses has ever been found.

The unfortunate Jaeger and fellow grape breeder T. V. Munson of Texas were better known in Europe than at home. Throughout the phylloxera crisis they both sent plant material to Europe to help the French develop rootstocks and Vinifera-American crosses. As a result, they were both honored with the French Legion of Honor in 1888. The depth and care with which Munson studied the American species are evident not only in his book *Foundations of American Grape Culture* but also in his herbarium specimens now found in the U.S. National Arboretum collection.

During the 1880s grapes and wine were produced in Ontario and every one of the United States except South Dakota and Wyoming. In New York State winegrowers along Lake Erie, the Finger Lakes, and the Hudson River were prospering. Some of those wineries are still active today. The oldest active winery in the United States is Brotherhood Winery in the Hudson Valley dating back to 1839 when it was called Blooming Grove. Its original owner, Jean Jaques, made altar wines.

Picking up where Nicholas Longworth left off was the Pleasant Valley Wine Company founded in 1860 in Hammondsport, New York. In 1865 Pleasant Valley made New York State's first champagne, a sparkling Catawba. How one of the East's most famous sparkling wines came to be called Great Western is related by author Leon Adams:

> In 1870, the Masson brothers [winemakers at Pleasant Valley] served a new sparkling blend of Delaware and Catawba to a meeting of the Pleasant Valley Grape Growers Association. Presiding at the meeting was famed horticulturist Colonel Marshall Wilder of Boston, who on tasting the wine exclaimed: "Truly, this will be the great champagne of the West." By "West," Wil-

Vitis candicans specimen collected by T. V. Munson. Living specimens of T. V. Munson's varieties may be seen today in his memorial vineyard in Denison, Texas. His splendid herbarium of native vine species is at the National Arboretum in Washington, D.C.

The historic entrance to the Taylor/Great Western winery. The majority of the other buildings in this vast winemaking facility are less picturesque, modern industrial in style.

der explained, he meant "our entire continent," the New World. His remark gave Great Western champagne its name, strange though it seems for a product of New York State.

Great Western champagne was the most renowned sparkling wine in America before Prohibition and won numerous awards abroad, including a gold medal at the 1873 Vienna Exposition. Urbana Wine Company, another champagne producer, was opened in Hammondsport in 1865 and was known until 1984 as Gold Seal Vineyards. Other large eastern wineries of that era include Renault Winery in Egg Harbor City, New Jersey (1868); Bardenheier in St. Louis (1873); and two Canadian wineries, Barnes (1873) and Brights (1874).

In terms of expansion and varietal discovery, the mid-nineteenth century was a golden era in eastern viticulture. A seed sown in 1843 in Concord, Massachusetts, would by its merits bring new prosperity to grape growers and by its faults have a depressing effect on the East's table-wine future. The mother vine of Ephraim Bull's seedling had been transplanted from field to garden. Whether the paternal pollen blew in from a neighboring Catawba or farther afield will never be known. In any event, the offspring was named Concord after its birthplace and made its debut at the Massachusetts Horticultural Society in 1852. By 1865 Concord was awarded the Greeley prize as the best all-around grape variety. Horace Greeley called Concord "the grape for the mil-

Brotherhood Winery, Washingtonville, N.Y.

Pressing grapes for champagne at the now-defunct White Top Wine Company in Hammondsport, N.Y.

Cynthiana

easy to grow. Late in the nineteenth century several premium Labrusca wine grapes, including Dutchess and Delaware, were developed for white wine. Their quality was immediately recognized but their acreage remained limited.

Toward the end of the century, the bottom began to fall out of the wine market. Overproduction in California precipitated a flood of low-priced wine into the East. The accelerating temperance movement created a negative and often prohibitive climate for local wine producers. With the introduction in 1870 of Prohibitionist dentist Dr. Thomas Welch's "Unfermented Wine," grape farmers planted increasingly more Concord instead of superior, but harder-to-grow, native wine grapes.

Strong as Labrusca character can be, it is overshadowed by the intensely fruity southern species Rotundifolia. Virginia Dare, a blend of

lions." This may be an understatement given that the strong Labrusca character of Concord has for North Americans become synonymous with "grape" flavor, whether as an accompaniment to peanut butter or as juice for breakfast. Americans take grape soda, jelly, bubble gum, popsicles, Jello, lip gloss, and candy for granted, but it is a uniquely American flavor unknown in many countries.

Much of Concord's rise to preeminence in the East is due to its hardiness, rusticity, and adaptability. Other native grapes such as Cynthiana and Norton surpass it for red wine, but few are as

Delaware

Virginia Dare was the most popular American wine before Prohibition.

Scuppernong, Concord, and neutral California Vinifera, was the most popular wine in the United States from the turn of the twentieth century to national Prohibition in 1919. The unique Muscadine flavor predominated. Virginia Dare's creator was North Carolinean Paul Garrett. Garrett's love of the Muscadine variety Scuppernong made him a millionaire with wineries in six states having a combined capacity of ten million gallons. Many of Garrett's trademarks and multistate blends are now being produced, not necessarily to original formulas, by the Canandaigua Wine Company.

Represented by Garrett & Co., North Carolina was one of six eastern states (Florida, Ohio, New Jersey, New York, Virginia) and the District of Columbia to win awards at the Paris Exposition of 1900. Quantitatively, the East did not keep pace with California's wine production, but the quality, diversity, and uniqueness of eastern wines earned them a place on wine lists nationwide.

3 PROHIBITION

Just when American winegrowing had spread to include nearly every state in the Union, Carrie Nation got Uncle Sam to bite on the notion of national Prohibition and precipitated a fall no less disastrous for wine lovers than Adam and Eve's departure from Eden was for all of us. Even a century before the Eighteenth Amendment was ratified, dry tyranny was claiming its first casualities among small-scale grape farmers in far-flung areas east of the Rockies. Indiana's 1816 law forbidding sales of alcoholic beverages on Sundays signaled the start. As early as the 1840s, counties and towns in many eastern and midwestern states were going dry. The evils of alcohol vied with the Ten Commandments as pulpit and soapbox topics.

The Prohibition Melodist, published in Philadelphia in 1888, enabled the drys to sing together such rousing hymns as "We have grappled with a monster in the fiend of rum and wrong" and "Oh look not on the sparkling wine, lest blind desire inflame thee." On the subject of desire, the drys had their own version of wine-women-and-song in their hymn "A Woman's No" copyrighted by the prolific melodist William J. Kirkpatrick:

She stood by her lover, in beauty and grace,
A sorrowful look on her brave, earnest face:
"No, Ralph, do not ask me; I can but refuse,
Unless, with God helping the right path you choose.
Your footsteps tend down to the valley of shame,
Where hopes are all blighted and sullied the name;
Now choose between me and the murderous wine,
For lips that touch liquor must never, never touch mine."
No, sir, no sir, no, no, no,
Not while downward still you go;
No, sir, no sir, not with the wine;
Lips that touch liquor must never touch mine.

Mr. Kirkpatrick showed no appreciation for the differences between the demon rum and the fruit of the vine. The consequences for eastern grapegrowers during this time were less than lyrical. Toward the end of the century, California wine was flooding eastern markets at such a rate that small wine producers, forbidden by local temperance ordinances to sell their wine locally, were forced out of business. Deprived of wineries to buy their fruit, the grape industry was in a desperate situation. When their counties and states went dry, farmers had no choice but to uproot their wine varieties and plant Concord or fruit trees.

In 1901 the State of Kansas published a bulletin called *The Grape* for the few grape growers remaining in business after twenty years of Prohibition. The inscriptions on the title page call the grape "a fruit too good to be made a chief source of the degradation of the race as an alluring (yet intoxicating) principle. To the glory of Kansas, 99 per cent of this luscious fruit which grows freely all over the state is used without fermentation." As for what to do with one's grapes, the bulletin helpfully gives two recipes for canned grapes, seven for jam, jelly, and marmalade, and one each for grape pie, pickled grapes, and grape syrup.

Carrie Nation

One can only imagine what Carrie Nation would have to say to the Belle of Ozark posing on this Missouri whiskey label. It should be noted that wine labels of the epoch were designed more decorously, and winegrowers found themselves caught in the struggle between two extremes—whiskey lovers and teetotalers.

On January 16, 1919, the Eighteenth Amendment to the Constitution was ratified by the required thirty-sixth state: "After one year from the ratification of this article the manufacture, sale, or transportation of intoxicating liquors within, the importation thereof into, or the exportation thereof from the United States and all territory subject to the jurisdiction thereof for beverage purposes is hereby prohibited. The Congress and the several States shall have concurrent power to enforce this article by appropriate legislation."

Had Congress defined "intoxicating liquor" as containing over 10 or 12 percent alcohol (which President Woodrow Wilson proposed), the history of North American wine would have been quite different. On October 28, 1919, however, the Volstead Act defined "intoxicating" as anything containing 0.5 percent or more alcohol and became law after Congress overrode a veto by President Wilson.

Given their efforts to separate church and state, our founding fathers would have been shocked by the Eighteenth Amendment to their Constitution. The abrogation of personal liberty was bad enough, but by not differentiating between wine and distilled spirits, the Prohibitionists compounded the affront. Thomas Jeffer-

son might well have insisted that to remove wine from society was to endanger the public health (an assertion that is increasingly supported by modern medical research). His belief in the healthful properties of wine is evident in his answer to an inquiry about his medical history at age seventy-six: "Like my Friend and Doctor [Dr. Benjamin Rush, Surgeon General to the Continental Army], I have lived temperately, eating little animal food, and that not as an aliment, so much as a condiment for the vegetables, which constitute my principal diet. I double however, the Doctor's glass and a half of wine, and even treble it with a friend; but halve its effects by drinking the weak wines only. The ardent wines I cannot drink, nor do I use ardent spirits in any form, malt liquors and cider are my table drinks."

Jefferson's political stance on the importance of separating wine from distilled spirits is clear from his writings. His trips to Europe had convinced him of the temperate nature of table wine. He therefore favored low taxes on wine as a means of encouraging consumption. On the other hand, he was disposed to tax whiskey in

The McCorn Winery went the way of the five-cent cigar—because of Prohibition, not inflation.

such a way as to discourage its use: "A tax on whiskey is to discourage its consumption; a tax on foreign spirits encourages whiskey by removing its rival from competition. . . . Whiskey claims to itself alone the exclusive office of sot-making."

Control of liquor consumption through differential taxation is one thing, but in outlawing the use of all alcoholic beverages, Prohibition caused dangerous side effects to the nation's well-being. The righteous "temperance" workers only stimulated the very devil they sought to destroy. Collusion, corruption, and criminal activity were widespread during the Prohibition years even among otherwise law-abiding citizens.

A few of the larger wine producers managed to stay in business in spite of the temperance plague until national Prohibition. The menu from an annual dinner of the American Wine Growers Association at the Waldorf-Astoria in 1914 has an all-American wine list to accompany a mouth-watering assortment of delicacies. There are eastern wines in each category, including Delaware, Virginia Dare, and numerous New York State champagnes. By 1920 gourmet and other diners had to be content with water, tea, or milk. If wine were available it had to be drunk from an opaque cup.

At age eighty-two, fifty years after her father, Van Buren McCorn of New York, had been forced to close his winery, Ruth McCorn Getz had this to say about Prohibition in an interview with Hammondsport historian Dick Scherer in 1969:

I will never forget the night Prohibition went into effect, which was a vast mistake. Most everyone went crazy trying to buy all the wine, beer, etc., that they could. I know most places stayed open as long as they could sell, but the McCorn Cellar closed at 11:00 P.M. forever. In the early days before Prohibition, Hammondsport was wet. Bath, Penn Yan, and Dundee were dry. Who were the drunks on our streets? From those towns. Prohibition was a very bad mistake. The morale of the people went down from that time. People who never drank before began to make home brew and there were many bootleggers. I know of one in particular, who came to town with a couple of chairs, table and bed, their only possessions, who became very wealthy by bootlegging.

Most wineries went under. A few limped through the era producing medicinal and sacramental wines. Italian home winemakers were joined by millions of other Americans suddenly interested in the art of fermentation. Thanks to the lobbying efforts of Virginia apple farmers, section 29 of the Volstead Act allowed for up to two-hundred gallons of "nonintoxicating, cider and fruit juices" to be made in the home. Most of the grapes for this hobby came from California.

The eastern wine industry was so effectively ruined by Prohibition and its aftermath that today the region's vineyards and estate wineries are objects of surprise and curiosity in areas where local wines were once taken for granted. After fifty years of "beverage control," many people still do not question the concept of state stores or limited licensing systems that restrict convenient access to table wine.

4 OUT OF THE ASHES: THE WINE REVOLUTION

On December 5, 1933, the Twenty-first Amendment to the Constitution was ratified by thirty-six states. It reads: "Section 1. The eighteenth article of amendment to the Constitution of the United States is hereby repealed. Section 2. The transportation or importation into any State, Territory, or possession of the United States for delivery or use therein of intoxicating liquors, in violation of the laws thereof, is hereby prohibited." The thirty-five years from Repeal to the 1968 passage of the Pennsylvania Limited Winery bill was for the most part a "dark ages" for American wine in general and for that of eastern America in particular. Just as many areas had gone dry before national Prohibition, many stayed dry long after Repeal. Kansas, Oklahoma, and Mississippi did not repeal statewide prohibition until 1948, 1959, and 1966, respectively. Within wet states, counties often stayed dry. Monopoly systems of liquor control were set up which strictly limited consumers' selections of wines and spirits.

An unholy alliance of teetotalers and liquor barons, neither caring for wine, effectively removed alcoholic beverages from the free enterprise system. A grapegrower's right to produce and sell wine was even more inhibited than a consumer's right to buy it. Most states, with the exception of California, placed exorbitant license fees and prohibitive restrictions on wine production, sales, and marketing. Expensive and limited licensing worked in favor of a few large companies and made family wineries a hopeless proposition economically outside California. The mere mention of the word "wine" in state and USDA research stations would jeopardize funding. Dry politicians effectively blocked wine research funds for the USDA and numerous state universities until the 1960s.

At the time of Repeal, the table wine industry was in disarray. Vineyards needed replanting with wine grape varieties. Wine producers themselves had lost respect for their own product. For them, wine had become little more than an alcoholic beverage made with unsold fresh table grapes, more a by-product than a product. Sweet, 20-percent wines were the stock-in-trade. That the clientele attracted to these "ports" and "muscatels" was not a credit to the industry is evidenced by the unfortunate term "wino" applied to those who consumed the greater quantity of them. At the opposite end of the spectrum were connoisseurs for whom the world of wine was an arcane foreign cult of sophistication. Prestigious labels, vintages, and prices were inseparable components of the pleasure of consumption. In America wine was viewed as either too lowbrow for respectable households or so esoteric you had to speak French in order to understand it.

Three geographically farflung journalists, Frank Schoonmaker, Philip M. Wagner, and Leon D. Adams, elected to champion American wines during this difficult period, and they deserve much of the credit for helping to bridge the gap between teetotalers and winos, home winemakers and label worshipers. They and several key winemakers including Adhemar De Chaunac, Charles Fournier, and Konstantin Frank, helped to catalyze the renaissance of American winegrowing which we have come to call the wine revolution or boom.

Although he was a New York City–based wine importer, Frank M. Schoonmaker was no foreign-wine cultist. In his *Complete Wine Book* (1934) and *American Wines* (1941), he predicted a great future for U.S. wines as soon as the right

grapes were planted in appropriate areas and dry influence dampened in legislatures. The well-traveled Princeton dropout wrote about and marketed wines from around the world. Working with the California industry, he pioneered the now common practice of varietal labeling. American wines among his signature selections bore the names of the predominant grape variety instead of borrowed foreign names such as Chablis, Sauternes, and Burgundy. That Schoonmaker was knowledgeable and discriminating when it came to eastern wines is evident in his comments about two native American varieties: "In good years, the wine made from the unblended juice of Elvira grapes, grown in the Finger Lakes region, is exceeded by none produced in the East. Pale straw in color, it has a delightful fragrance, recalling that of a young Moselle, with enough of the native American character to give it individuality and distinctiveness. Its acidity is high; a factor which contributes to the refreshing quality of the wine." About Concord, however, he was less enthusiastic. "As a true winegrape, it has almost nothing to recommend it: it can hardly be made into wine at all unless heavily sugared, and

Some examples of modern labeling in the East: Glenora Wine Cellars Riesling (New York); Montbray Wine Cellars Chardonnay (Maryland); Allegro Vineyards Cabernet Sauvignon (Pennsylvania); Commonwealth Winery Seyval Blanc (Massachusetts)

a dry Concord table wine is assertive in flavor and extremely common."

While Schoonmaker provided perceptive commentary about various grape varieties and their wines, Philip M. Wagner of Baltimore, Maryland, went a step further by becoming a winegrower himself. Winemaking began as his hobby, a diversion from his work as editor of the *Baltimore Sun*. His first book, *American Wines and How to Make Them*, was the only book on winemaking in print in English when it was published in 1933. Wagner grew up in a wine-drinking family. During Prohibition he bought California grapes, favoring Zinfandel and Carignane. After Repeal these grapes were needed by California wineries and Wagner had to discover a source closer to home. Finding abundant Concord and little else, he planted pre-Prohibition native eastern wine grapes such as Delaware, Norton, and

Philip Wagner enjoys his eightieth birthday celebration given by the Maryland Grape Growers Association for eighty of his best friends.

Some examples of nineteenth-century labeling: Monticello Wine Company's Extra Virginia Claret and Virginia Delaware. Note the bottle shapes, which indicate wine styles.

Clinton. These did not provide him with the neutral table wines he desired, and in 1935 he obtained grafted Vinifera vines from California. Many years later, speaking with characteristic irony, Wagner described the results of his home research vineyard:

Maryland conditions are ideal for experimental work with grapes. We are in the direct path of the Caribbean hurricanes, which usually drop 3 or 4 inches of rain on us the day before starting harvest. We are on the eastern, not western edge of the Continental Mass, meaning that we get all extremes of continental weather, which can favor us with from −14 degrees to 75 degrees Farenheit in the same January. We alternate flood and drought and enjoy high humidity. Most of the diseases thrive here. We have no need to saturate a greenhouse with peronospera as they do in Geilweilerhof, to check mildew resistance, because the atmosphere is already

Joceyln Wagner bottling wine at Boordy Vineyards in the early days

saturated with it. We are perfectly equipped at no expense to test disease resistance, winter hardiness, hail resistance, phylloxera of course, bird damage, the effect of high winds, ripe rot and splitting—and at that time we were also about to become the focus of the Japanese beetle invasion. No experimenter could ask for more. Anything that survives in Maryland is worth trial anywhere this side of the Arctic circle.

After a short time it became clear to Wagner that Vinifera varieties were not going to provide his hobby *vino de casa* with reliability in Maryland. While perusing French viticultural literature, Wagner found references to "hybrides producteurs directs" (*h.p.d.*'s), crosses between American and Vinifera wines made in France. An assignment in Europe in 1936–37 gave him an opportunity to verify firsthand that there were indeed such crosses and that they were being used almost exclusively for wine.

Upon his return Wagner discovered that various French-American varieties had already crossed the Atlantic and could be found in several research collections. These new varieties, however, were at that time being ignored in the East because they lacked "grape flavor," the very characteristic that makes them particularly suited for table wine. Wagner and his wife, Jocelyn, began collecting these new wine-grape varieties from wherever they could find them: New York, California, North Carolina, and even, in the case

of Baco noir, directly from Maurice Baco in France.

The Wagners began to propagate interesting varieties for friends. By 1942 they had established a small commercial nursery. For years they were the only commercial source of the French-American varieties that were to make the winegrowing revolution possible in the East. In 1945 the Wagners bonded a small winery at their home so that they could legally produce wines from the increasing yields of their "hobby" vineyard; they called it Boordy Vineyards.

Having written about how to make wine, Wagner next undertook to explain grape growing to an ever-expanding group of Easterners who wished to establish their own vineyards. He published *A Wine-Grower's Guide* in 1945. Writing from experience and with a journalist's clarity, Wagner opened the world of viticulture to thousands of would-be vignerons. One would be hard-pressed to find an eastern winegrower today who does not begin his or her story with, "Well, I read Wagner's book(s) and. . . ." Many farm wineries that seemed to spring out of nowhere in the 1970s were in fact part of a vast network of Wagner readers armed with Boordy vines and home-winemaking experience.

Although he had maintained close contact with grape scientists and winemakers in the East for some years before, Wagner considers a gathering of eastern winemakers in Fredonia,

Philip and Jocelyn Wagner in a typical wine conference pose, at the head table

New York, in September 1945 to be a critical juncture in the evolution of eastern wines. At this meeting of industry leaders, he placed a bottle of his Maryland-grown, French-American wine amidst various samples of native American varietals from Canada and New York. All present agreed that Wagner's wine demonstrated potential for a new dimension in eastern wines. One of those most impressed by Wagner's French-American wine was Adhemar De Chaunac, winemaker for Brights of Ontario. During the post–World War II period, Brights produced only Labrusca dessert wines. In these new French-American grapes, De Chaunac saw a way to produce Canadian-grown dry table wine. He immediately ordered quantities of both French-American and Vinifera vines from France, including Maréchal Foch and Léon Millot from Alsace. Working with viticulturist George W. B. Hostetter, De Chaunac began to improve Canadian wines. In 1959 Brights released Canada's first Vinifera champagnes using Chardonnay and Pinot noir grapes from their own vineyards.

Nearly ten years before De Chaunac began making innovations in Canada, a debonair French winemaker had begun to seek alternatives to the native American varietal selection in New York. In 1935 Charles Fournier left his post as chief winemaker for Veuve Cliquot-Ponsardin in Reims to work for the Urbana Wine Company (later Gold Seal) in Hammondsport. With him, Fournier brought French yeast strains. Recognizing that champagne is not made with yeast alone, he imported, in 1936, French-American varieties Seibel 1000 (Rosette) and Ravat 6 (Ravat

Charles Fournier, one of the East's most beloved winemakers

blanc). Gold Seal's best champagnes, usually blends of different varieties, received Fournier's signature. In 1950 wines from other states and abroad were invited to compete for the first time in the wine competition of the California State Fair. When the only gold medal that year went to Charles Fournier New York State Champagne, the organizers decided it would be better to restrict entries to California wines for future competitions.

In addition to demonstrating that excellent wines could be made with native and French-American grapes, Fournier made a further contribution to Eastern winegrowing by hiring Konstantin Frank, a viticulturist emigrated from Russia, to plant Vinifera vines for Gold Seal. Frank succeeded in producing Vinifera grapes in New York, and Fournier vinified the first commercial Vinifera wines in the eastern United States. Leon Adams recounts: "I was one of those present at the Winter 1961 dinner of the San Francisco Wine and Food Society in historic Jack's Restaurant, when Gold Seal New York State 1959 Chardonnay and Johannisberg Riesling were served for the first time in the West. To the several California vintners in attendance that memorable night, it was a shock to realize that their long-acknowledged monopoly on the production of fine Vinifera wines in North America might at last be at an end."

Konstantin Frank, born in 1899, arrived in America in 1951 with a wife, three children, and no English. Frank had once directed an agricultural research institute in his native Russia and specialized in viticulture and enology. He was working at New York State's Agricultural Experiment Station in Geneva as an unskilled laborer when he began consulting with Fournier in 1953.

Frank went on to establish his own Vinifera vineyard and winery, selling his first wines in 1965. His vintage 1961 Trockenbeerenauslese sold for $45 per bottle and became legendary among connoisseurs. Because most wine writers

are more familiar with Vinifera wines and because Frank achieved the impossible dream of growing European vines in the East, his name and New York State wines appeared in connoisseur guides that might otherwise have ignored the East entirely. Although he has not published any books, Frank's nursery of grafted vines, his articles, and the notoriety of his wines have helped him to proselytize the cause of Vinifera culture ("Noble" vines or nothing) in the East as vigorously as Wagner has promoted French-American grapes.

Konstantin Frank, Charles Fournier, Adhemar De Chaunac, Philip Wagner, and Frank Schoonmaker are each central figures to different aspects of the post-Prohibition winegrowing reformation in the East. Journalist–wine historian Leon Adams has only recently taken his place among them after working anonymously for many years as a crusader for wine. Troubled by the problem of alcohol abuse in the United States, which had been exacerbated by Prohibition, Adams has dedicated his career to the advocacy of wine for public health. Like Thomas Jefferson, he considers wine a beverage of moderation. American drinking habits can, he feels, be civilized if light table wines become a part of the national diet.

Adams founded the California Grape Growers League in 1931, which was a forerunner of the Wine Institute incorporated in 1934 and the Wine Advisory Board established in 1938. He ran these agencies for twenty years and through them endeavored to put wine on American dinner tables. Given the dismal state of affairs after Repeal, the task was enormous. In the 1930s leading liquor stores would hide wine under the counter; only the cheaper stores would display wine. Slow movement from the shelves meant that the bottles would gather dust and the labels become fly-specked. Adams armed his twenty-eight-man dealer-service staff with feather dusters for them to use when educating wholesalers and retailers about attractive wine displays. Wine Advisory Board funds were channeled to California universities for research; standards set for wine quality; and lobbyists hired to obtain

Dr. Konstantin Frank, father of Vinifera culture in the East

Leon D. Adams, father of the farm winery movement

"appetizer" or "dessert," and "light" changed to "table" wine in federal and state regulations. Although he wrote and edited thousands of speeches, pamphlets, and books, including the home *Wine Study Course* taken by millions of people since 1942, Adams remained anonymous (his 1952 classic, *Striped Bass Fishing in California and Oregon*, notwithstanding) until 1958, when he published the *Commonsense Book of Wine*. His *Commonsense Book of Drinking* followed in 1960. Adams's oft-quoted landmark work, *Wines of America*, appeared in 1973, followed by revised editions in 1978 and 1985.

In the twenty years he spent researching *Wines of America*, Adams crisscrossed the country searching for each wine-grape vineyard that had been, was, or would be in every state of the Union, Canada, and Mexico. With the thoroughness of an investigative reporter, he tasted every available wine made with local grapes, homemade or commercial, to evaluate their potential for winegrowing. At first novice eastern winegrowers were amazed by the interest that this California writer had in their tiny vineyards and wine cellars. Today few eastern winegrowers would be surprised to find Adams with

fair treatment for wine at state, federal, and international levels.

Big California wine producers were not always sympathetic to Adams's zeal for table wine. Many felt the Wine Institute should promote the sweet wines with higher alcohol content which comprised the majority of their sales. His special support of the small wineries that payed much lower dues was not always understood.

Adams appreciated the importance of semantics, and he had the term "fortified" changed to

State wine marketing specialist Lou Ann Whitton tending the wine booth at the state fair, 1980

48   *A Brief History of Eastern Viticulture*

his pipe, bow tie, and beret in their winery asking, "What's new?"

Knowing that most states had a history of winegrowing, Adams could see no reason why they should not have a future. He encouraged grape growers to unite with their state representatives and agricultural commissioners to obtain legislation that would enable them to establish wineries at their vineyards. He reminded them that "agriculture can defeat liquor in any legislature." Guided by Adams, who is now hailed as the father of today's farm wineries, Pennsylvania was the first state to pass a "Limited Winery" law in 1968; the number of wineries there increased from none in that year to over forty by 1985. This pattern has been repeated in many other states. Coincidentally, in 1968 sales of table wines exceeded those of dessert wines for the first time since Prohibition. It was in 1968, then, that the wine revolution in America, which Adams and other leaders had been fostering, had its start.

Part Two

Nature Sets the Stage

5  CLIMATE SEPARATES EAST FROM WEST

Wine is an expression of a place. This is why experienced tasters can identify wines by their aromas and flavors alone without seeing the labels. It is climate, first of all, that separates Burgundy from Bordeaux, northwest Pennsylvania from southeast Pennsylvania, and, within the scope of this book, the East from the West.

Easterners can look to Europe rather than to the West for climate similar to their own. Most of Europe and eastern America have a temperate climate with rain during the summer, whereas in the Mediterranean region and in California, there is virtually no summer rain. One emerging U.S. wine region, the Pacific Northwest, encompasses both temperate and Mediterranean climate conditions.

A traditional belief about the relationship between climate and quality is that cool climes produce light, flowery wines, whereas warm regions produce less fruity, heavier wines. Today, modern technology (including nighttime harvesting, field crushing, and almost instant refrigeration) has in large measure modified climate-related conditions in wine production. Fruity white, rosé, and light red wines are now emerging from very warm climates. On the other hand, no degree of technology can lessen the influence of temperature and precipitation on the character and ripening rate of mature fruit. Matching grape variety with climate is the ultimate achievement in regional winegrowing. In most areas of the East this process is just beginning.

Topography

Dramatic changes in topography as well as climate occur as one moves eastward from the Pacific. High mountains and plateaus in the West contrast sharply with the low-lying plains of the East, where the flat profile is interrupted slightly by the Ozarks and by the modest (compared with the Rockies) Appalachian range. Pinpointing an exact boundary between West and East is difficult, but the line runs through the Great Plains: from North Dakota through South Dakota, Nebraska, Kansas, Oklahoma, and Texas. Through these states run the 100th meridian, the Mountain/Central Time Zone line and, more important from a viticultural point of view, the moisture index. Conditions change here from arid to humid.

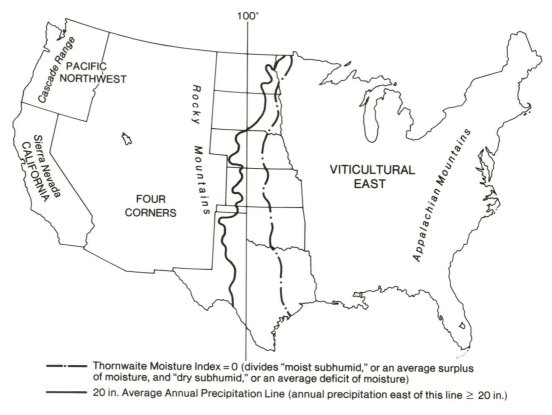

Thornwaite Moisture Index = 0 (divides "moist subhumid," or an average surplus of moisture, and "dry subhumid," or an average deficit of moisture)

—————— 20 in. Average Annual Precipitation Line (annual precipitation east of this line ≥ 20 in.)

The East/West Dividing Line

Most of the eastern United States is characterized as "warm and moist with warm summers" by the Köppen-Geiger system of climate classification. The East shares this classification with other parts of the world including:

Africa   eastern South Africa (Durban
              area)
Asia   eastern China (Foochow,
              Shanghai, Hankow)
              southern Japan (Tokyo south)
              South Korea
              northeastern Taiwan (Taipei
              area)
Australia   east coast (MacKay south to
              Sydney, inland to
              Bendingo)
Europe   northern Italy (Veneto area
              on Adriatic coast)

              Rumanian and Moldavian
                coasts on Black Sea
S. America Brazil (from Rio de Janeiro
                south)
              Uruguay
              Argentina (Bahia Blanca north)

Eastern American tourists to these foreign places are likely to encounter some familiar-looking grapevines. Native American vines imported to these areas have found favor because of their resistance to fungus diseases that thrive in this type of climate.

The two main soil classes in the United States respect the arid-humid division between East and West. Pedalfer soils in the eastern half of the country have aluminum and iron compounds that result from the action of acids on clay. Pedocal soils in the West contain calcium compounds and are alkaline.

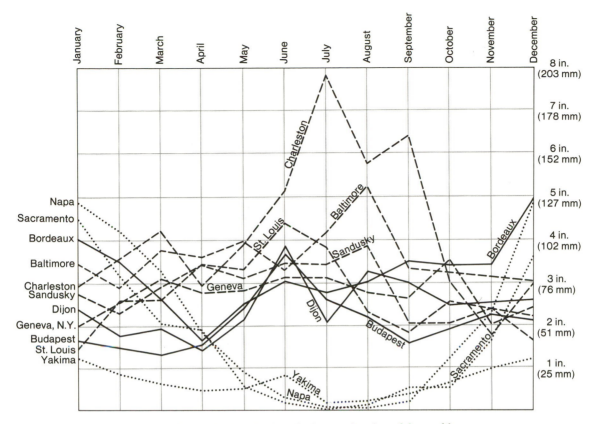

Annual precipitation of selected winegrowing sites of the world

Precipitation

Precipitation is the chief weather factor that distinguishes the East from California. Very few eastern vineyards are dependent on irrigation for survival. Twenty inches of annual precipitation is considered a minimum for "dry farming" vines, and most eastern vineyards comfortably exceed that minimum. Heat waves accompanied by drought have been enough of a problem in parts of the Midwest to warrant irrigation; water-saving drip systems are the most widely used.

While there are advantages to independence from irrigation, precipitation during the growing season, on the other hand, can result in costly problems. Rain during flowering, for example, can cause poor fruit set, reducing the number of berries per cluster. Harmful fungi such as black rot and downy mildew thrive in rainy weather

(fortunately, modern science and technology provide effective methods for dealing with these plagues). Rain during harvest (a threat both East and West) dilutes sugar concentration and causes fruit deterioration, splitting, and rot. Although there have been excellent sweet table wines made in the East from late-harvested, "noble-rotted" grapes (that is, grapes dehydrated by a favorable development of *Botrytis cinerea*), such cases are rare, and growers prefer to harvest clean, unblemished fruit.

Outside of Texas, hail is rarely a serious threat to eastern growers. A severe hailstorm in spring or early summer can strip a vine of most of its shoots, leaving it with a few ragged leaves and no crop. Hail damage to the shoots of young vines causes growers to lose a year in establishing permanent trunks and cordons.

Snow is the one type of precipitation welcomed by growers. In areas with very cold win-

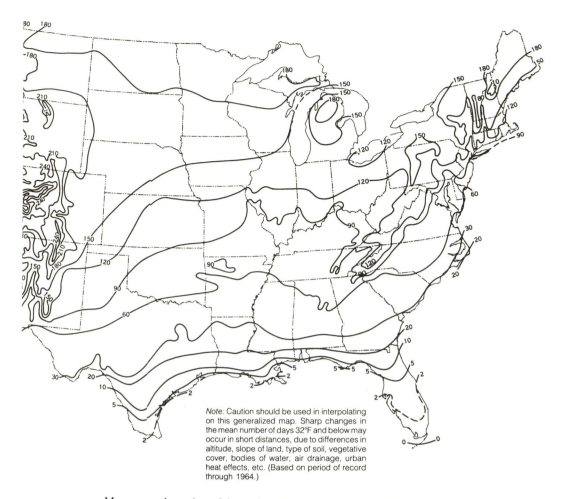

Note: Caution should be used in interpolating on this generalized map. Sharp changes in the mean number of days 32°F and below may occur in short distances, due to differences in altitude, slope of land, type of soil, vegetative cover, bodies of water, air drainage, urban heat effects, etc. (Based on period of record through 1964.)

Mean annual number of days of maximum temperature 32° F and below

ters, snow helps to insulate the vines, protecting the trunks and graft unions from the damaging effects of excessively low temperatures.

Temperature

Temperature extremes can spell life or death for vines, and late spring frosts can reduce individual vintages. Temperature has a major effect, too, on wine quality, as both daytime and nighttime temperatures influence the fruit's ripening rate, how much sugar the grapes accumulate, and how much acid they retain. In general, fruit character is maximized when weather permits the grapes to mature slowly. It takes many years to understand the effect that a given set of cli-

matic conditions will have on fruit and wine character, but growers must also consider the basic health and survival of the vine itself.

Grape growers in the United States commonly refer to their climate areas in terms of growing degree-days measured as the sum of the monthly mean temperatures over 50°F from April 1 to October 31. The choice of 50°F is somewhat arbitrary but is made because at temperatures below it there will be little if any shoot growth. When, for example, the monthly mean temperature in Baltimore during July is 76°F, then the heat summation for the month would be 76° − 50° = 26° × 31 days = a heat summation of 806 degree-days.

In general, eastern climates are subject to greater extremes—that is, hotter summers and

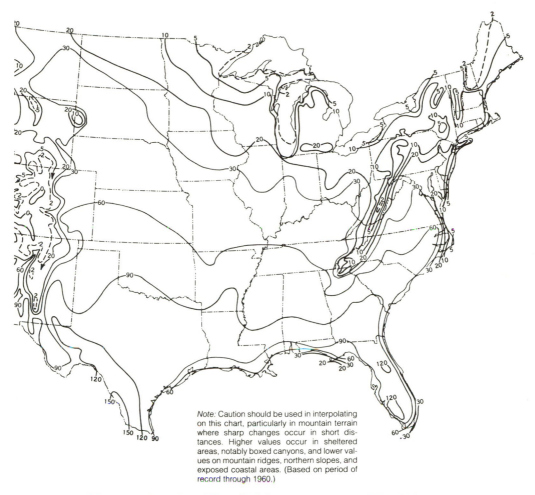

Mean annual number of days of minimum temperature 90° F and above

colder winters—than are those of either Europe or California. The tendency of winter conditions in the East to change unpredictably from mild to arctic also causes real difficulties for growers. Sudden drops in temperature injure vines, whereas the same low temperature arrived at gradually would do no harm. Serious injury was sustained in New York vineyards in December 1980 when the thermometer registered 34°F one day at noon and −18°F only eighteen hours later. Similarly, a week or so of balmy (60°F) weather in February or March followed by a drop back into the teens and low twenties can literally nip young grape clusters in the bud.

Vinifera varieties are especially vulnerable to injury from fluctuating winter temperatures. American species and most of their hybrids are protected by a natural safeguard: they require exposure to temperatures ranging from 32° to 41°F for approximately one thousand hours before breaking dormancy and are not easily coaxed into prematurely pushing sap during an unseasonably warm spell in late winter. The European species, *Vitis vinifera*, however, lacks this natural protection and can be fooled into a fatally early emergence. Such species-related physiological mechanisms as dormancy requirements reflect the climate conditions in which the plants evolved. Easterners must be aware of the risks posed by endemic low winter temperatures when they decide which grape varieties to plant. New York State viticulturists issued the following temperature guidelines for rating a vineyard site:

Crown gall (*Agrobacterium tumefaciens*) is the dreaded bacterium that invades cracks in the trunk of the vine and causes unsightly and eventually deadly galls. The most common cause of trunk splitting in the East is low winter temperatures.

EXCELLENT. Winter temperatures reaching −5°F 3 times or less in 10 years; winter temperatures reaching −10°F no more than once in 10 years, with the long-term minimum temperature not lower than −10°F. Suitable for all current commercial varieties.

GOOD. Winter temperatures reaching −5°F 5 times or less in 10 years; winter temperatures reaching −10°F no more than once in 10 years, with the long-term minimum temperature not lower than −15°F. Suitable for all current commercial varieties, but cold-tender varieties can be expected to sustain severe damage at least once in 10 years and lesser damage more often.

ACCEPTABLE. Winter temperatures reaching −5°F almost every year; winter temperatures reaching −10°F 4 times or less in ten years, and the long-term minimum temperatures of −15°F or less occurring no more than once in 10 years. Suitable commercially only for varieties of medium or greater hardiness.

POOR. Winter temperatures reaching −10°F 5 or more times in 10 years; winter temperatures reaching −15°F 3 or more times in 10 years. Not suitable for commercial grape production.

New York's major grape-growing districts, with the exception of Long Island, are in the "acceptable" category, as are many of the northerly areas of the East and Midwest. By careful site selection and attentive vine management, however, one can overcome some of the difficulties presented by an area's climate. Vinifera varieties have recently been planted in areas traditionally regarded as unsuitable. Some growers are willing to undertake more expensive cultural practices in the vineyard (multi-trunks, double pruning, burying, and so forth) and to accept occasional years with little or no crop, averaging their costs over favorable and unfavorable years.

Just as winter lows are generally lower, summer temperatures are generally higher in the East than in many of the other of the world's wine regions. For this reason the harvest season begins as early as July in the South and southern Midwest and August in the Mid-Atlantic states. As temperatures rise above 86°F, the rate of photosynthesis declines. Ripening is impaired by excessive heat (upper nineties and above). In other words, as the temperature rises acid levels may become disproportionately low, sugar production stalls, and the danger of sunburned fruit increases. In addition to making a careful choice of varieties, a grower can help vines coexist with hot weather by using appropriate training and trellising methods.

Microclimates

Latitude and altitude affect the amount and strength of sunlight during the day and the relative coolness of nighttime temperatures. For every thousand-foot rise in elevation there may be an average drop in temperature of 3.5°F. Northern latitudes and higher altitudes have shorter growing seasons (the amount of heat accumulation between frosts tends to be small) and as a result, the rate at which grapes accumulate sugar and lose acid is slower than in more southerly regions or lower altitudes. For white wines, long, slow maturation has often proved advantageous for the production of fruity, perfumy wines. Growers look to hillsides and higher ele-

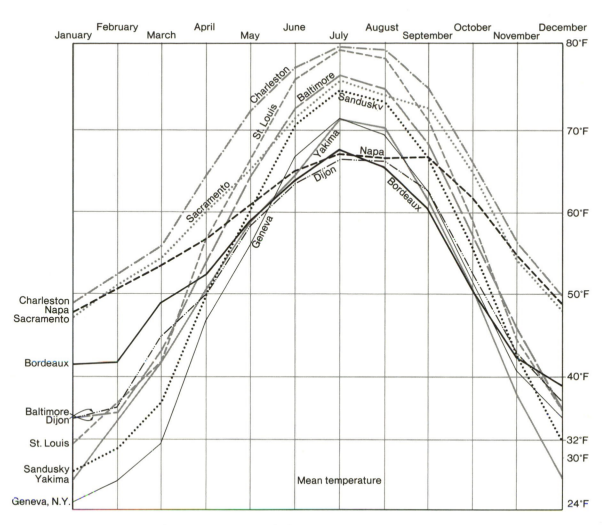

Annual mean temperatures of selected winegrowing sites of the world

Temperature labels on the chart (left axis):

Charleston
Napa
Sacramento

Bordeaux

Baltimore
Dijon

St. Louis

Sandusky
Yakima

Geneva, N.Y.

Right axis: 80°F, 70°F, 60°F, 50°F, 40°F, 32°F, 30°F, 24°F

Month labels (top): January, February, March, April, May, June, July, August, September, October, November, December

Line labels on chart: Charleston, St. Louis, Baltimore, Sandusky, Yakima, Napa, Dijon, Bordeaux, Geneva, Sacramento

Mean temperature

vations for less frost-prone planting areas because cold heavy air masses tend to settle in valleys and bring unwelcome late spring frosts. Mountain ranges, with their cooling altitudes and warm sunny slopes, are rich sources of vineyard sites. The southeastern section of the Appalachians, including the Blue Ridge and foothills, contains prime vineyard sites from Pennsylvania to Georgia. In the South, the hills offer the special benefit of apparent refuge from Pierce's disease.

There is debate among grape growers over whether to follow the example of orchardists who plant on north slopes to inhibit premature budding and consequent spring frost damage. In places where summers are hot, the cooler temperatures of a north slope can slow ripening and thus possibly improve fruit quality. Planting on a northern exposure does, however, involve the risk that absolute temperatures may be lower (that is, no warmth radiating from the soil) at a critical period than those with a slope having a southern exposure in the same locale would be. Another hazard of north-slope planting is the potential for increased rot and mildew development if there is less solar drying of morning dew and rainfall.

Grapevines have thrived on Isle St. George, Ohio, in Lake Erie for more than a century.

Most of Europe's great vineyards were planted along major rivers or the Mediterannean. Early American vineyardists followed suit along the Ohio, Hudson, and other waterways. Vinifera culture in the eastern United States (and Canada) began around the Great Lakes, near the Finger Lakes, along the New England coast, on Long Island, and in other water-induced microclimates. Because they gain and lose heat much more slowly than the surrounding air, large bodies of water have a profound moderating influence on temperatures near their shores and affect nearby vineyards. By cooling the spring air that passes over them, water masses help delay budbreak, thereby reducing the danger of loss from late frosts. Conversely warming the air temperatures in fall, water helps delay the first frost, allowing more time for grapes to mature. Further, this moderating effect can be critical to the winter survival of vines.

Understanding weather from a vineyard owner's viewpoint is important when visiting eastern vineyards. The choice of grape varieties will reflect local conditions—whether those of frigid Minnesota, tropical Florida, or one of the many regions in between. Climate's influence on wine should not be underestimated.

6 GRAPE FAMILIES

Introduction

A grape berry is the world's smallest grape juice container. Grape variety determines the flavor of the juice and the character of the wine made from that juice. On the subject of our perception of fruit flavors, biochemistry professor Terry E. Acree has observed:

> Any complex natural product like a fruit flavor arises because humans can smell individual chemicals. Each of these chemicals produces a different sensation. At the instant they are consumed, all the chemicals and all the sensations are experienced by humans simultaneously and the human mind integrates them into a single impression. The most interesting fact is that all of these differences that humans experience when they consume a natural product arise as a result of a very small number of chemicals present in very low concentration. You are tasting the genetic fingerprint of that fruit.

For most of the grape-growing world, the "genetic fingerprint" of commercial grape varieties has come about in the evolution of the Eurasian vine species, *Vitis vinifera*. In eastern America, there are several other *Vitis* species which, indi-vidually or combined through breeding with Vinifera, make important genetic contributions to the fruit flavors of grape varieties and the wines made from them. There are two major classes of grapes grown in the East in addition to European Vinifera: native American (Labrusca, Muscadinia, and other *Vitis*) and European-American (crosses between Vinifera and native American). In California all the major wine grapes are Vinifera (although there are several European-American crosses used as teinturiers or color grapes). In the eastern states a single winery may produce wines from Vinifera, European-American, and native American grapes. In this regard, eastern wineries are unique.

A diversity of grape varieties provides a wide range of wine flavors. An individual's taste preferences, however, are often considerably narrower. Familiarity with the three main grape classes is important if we are to understand the spectrum of eastern wines. Book learning should be reinforced by tasting selected varieties in each class.

In France grape varieties used in Appellation d'Origine Contrôllée wines are legally wed to specific geographic areas. By law, premium red

Interior view
of berry

wines in Burgundy must be made from Pinot noir; wines labeled Beaujolais must be made from Gamay noir; white Bordeaux wines called Graves must be a blend of Sauvignon blanc, Sémillon, and Muscadelle; and red wines labeled Châteauneuf-du-Pape are a blend of up to fourteen designated varieties. The same is largely true in Italy: Barolo and Barbaresco wines are 100 percent Nebbiolo; Soave is Garganega blended with Trebbiano di Soave; and the re-

cently revised Chianti formula specifies the proportions of a blend of red and white grapes.

Wine production in Germany, although highly regulated, allows for a free evolution of grape varieties as long as they are pure Vinifera. For example, Müller-Thurgau, a Riesling-Sylvaner cross made in 1882, has surpassed both of its popular parents to become the leading grape variety in West Germany. New intraspecific (*V. vinifera* × *V. vinifera*) crosses such as Ortega, Kerner, and Scheurebe are now appearing on German wine labels. Disease resistant, interspecific (*V. vinifera* × other species) crosses, which make wines indistinguishable from pure Vinifera in blind testings, are now being produced at German viticultural institutes. Although interspecific wines are not presently approved for commercial use in Common Market countries, they may be in the future.

In the United States there are no governmental restrictions on what varieties may be grown where. Vineyard performance and the marketplace determine the fate of all grapes. The

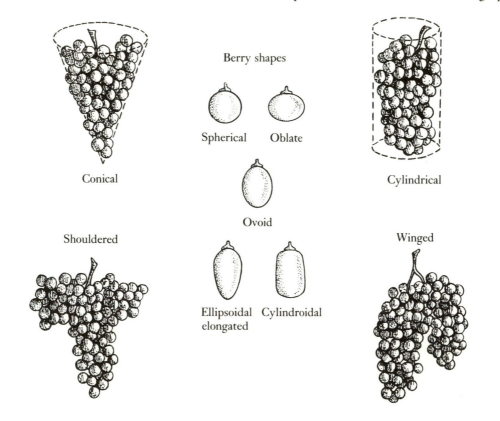

Conical

Berry shapes

Spherical Oblate

Cylindrical

Ovoid

Shouldered

Ellipsoidal Cylindroidal
elongated

Winged

federal appellation-of-origin regulations are concerned solely with determining boundaries for viticultural areas, such as Lake Erie, Lancaster Valley, and Leelanau Peninsula, for wine-labeling purposes. Federal authorities are tangentially attempting to establish an official wine-grape nomenclature list that will standardize varietal names, for example, "Chardonnay" and not "Pinot Chardonnay," "Colombard" and not "French Colombard."

In a region as diverse as the East, it is vital that there be freedom to experiment with as many promising varieties as possible, which must include freedom to import grapes from overseas as long as they have been inspected for pathology. Strict sanctions in the United States on vine importation in the past decades have not inhibited the spread of grapevine viruses, but they have greatly limited selection of both fruiting varieties and rootstocks.

Grape variety, environmental conditions, and vinification techniques are primary factors in a wine's identity. There is currently no definite correlation between the origin of an eastern wine and its taste. Two Seyvals from different regions may have more in common than two from neighboring wineries because of the very different styles in which the wines are produced. One may be sweet and fruity and the other bone dry and woody. Because most eastern wineries and supporting vineyards are young, the character of their wines is still continually evolving. Over time, more consistent styles for specific varieties in a given eastern area can be expected to develop, as they have in most of the world's wine-growing regions. For the moment, however, a benign anarchy reigns as growers strive to find the most suitable matches for their soils and climates. Winemakers in turn are searching for those vinification methods that will maximize the qualities that a particular local variety or a blend of varieties can offer.

Vinifera: The Eurasian Grape

Vitis vinifera is the vine species native to the Caspian Sea area which has accompanied men and women on their journey through recorded history. Fossil imprints of vine leaves and seeds show that the diet of prehistoric people was enriched with grapes and probably wine. Sealed amphorae of wine, vintage dated to circa 3,000 B.C., have been found in Egyptian tombs, and archaeologists continue to turn up evidence of commercial vineyards from ancient times.

Zone	Minimum (percent of volume)	Maximum added (percent of volume)	Special circumstances (percent of volume)
A	5	3.5	up to 4.5
B	6	2.5	up to 3.5
C-Ia	7.5	2	
C-Ib	8	2	
C-II	8.5	2	
C-III	9	2	

European Economic Community regulations concerning the permissible amount of sugar that may be added to wine-grape must are based on the climate-zone delimitations. The table above shows the minimum acceptable *natural alcohol* levels of the must (which occurs from fermentation of the grape juice as it comes from the vineyard) and the maximum permissible levels of alcohol adjustment by the addition of sugar. During years of extremely poor weather, in zones A and B, winemakers are permitted to add substantial amounts of sugar to the must.

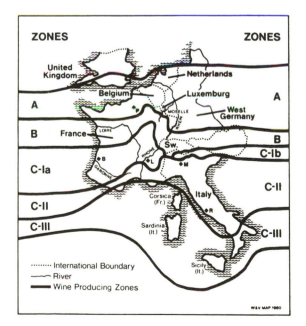

Viticulture was the subject of learned treatises at the time of Christ. As Christianity spread throughout Europe so did Vinifera viniculture, providing a source of sacramental wine.

After thousands of years of selection, Vinifera fruit has evolved into various specialized forms: small, highly flavored clusters for wine; large tough-skinned grapes for table use; and seedless varieties for raisins. *Vitis vinifera* remained Western civilization's unique grape species until the discovery of the New World. When, in the mid-nineteenth century, phylloxera, downy mildew, powdery mildew, and black rot all migrated from eastern America to Europe, Vinifera culture was radically changed. The need for grafting on native American rootstocks and for spraying to control fungus diseases suddenly made grape growing much more expensive and difficult in Europe.

Vinifera vines may be found on every continent (except Antarctica) and still comprise nearly all of the world's grape economy. The fact that Vinifera wine grapes are well endowed for their purpose does not mean that the juice never needs amendment. Depending on the climate where they are grown, Vinifera musts may need additional sugar, acid, and even water to make a better-balanced wine. Where the climate is cool, sugar is sometimes deficient, and in warm climates, acid may be low. Such additions, in moderation, are accepted practice (although usually done by "the other" wineries or region, "not here").

Successful commercial Vinifera culture in the East is a very recent phenomenon in spite of the fact that Vinifera plantings here date back to colonial days. Much has been learned in the past decades about how to manage Vinifera vines under various growing conditions, and where there is a will to plant Vinifera varieties, a way is being found. A better understanding of how to control the fungus diseases, even in very warm, humid areas, has emerged. Some growers in very cold areas have developed practical methods for burying canes after leaf fall and uncovering them in spring. Multiple-trunk training and double pruning (leaving extra buds at first pruning) allow growers to sustain a moderate amount of cold

damage and still be able to produce commercial crops. Rootstocks are carefully selected by growers in an effort to reduce excessively vigorous vegetative growth, which has been found to increase the likelihood of winter injury.

Acreage in this class is expanding rapidly and excellent Vinifera wines from the East are already receiving international acclaim.

Some Vinifera varieties described in Chapter 7: Aligoté, Cabernet franc, Cabernet Sauvignon, Carmine, Chardonnay, Gamay, Gewürztraminer, Merlot, Muscat blanc, Pinot noir, Riesling, Sauvignon blanc, Sémillon.

The Native American Grapes

The forests and hedgerows of eastern America are resplendent with wild grapevines belonging to a score of different species, most of which are useless for wine. The majority of cultivated native American grapes are in fact crosses between two or more species, and the exact bloodlines of some of these vines are the subject of much academic debate. There are those experts who insist that Concord is a pure *Vitis Labrusca* variety and others who contend that it must have some Vinifera (or other species) blood because it has perfect flowers, sweeter berries, and larger clusters than those found in the wild. (Another name for Labrusca grapes of questionable purity is *Vitis labruscana*.) In order to avoid getting bogged down in botanical detail, we will group native grapes according to the species that predominates their appearance and taste.

Due to the longtime dominance of Concord east of the Rockies, the native American class as a whole, and the *Vitis Labrusca* family in particular, suffers from a one-dimensional image. In fact, many varieties within the native American class are far better suited to winemaking than Concord, which is not suited at all.

Native American vines may be found around the world. The curriculum vitae of some American grapes show service in Asia, South America, and Eastern Europe. Big, leathery, dark green leaves with the distinctive felty white or rust backs are recognizable anywhere, whether in Hungary, Venezuela, or Japan. Savvy tourists can spot them providing shade over trellised doorways in France, Italy, and Greece.

In the 1920s many European governments took legislative action to curb expanding use of native American varieties that had entered their countries during the phylloxera debacle. Six native American varieties were officially prohibited in France. After 1935, Noah, Clinton, Othello, Herbemont, Lenoir, and Isabella could no longer legally be propagated, planted, or commercially vinified. Twenty years later there were still over 150,000 acres of these six "prohibited" varieties; it took a combined carrot-and-stick (subsidies and fines) program by the government to definitively reduce acreage in France.

Labrusca

The majority of vines growing in American backyards are from the Labrusca family—Concord is the blue grape and Niagara the white. One of America's most famous culinary marriages is that of Labrusca jelly and peanut butter. Labrusca fruit flavor has been chemically synthesized for use in items ranging from bubble gum to lip gloss. On the wine front, Labrusca grapes have been used successfully in sherries, ports, champagnes, and Kosher wines. Labrusca table wines have been made in the East for many years, but in very small quantities relative to Vinifera table wines from California and abroad.

Sweet Concord, Niagara, and Pink Catawba still enjoy a loyal following; however, they are no longer the flagship wines of this family and certainly do not characterize the eastern table wine scene today. Labrusca wines are not always sweet: dry or nearly dry Catawbas and Delawares are increasingly available. A visit to a modern farm winery producing Catawba, Delaware, or Dutchess in modern stainless steel tanks will demonstrate that.

Labrusca flavor has been studied by Terry Acree at New York's Geneva Experiment Station. Acree has found that Labrusca flavor is complicated because it has several components that may be strongly present in one variety and nonexistent in others. The four categories of La-

brusca flavor used by Acree are: foxy (wet dog), perfumy (floral), strawberry (cotton candy), and methyl anthranilate (bubble gum). Niagara is considered foxy, whereas Catawba is not. Concord is strong in methyl anthranilate, whereas Catawba is not. Catawba is high in perfumy character. Ives, high in strawberry flavor and all the other flavors as well, is considered the "paradigm of Labrusca flavor."

Fresh Labrusca grapes have a distinctive "slipskin" under which lies a layer of very sweet, mild juice. Much of the acid is in the pulp, centered around the seed. Compared as a class with Vinifera grapes, Labruscas have a lower sugar concentration and higher acid level. The practice of adding sugar and/or water ("amelioration") to Labrusca juice for wine is often desirable for improved wine quality, depending on the grape variety.

Niagara has a low sugar content in relation to its acid (example, 14° Brix/0.8 percent Total Acid). Catawba tends to average higher in both sugar and acid (example, 18°/1.14 percent Total Acid). Delaware has a natural balance between sugar and acid which may need no adjustment (example, 20°/.9 percent Total Acid). Although vineyard practices and weather cause substantial variation in the performance of any grape variety, relative differences among varieties in the same vineyard remain fairly constant.

Because Labrusca flavor attenuates naturally with age, "baked" sherries and ports made with 100-percent Labrusca grapes do not have a Labrusca aroma. Even Concord wine left in a barrel long enough will eventually lose its Labrusca character.

By using cold fermentation and picking the fruit before it has developed an overly strong Labrusca aroma, winemakers can produce wines that would be called fruity but not "foxy" in a derogatory sense. Some wineries are decidedly more progressive than others in this regard (including several of the biggest which now have small "pilot" facilities within their giant plants). If you have tasted one Catawba, you have *not* tasted them all.

Some Labrusca family varieties described in Chapter 7: Beta, Catawba, Concord, Delaware,

A cluster of Muscadine grapes

Diamond, Dutchess, Edelweiss, Elvira, Fredonia, Iona, Isabella, Ives, Missouri Riesling, Niagara, Steuben.

The Muscadines

Muscadines are at home along the Gulf of Mexico, the Coastal Plain, and lower Piedmont areas of the Southeast. If you are in the area in late summer or fall, take a walk in the forest and, using your nose as a guide, look on the ground for marble-sized berries of wild Muscadines. The taste of that moment can be brought back by a sip of Muscadine wine.

Muscadine grapes have a pronounced fruit flavor and unique aroma that is very difficult to describe to the uninitiated. It is different from, but similar to, Labrusca flavor and has traditionally been known as the Southern "fox" grape. Biochemists have found ethyl anthranilate in Muscadines in place of the methyl anthranilate found in Labruscas. Non-Southerners are likely

Mason jars symbolize the homemade origins of Southern Muscadine wine.

to associate the Muscadine flavor with that of an unfamiliar exotic fruit. Europeans liken sweet Muscadine wine to flavored aperitif or dessert wines. For Southerners, wherever they are living, it is a fragrance of home. Homemade wine from the backyard arbor is such a tradition that some Muscadine wine is still marketed in Mason jars.

The production of nondessert—that is, drier—table wines in the Cotton Belt is a very new phenomenon. Various vinification techniques, such as blending with neutral, non-Muscadine varieties, are being developed both at universities and at southern farm wineries. Florida researchers are selecting Muscadine varieties with nearly neutral fruit aromas.

Botanically, Muscadines are so different from other *Vitis* species that scientists have proposed a separate genus for them, called *Muscadinia: Vitis rotundifolia* would become *Muscadinia rotundifolia*. The wood of *Muscadinia* vines closely resembles a tree branch—hard, with adherent bark and continuous pith through the nodes. The leaves are small, round, and hairless. Tendrils are simple (not forked). They are so difficult to root that they are useless as rootstocks; propagation is done by layering. They need a minimum 200-day growing season, with at least 30 inches of rain, and can be damaged by temperatures below 10°F.

Since Muscadines have a high resistance to nearly all indigenous diseases including the redoubtable Pierce's disease, scientists have long dreamed of developing *Muscadinia* × *Vitis vinifera* crosses. Owing to differences in chromosome numbers between the two (for *Vitis* n = 19, for *Muscadinia* n = 20), hybridization is a difficult but not impossible feat. The first fertile, fruiting *vinifera* × *rotundifolia* cross, the DRX-55, was reported by North Carolina breeder Robert T. Dunstan in 1955. California and French breeders have since succeeded in producing these unusual vines, but so far no commercial varieties have been released.

In a USDA farmer's bulletin entitled *Grape Growing in the South* (published in 1900), S. M. Tracy gives the following advice to home Muscadine growers: before planting the vine place several pounds of bones in the bottom of each hole and cover with a little soil, build an arbor, train a single cane to the top, and from then on allow it "to branch and run at will." Tracy further recommends putting a half bushel of hardwood ashes around each vine and growing crimson clover as cover. Any cultivated Muscadine would have been female in 1900, but there were large numbers of wild vines back then (over half of which were male) and enough insects to do the job of pollination.

Things have changed since 1900 for Muscadine growers. Forests and insects have been cleared away: a lone female Scuppernong would now have a tough time producing fruit. Fortunately, progress sometimes begets solutions to the problems it causes. In the early part of this century, plant breeders in the South attempted to create perfect-flowered Muscadines. The old system of planting male vines ("every third row, every third vine") is necessarily wasteful of land and trellis space, and resultant fruit set is often irregular. Today there are numerous perfect-flowered Muscadine varieties that can both set their own fruit and serve as pollinators for female varieties.

A Muscadine cluster has only a few (6 to 24) berries, which ripen very unevenly and drop off individually when ripe. The large berries have thick skin and a thick, slippery pulp that is difficult to press. A light pressing, yielding a mere 120 gallons of juice per ton, helps to avoid extracting bitterness from the skins and produces the best quality table wine. Of all the grape species, Muscadines tend to be the lowest in sugar concentration, requiring additional sugar at fermentation. Acid levels are also low relative to other species.

Until recently, the whole Rotundifolia family went colloquially by the name of Scuppernong, which actually designates a single variety. Today, other Muscadine varieties are named on wine labels, and new ones will continue to appear.

Some Muscadine varieties described in Chapter 7: Carlos, Magnolia, Noble, Scuppernong.

Other *Vitis* Wine Grapes

Whereas both Labruscas and Muscadines have easily identifiable grape flavors, there are other *Vitis* species whose fruit has a more aciduously anonymous character (sweet Bing cherries versus sour pie cherries are analogous). Among these other *Vitis* species, *V. riparia* and *V. aestivalis* have long been considered excellent for the production of dry, usually red, table wine.

Wild vines of *Vitis riparia* have been selected for cultivation in Minnesota both for red wine and for breeding stock. Riparia is the earliest ripening and most winter-hardy of native American vines. The grapes contribute dark color, high sugar, high acid, and a herbaceous (grassy), berrylike flavor to wine. One of the most successful French-American crosses, Baco noir, is a first-generation cross between Riparia and Vinifera.

Vitis aestivalis grows wild in most of the eastern region. The grapes are small, dark, and have relatively little juice. They produce a rich red wine with an astringent, "coffeelike" character. In a 1911 USDA bulletin (no. 145), "enological chemist" William B. Alwood reported the following about Norton, an Aestivalis variety grown near Charlottesville, Virginia: "These show a very high average sugar content and an average acid content of less than 1 per cent. This is certainly a high quality and warrants the statement that such a juice needs very little change in composition for wine making. The maximum sugar content found, of 22.34 per cent, with 0.902 of total acid, is phenomenal for a strictly American grape." Norton and its close relative Cynthiana today produce excellent red wines, primarily in the Midwest.

Several new wine varieties have been bred in Florida, including the red Conquistador and the white Stover. Their genealogy includes such little-known native species as *V. smalliana*, *V. Simpsonii*, and *V. Shuttleworthii* crossed with European-American varieties. These grapes are remarkable for their resistance to both Pierce's disease and the fungus diseases that thrive in the tropical Deep South.

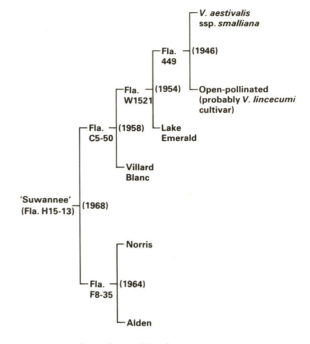

Genealogy of the Suwannee grape

Some other *Vitis* varieties described in Chapter 7: Conquistador, Cynthiana, Herbemont, Lenoir, Norton, Stover.

European-American Wine Grapes

In the European-American class are wine grapes bred to overcome the numerous obstacles presented by nature and still produce wines with Vinifera character and quality. Many varieties are already in use and there is a steady flow of new crosses, making this a dynamic group. From an ecological standpoint, naturally disease-resistant vines mean less need for fungicides and less fuel for the tractor. This in turn improves the economic viability of vineyards.

Both eastern and western European scientists are breeding for mildew and cold resistance in grapes. The USDA has a breeding program for black rot resistance. California and several southern states are creating new wine grapes that are resistant to Pierce's disease. There is grape-breeding and -testing activity, both amateur and

Removing the flower cap and emasculating the anthers

professional, in almost every eastern state. Improved grape varieties are of real importance to the future of grape growing in the eastern United States and Canada.

The largest sector of the European-American class is presently comprised of the French-American varieties, also known as "French Hybrids" or "Hybrid Direct Producers." These grapes are the viticultural children of amateur breeders in France who, from 1880 to 1960, created their own answer to the phylloxera-mildew crisis. There were enough growers in France who were satisfied with the wines of the *hybrides producteurs directs* to plant nearly one million acres of them. In 1958, the *h.p.d.*'s represented one-third of France's three million acres of vines.

These modern crosses between American species and *Vitis vinifera* were an innovation in a centuries-old, world-renowned industry, and many French winemakers saw them as a threat to established traditions. The fact that these varieties had new and different flavor elements created a dilemma for those in charge of maintaining the traditional quality and character of French

Pollinating the pistils of a mother vine

Bagging a mother cluster to protect it from stray pollen

wines. Beginning in 1927, all American and French-American varieties were officially barred from Appelation d'Origine Contrôlée wines, although they were permitted in nonappellation table wines or "vin ordinaire."

French-American varieties in France nearly doubled in acreage—from 534,000 acres to 994,000 acres—from 1929 to 1958. These were difficult times economically for Europe, exacerbated by the ravages of World War II. The crosses of Messieurs Seibel, Seyve-Villard, Baco, and others produced larger crops with less work than did pure Vinifera vines. The French people, especially those in areas where growing conditions were climatically difficult, were willing to accept wines that were different from their traditional fare but more easily affordable to produce.

In the 1950s, because of the economic problems posed by serious and chronic overproduction of table wine (for which Algeria was largely responsible), the French government instituted a nationwide variety classification system designed to reduce the number of highly productive but lesser valued grapes. Most of the French-American and half the Vinifera varieties were named for gradual phasing out of the national vineyard.

Since 1958, acreage of direct producers in France has declined approximately 200,000 acres every ten years. At that rate, there will still be French-American vineyards in France in the next century. Official nursery statistics for 1975–76 show that French nurserymen planted 8.5 million own-rooted and 3.5 million grafted *h.p.d.* cuttings (about 3.5 percent of the official total nursery planting for that year).

The process of selecting the best French-American varieties for eastern conditions began in the 1930s and accelerated substantially in the 1970s. It takes a minimum of ten years after planting to be able even to glimpse a variety's commercial value. Chelois, Cascade, and De Chaunac, formerly in the vanguard of the eastern wine boom, are now yielding ground to Seyval, Vidal, and others. Some of this change is due to the inherent qualities of the varieties themselves and some to the shifting market demands, most recently the "white wine boom."

The European-American class is growing with new crosses from breeding stations both here and abroad. One recent European-American variety that has entered commercial channels from the Geneva (N.Y.) Station is Cayuga White. Its debut as a varietal wine came in 1977 when it was marketed by Widmer's Wine Cellars. In 1984 over twenty wineries were producing Cayuga Whites. A similar destiny awaits a select few new varieties now under trial in experimental vineyards around the world.

Fortunately, the 1970s' wave of "grape-variety racism" that tended to prevent fair assessment of European-American wines is receding, as is the snobbism that was once a prerequisite for wine criticism. Thanks to the widespread inauguration of "blind" wine tastings, a new wave of wine consumers and even critics is now judging wines according to merit rather than seniority. Even Europeans are reassessing the politics of "racial" discrimination in the Common Market now that there is a new generation of complex crosses

Chambourcin rosé wine sold at roadside stand in France's Loire Valley, 1980

between Vinifera and French-American varieties that are too good to ignore.

In truth, most wine consumers are no more concerned with the genetic background of their wines than with that of their dinner steak. Did it come from an Angus, a Hereford, or an Angus-Hereford cross? As long as the meat is tender, flavorful, and cooked according to instructions, no one really cares (except perhaps a person planning to raise cattle). There are three places where the genetic makeup of a vine is important: in the vineyard, in the bottle, and in the pocketbook. The protocol of placement on the varietal totem pole is strictly a private affair.

Some European-American varieties discussed in Chapter 7: Aurore, Baco noir, Canada Muscat, Cascade, Cayuga White, Chambourcin, Chancellor, Chelois, Colobel, Couderc noir, De Chaunac, Florental, Horizon, Maréchal Foch, Léon Millot, Ravat noir, Rayon d'Or, Rosette, Rou-

Callusing boxes of grafted Vinifera vines

caneuf, Rougeon, Seyval, Siegfried, Veeblanc, Verdelet, Vidal blanc, Vignoles, Villard blanc, Villard noir.

Rootstocks

In the East many native varieties are grown for their fruit, whereas in most of the rest of the world the native vines serve in the vital role of rootstock. By grafting traditional Vinifera varieties onto American stocks, Europeans were able to save their wine industry. Most rootstocks used today were developed nearly a century ago at the time of the phylloxera crisis. The three phylloxera-resistant species which have proved the most useful are *Vitis riparia*, *Vitis rupestris*, and *Vitis Berlandieri*.

Jay Truluck and Doug Flemer trim wild Riparia wood found growing along the Greyton H. Memorial Drive in Hammondsport, N.Y., for use as rootstock.

Close-up of an emerging grafted Vinifera shoot

Riparia

As its name implies, Riparia prefers the rich, humid soils found along riverbanks. It is a rampant grower, with long, trailing canes and fine roots that spread laterally and not very deep. A short-season vine, it roots and grafts readily. The large, dark-green leaves and lush growth of a Riparia vine are deceptive in terms of its performance as a rootstock, in which it is rated as weak. Riparia roots seem to restrain the growth of Vinifera vines grafted to them, a characteristic that is considered useful on rich soils with such vigorous growers as Cabernet Sauvignon, Sauvignon blanc, and Gewürztraminer. Eastern growers have found that canes (green shoots that have gone dormant) of pencil-size or slightly larger diameter survive cold winters better than "bull canes" with thumb-size or larger diameters, and a weak rootstock is one way to put the brakes on vegetative vigor. Riparia Gloire de Montpellier is the only commercially available pure Riparia stock. Those who live north of the South and

Gulf states, however, can find abundant Riparia wood entwined in nearby trees.

Rupestris

For everything said above about *Vitis riparia*, the reverse is true of *Vitis rupestris*. This midwestern species grows more like a bush than a vine, with short, spindling shoots and a root system that is strongly vertical, reaching far into deep soils for water and minerals. It has a very long vegetative cycle (circa 260 days). Because of its extreme vigor, late maturity, and dislike for humid soils, it is not recommended in the East. The most widely cultivated pure Rupestris stock is Rupestris St. George (called Rupestris du Lot in France). However, 3309 Couderc, a Riparia × Rupestris cross, is a standard eastern rootstock variety. Rupestris is a rare find in the wild today; its habitat is in the southwestern quadrant of the East.

Berlandieri

Native to Texas, Berlandieri has a long vegetative cycle, good resistance to phylloxera, and excellent resistance to iron deficiency caused by high pH soils. Pure Berlandieri vines are very difficult to root, which makes hybridization with other species necessary for commercially viable rootstocks. Although eastern soils are on the acid side, two of the most prevalent stocks in the East, SO4 and 5BB, are Riparia × Berlandieri crosses.

Eastern growers are often not sure what rootstock to use. Where to find it can be even more problematic. One common method of choosing rootstocks is by default—that is, taking what a nursery can supply right away. A preferable way is to place an order with a nursery in the fall, having the nursery graft the specified varieties, grow them for a season, and deliver dormant-rooted plants for planting the following fall or spring a year later.

A great deal more time will have to pass and experience gained before we will be able to determine optimal rootstocks for various varieties grown in various places. Those Vinifera growers who must be concerned with properly maturing their vines in order to avoid winter injury should consider the following stocks, listed according to the amount of vigor they impart to the scion:

Weakest:	Riparia Gloire
Weaker:	101–14 Millardet et de Grasset., 420 A, 1616 Couderc
Medium vigor:	3309 Couderc, SO 4, 5 BB

7 ABC GUIDE TO EASTERN WINE GRAPES

The following list of varieties and key grape breeders (asterisk), some of whose wine grapes are yet unnamed, is designed to help orient the reader who gets a present of an eastern wine with an unfamiliar name on the label. It does not pretend to be a definitive compendium of every grape that grows east of the Rockies but is intended more as a Who's Who in Eastern Wine Grapes compiled from my personal experience. Some Vinifera varieties that are well described in the great body of international wine literature are not listed below because their plantings in the East are still very small. On the other hand, esoteric, exclusively eastern grapes may be included despite equally small acreage.

Aligoté	Cayuga White	Diamond	*Kuhlmann	Norton	*Seyve-Villard
Aurore		Dutchess	LaCrosse	Pinot noir	Siegfried
Baco noir	Chambourcin	Edelweiss	*Landot	Ravat noir	Steuben
Beta	Chancellor	Elvira	Lenoir	Rayon d'Or	Stover
*Burdin	Chardonnay	Florental	Magnolia	Riesling	Suwannee
Cabernet franc	Chelois	Foch/Joffre	Merlot	Rosette	*Swenson
	Colobel	Fredonia	Millot (Léon Millot)	Roucaneuf	Veeblanc
Cabernet Sauvignon	Concord	Gamay	Missouri Riesling	Rougeon	Ventura
	Conquista-dor	Gewürztraminer	*Munson	St. Croix	Verdelet
Canada Muscat	Couderc noir	Herbemont	Muscat varieties	Sauvignon blanc	Vidal blanc
		Horizon	New York 65.533.13		Vignoles
Carlos		Iona		Scuppernong	Villard blanc
Carmine	Cynthiana	Isabella	Niagara	*Seibel	Villard blanc
Cascade	De Chaunac	Ives	Noah	Sémillon	Villard noir
Catawba	Delaware	Kay Gray	Noble	Seyval blanc	

Classification Symbols for Grape Varieties

[V]   = Vinifera
[NA/L]   = native American/Labrusca
[NA/M]   = native American/Muscadine
[NA/OV]   = native American/other *Vitis*
[EA/C]   = European-American/Canada
[EA/F]   = European-American/France
[EA/G]   = European-American/Germany
[EA/US]   = European-American/United States

Eastern Grape Varieties

Aligoté.   Although a few agreeable wines have been produced, Aligoté is rare in the East. Where this white variety is grown, notably in the Burgundy region of France, it produces abundant crops of everyday table wine that is best consumed young. [V]

Aurore.   This early ripening white wine grape is a mainstay in New York and other northern states. It is a reliable producer of mildly fruity wine often used to blend with native American varieties. Alone it does well fermented German-style, producing wines of moderate alcohol, fruity, with varying degrees of sweetness. Buy a bottle for lunch or a picnic.

Because of its susceptibility to black rot and bunch rot, Aurore has little future in warmer regions where its early ripening ability is of no advantage. New crosses such as Horizon may eclipse Aurore in the future. [EA/F]

Baco noir.   Avid red-wine fans looking for something to enhance meat and potatoes will enjoy a bottle of Baco noir. If it is a recent vintage, it will have a strong, grassy character reminiscent of young Cabernet Sauvignon. There is nothing "soft" about Baco. Even when picked very ripe, it has high acidity. A Baco with good color and body (in poor years it can be thin) will benefit from a few years of aging.

Baco is found from Mississippi to Wisconsin. Its future appears stable but not expansive, at least not until there is increased demand for hearty reds. In the vineyard, Baco provides growers with the wildest, most prolific amount of foliage in the trade—excellent for dolmas (stuffed grape leaves) and shade, but a nuisance otherwise. [EA/F]

Beta.   This red Riparia-Concord variety was bred by Minnesota hybridizer Louis Suelter in the late nineteenth century. The vines withstand −30°F to −40°F, and the fruit ripens early with a large amount of acid. Beta is not likely to rise above the "when all else fails" class, especially now that new wine grapes with little or no Labrusca flavor are available from cold climate hybridizer Elmer Swenson. [NA/OV]

*Burdin.   The Burdins, father and son, had their best successes with crossing French-Americans with Gamay noir in the Beaujolais region between World Wars I and II. Burdin crosses (see Florental) are planted in a few eastern vineyards (Pennsylvania). They are regarded as moderate producers of superior wine. [EA/F]

Cabernet franc.   One of the famous red Bordeaux and Loire Valley varieties, Cabernet franc is currently grown on a very small scale in the East. Some Virginia growers report superior winter hardiness compared with Cabernet Sauvignon, its traditional blending partner. Wine quality is excellent both for reds and rosés. In long-season areas where Vinifera vines prove successful, this variety certainly has a place. [V]

Cabernet Sauvignon.   The most prestigious red wine grape in the world, Cabernet Sauvignon is widely but not extensively grown in the East. Blending Cabernet with French-American varieties such as Chambourcin and Chancellor has produced excellent results. Most Cabernet and Cabernet blends are aged in wood to add to their bouquet, body, and complexity. This additional cellar aging increases the cost of the wine, but also its longevity.

The problem of winter damage to trunks (which become infected with crown gall) is best controlled by curbing this variety's naturally vigorous growth. Of all the Viniferas now planted in

Cabernet Sauvignon

the East, Cabernet has the least problem with fungus diseases or rot on the fruit. Its late bud-break in the spring helps it avoid damage due to late frost. Cabernet flourishes on New York's Long Island and locations throughout the East where the growing season is sufficiently long to ripen the fruit. [V]

Canada Muscat. Released by the Geneva station in 1961, this late-ripening Muscat Hamburg (× Hubbard) cross has not been widely planted and does not appear to have a future in the premium wine class. [EA/US]

Carlos. Introduced in 1970 by the North Carolina Agricultural Experiment Station, Carlos is a perfect-flowered Muscadine bearing bronze fruit with a flavor similar to Scuppernong. Carlos may be found as a varietal white wine in several southern states. It is rarely vinified completely dry. [NA/M]

Carmine. Harold Olmo, plant geneticist emeritus at the University of California, Davis, released this Cabernet-Carignane-Merlot cross in 1976. I saw this variety flourishing in a vineyard in Georgia and was most impressed with the wine made from it, which tasted like a rich Cabernet-Merlot blend. This is a grape worthy of

further trial in suitable areas of the East as long as clean (virus-free) stock is available. It could give Cabernet Sauvignon some competition for vineyard space. [V]

Cascade. This early-ripening Seibel red is for the most part a "has been" on the eastern scene. Vineyard performance can be seriously undermined by the ring-spot viruses, to which it is very susceptible. Other than its low acidity, Cascade contributes little to a blend. It makes a fair rosé. [EA/F]

Catawba. America's foremost wine grape of the nineteenth century is still alive and well in eastern America, most notably in New York and the Midwest. For a while, strong Labrusca character and a large dose of sugar, especially in "Pink" Catawbas, had connoisseurs running the other way. Today, progressive eastern winemakers are coming up with entirely new winemaking techniques for this veteran grape. Dry varietals and brut champagnes made with 100 percent Catawba juice are appearing which will suit many modern palates. Catawbas are made in a diversity of styles, so it is a wine to taste before you buy. [NA/L]

Cayuga White. Since its release from New York's Geneva station in 1972, this Seyval by Schuyler (Zinfandel × Ontario) cross has gained a substantial following. It is a good producer with excellent disease resistance. It is only moderately winter hardy, however: a factor that will ultimately determine its boundaries. Cayuga has a delicate, fruity flavor complemented by an especially pleasant aftertaste even when finished dry. [EA/US]

Chambourcin. Of undisclosed parentage, Chambourcin is one of the finest eastern red varieties. It is popular in the Loire Valley–Touraine region of France possibly because it has the similar ability of that region's traditional Vinifera variety, Cabernet franc, to make both rich red and fruity rosé wines. In 1980 I was able to purchase Chambourcin rosé at a roadside stand in the Muscadet region. A late-ripener, Chambourcin is suited to long-season areas; it is sparsely planted in a number of states. [EA/F]

Chancellor. A favorite Seibel red "direct producer" in France, Chancellor covered nearly 100,000 acres there in 1958. Its popularity was owing to its ability to yield large crops of well-balanced fruit that made deeply colored wine. Chancellor is often fermented in a traditional claret style with wood aging. It is considered compatible with most other red varieties in a blend. Mildew susceptibility has limited its popularity in some vineyards, but in the event of an eastern red wine boom, acreage of Chancellor is likely to increase. [EA/F]

Chardonnay. Presently enjoying an international vogue, this noble Burgundian grape is represented at more U.S. wineries than any other white. Any eastern winery producing Vin-

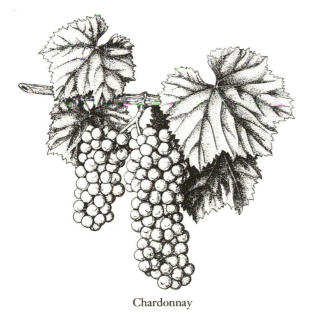

Chardonnay

ifera wines will almost certainly produce a Chardonnay. There is tremendous variation among Chardonnay wines throughout the East, owing to young vines, different vineyard climates, and varying winemaking techniques. One can find light, fruity Chardonnays; big, buttery "California"-style Chardonnays; or classic, austere French-style Chardonnays (also found in California). Because they are—regardless of style—selling out before the label glue dries, many Chardonnays are sold and consumed before they have had time to develop to their maximum quality.

Chardonnay is one of the more winter-hardy Vinifera varieties in terms of ability to withstand low temperatures. Unseasonably warm periods during winter, however, can fool Chardonnay buds into pushing prematurely and cause them to be killed when the weather turns cold again. Because it buds out early, it is especially threatened by spring frost damage as well. [V]

Chelois. Pronounced shell-wah, this Seibel variety does well as a Burgundy-style red that will age gracefully. When fully ripe, the grapes supply good fruit and body to any blend. In well-drained, preferably deep soil, the vines grow luxuriantly and produce abundantly. Unfortunately, there have been reports of virus problems causing early decline in Chelois plantings. Acreage is not now expanding, but healthy Chelois definitely have a place in hearty eastern reds, especially where early mid-season ripening is needed. [EA/F]

Colobel. It is rare to find a Colobel wine because this grape's real purpose is to be a *teinturier* or color grape. Having approximately ten times the color intensity of average red wine, Colobel is needed only in small amounts in blending. Where this variety was authorized in France, the legal limit of Colobel addition was 5 percent. Most eastern reds have ample color, so there is little need for the cultivation of Colobel. Another Seibel *teinturier* cross, Salvador, is grown on a commercial scale in California but not in the East. [EA/F]

Concord. Specialty items such as port, sherry, and Kosher wine are valid uses for ripe Concords. Unripe or "green" Concords make serviceable champagne blending stock. Sweet Concord wine is still a popular seller at many eastern wineries. Concord is poorly qualified for dry table wine, but pure Concord juice makes a fine children's "varietal." [NA/L]

Conquistador. Released in 1983 by the University of Florida, this is a purple bunch grape recommended by the university for wine. The fruit tastes like one of its progenitors, Concord, but the wine is said to be superior. It is resistant to Pierce's disease. [NA/OV]

Couderc noir. This Rupestris-Aestivalis × Vinifera cross was one of the earliest to appear in France. It is a vigorous, high-yielding variety suited to warm regions because of its late maturity. To date it is grown only on a few acres in the Midwest. The wine has good color, Aestivalis character, and is said to make a good rosé. Georges Couderc (1850–1928) planted 480,000 grape seeds over forty-two years. Couderc noir and the rootstock 3309 Couderc are the most enduring progeny. [EA/F]

Cynthiana. There is an ampelographic (grapevine identification) question that has been kept alive for well over a century as to whether Cynthiana and Norton are in fact identical. No one doubts that they are almost indistinguishable from each other in the vineyard, but most viticulturists of the nineteenth century concluded that these "twin sisters" are genetically distinct individuals.

Cynthiana was discovered growing in Arkansas and was first popularized by nurseryman William Prince of Long Island, New York, circa 1850. Prince sent cuttings to George Husmann in Hermann, Missouri, in 1858. According to Husmann, despite similar foliage, the fruit and wine of Cynthiana were different from those of the Norton then already under commercial cultivation in Missouri.

Cynthiana has a somewhat larger, earlier maturing fruit said to be less tannic and "coffeelike"

than Norton. The wine, considered spicy and delicate, won the top award as "best red wine of all nations" at the 1873 Vienna World Exposition. Both Cynthiana and Norton, useless as table grapes, were considered peerless as red wine grapes in the United States by all who were familiar with them. They are currently grown commercially only in Missouri and Arkansas, but other regions with long growing seasons are beginning to take notice of the potential of these former champions. [NA/OV]

De Chaunac. Pronounced de-*show*-nack, this is an early ripening, productive, disease-resistant vine. In any experimental plot, no matter how neglected, this Seibel cross stands out. When the table-wine boom came east, many of the large wineries felt De Chaunac would meet their needs for a basic red wine grape. Thousands of acres were planted, largely in New York and Ontario, in the early 1970s.

By the time this acreage came into production, it was already becoming clear that a serious case of overplanting had occurred. Large tonnages of mediocre red fruit flooded a market thirsty for whites. In the grape industry, surplus is the mother of invention. There are sparkling, rosé, nouveau, dessert, and even white De Chaunac wines on the market as well as many styles of red. As winemakers gain experience, increasingly good wines are coming from a grape whose fan club is somewhat limited. (Even Canadian enologist Adhemar De Chaunac himself is said to have preferred Chelois.) [EA/F]

Delaware. Now that quick transport to a winery equipped with temperature-controlled tanks has become the rule rather than the exception, Delaware should be able to retain its position as a fine eastern variety even in the face of stiff competition from newer grape varieties. This high-sugar, attractive pink grape, when properly handled (that is, not allowed to oxidize) can make an excellent dry white wine. Light, flowery, slightly sweet, Delaware dessert wines are currently good sellers for the wineries that produce them. Delaware has long been used in premium champagne blends.

Delaware's hazy origins (Labrusca-Aestivalis-Vinifera) trace back to Frenchtown, New Jersey, in 1849, but its name comes from a small town in Ohio where it was first popularized. Although it is winter-hardy, it is not one of the easiest grapes to grow: it is finicky about soil conditions and sometimes requires grafting. The mildews are attracted to the delicate leaves and fruit and must be vigilantly kept at bay. Delaware has long occupied a special place among the native American varieties with moderate Labrusca character and shall no doubt continue to do so. Delaware, by the way, is a popular table grape today in Japan. [NA/L]

Diamond (Moore's Diamond). Born in 1873 of Concord and Iona parents at the hand of Jacob Moore in Brighton, New York, Diamond ranks among the better native American varieties for white wines. It survives today only on a very limited scale, produced by a scant handful of wineries. [NA/L]

Dutchess. Dutchess is the third of the "Three D's" of premium native wine grapes. Hybridized in 1868 by A. J. Caywood of Marlboro, New York, there is Delaware in its parentage. According to Pennsylvania winegrower Douglas P. Moorhead, this is one of very few whites to improve with age, easily for ten years. It does well with oak aging and makes good dry wine, although it is usually finished sweet. There is almost no Labrusca in the aroma. Dutchess is a good candidate for light or low-alcohol wines since the acid levels are relatively low at low sugar levels. Today Dutchess is found chiefly in New York and Pennsylvania, where it should be grown only in well-drained, moderately fertile soils. [NA/L]

Edelweiss. A large-clustered, early maturing white grape with Labrusca character, Edelweiss was bred by Elmer Swenson and released by the University of Minnesota in the late 1960s. New, more neutral-flavored crosses, which have even better winter hardiness than Edelweiss, are being developed by Swenson and other Minnesota breeders. [NA/L]

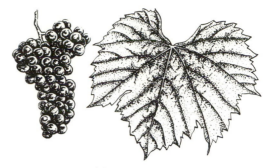

Maréchal Foch

Elvira. Ranking as one of the better of the native Americans, Elvira is still grown commercially in New York and Ontario. Rarely found as a varietal, it is mostly used for blending by large wineries. Elvira is a white-berried offspring of Taylor (Labrusca × Riparia) introduced by Jacob Rommel of Missouri in 1869. [NA/L]

Florental. The Gamay noir parentage of this Burdin cross is said to be readily apparent in the "Beaujolais" character of its wine. It might be a valuable addition to cool-region vineyards because of its productivity and early maturity; however, it is a delicate vine requiring grafting and a vigilant spray program. Further experimentation is warranted. [EA/F]

Foch (Maréchal Foch)/Joffre. Some of the East's finest reds have come from this very small-clustered Kuhlmann cross. As one of the earliest ripening varieties, it can be grown in the most northerly regions and in cool, mountainous areas with short growing seasons. Early in the dis-

Joffre

tribution of the French-American crosses in the United States and Canada, two Kuhlmann varieties came out under the name of Foch and two under Millot. All have identical parentage. Often a small percentage of Maréchal Joffre is unwittingly planted in with Foch and is detectable in the vineyard by its earlier ripening and different appearance.

The wines of both "Foch" varieties are similar, with strong flavor and intense color. The strong Foch character is agreeably attenuated by wood aging or, in a nouveau style, by carbonic maceration. [EA/F]

Fredonia. Rarely produced as a varietal, Fredonia is used mainly for sherry production. It is a standard native American cross released by the Geneva station in 1927 and grown primarily in New York and Ontario. [NA/L]

Gamay. Ontario is the most likely place to find the true Gamay noir of France's Beaujolais region. Canadians have been importing vines directly from Europe, whereas U.S. propagation stock has effectively been limited to a single source in California by USDA import regulations. There are two other "Gamays" in California: Gamay Beaujolais, a Pinot noir clone, and Napa Gamay, known in France as Valdiguié.

Each of these Gamays is capable of making fine wine, but a vineyard inspection will be needed to determine which of the three possibilities has been vinified. None of the three Gamays is as yet cultivated on a large scale in the East. [V]

Gewürztraminer. A favorite of the Alsace region of France, this spicy pink grape has brought both good and bad news to the eastern United States. The good news is the fine wine with excellent character it has made here; the bad news is the high incidence of winter damage to the vines. If its vigorous vegetative growth can be controlled by a low-nitrogen diet or by other means, Gewürztraminer's chances of survival may improve. [V]

Herbemont. This is one of those thoroughly American varieties that caught on so well during the phylloxera crisis in France that in 1934 the French government prohibited further planting and paid stipends for its removal. By 1958 only 6,650 acres remained, and today acreage is undoubtedly far less. It is a spontaneous Aestivalis-Cinerea-Vinifera variety known since 1788, when it was propagated from an old vine in Columbia, South Carolina, by Nicolas Herbemont. The same grape was cultivated in Georgia under the name Warren.

Unlike its sister variety, Lenoir, this black-skinned grape has white juice and has been used to make white wine. Its resistance to Pierce's disease enables it to flourish in many parts of the South. Only by taking a trip to Del Rio, Texas, can we taste a commercially grown Herbemont where it has been cultivated by several generations of the Qualia family. [NA/OV]

Horizon. Formerly G.W. #7, this is one of the newest releases of the Geneva station, the forty-seventh in the station's first century of activity. Horizon is a sister seedling of Cayuga White (Seyval blanc × Schuyler). Wine quality has been rated somewhat inferior to Cayuga but superior to Aurore. Given its better performance over both in the vineyard, Horizon may become the choice of cool-region growers for a low acid, neutral-flavored white grape used for blending. [EA/US]

Iona. This Labrusca family seedling of Diana (itself a seedling of Catawba) originated in 1855 on the Hudson River's Iona Island in New York. The pale red grapes have historically been credited with good vinous character (and are reputed to have excellent keeping qualities in a root cellar). The vine thrives only in very well-drained soils and non-humid climates. Iona lives today in a few New York vineyards and is favored for rosé at one winery in Conesus–on–Hemlock Lake. [NA/L]

Isabella. Only rarely produced as a varietal wine, this early American variety does not rank in the forefront of native Americans for wine. According to Frank Schoonmaker, it was through "sheer stupidity or bad luck" that Isabella was fairly widely planted in southern Switzerland and northern Italy, where it was known as the *uva fragola* or strawberry grape. In fact, Isabella has been planted on nearly every continent, an honor not merited by the wine quality of this thick-skinned, dark purple grape with a musky aroma. [NA/L]

Ives. Strong red color and good disease resistance have kept Ives under cultivation since it was raised from seed by Cincinnatian Henry Ives in the 1840s. With its strong, unrefined Labrusca character, Ives's present and future utility for table wine is nonexistent. [NA/L]

Kay Gray. A recent Swenson release that survives Minnesota winters very well, even at less than −30°F, Kay Gray produces a pleasant, mildly fruity white wine. [EA/VS]

*Kuhlmann. When Alsace was returned to France after World War I, Eugene Kuhlmann (1858–1932) put several of his interspecific crosses on the market. Genetic siblings (Riparia-Rupestris-Vinifera) Foch, Millot, Joffre, and Lucie Kuhlmann have been the most popular. All four have entered U.S. vineyards, but there is some confusion as to which is which. Whereas Foch, Millot, and Joffre have a Burgundy-like character, Lucie Kuhlmann is said to more closely resemble Bordeaux. These varieties need to be positively identified in the vineyard before their individual performances in the bottle can be properly evaluated. [EA/F]

LaCrosse. Elmer Swenson used Seyval blanc as one of the parents to produce this white wine grape suited to cold northern climates. LaCrosse will withstand much colder temperatures and ripens earlier than Seyval. The wine is not unlike that of Seyval but has a trace of muscat in the aroma. [EA/US]

*Landot. Two of Pierre Landot's (1900–1942) crosses, Landal (Landot 244) and Landot noir (Landot 4511), are grown on a limited, but commercial basis today. The wine quality is usually excellent. [EA/F]

Lenoir. About 1859, under the name of Jacques, Lenoir traveled from Georgia to southern France. While phylloxera was killing off all the vines around it, Jacques continued to thrive and produce dark, highly sugared, black-currant-flavored wine. Eager for more vines, the French were told that Jacques had been abandoned and was unobtainable. Several years of investigation by Missouri nurseryman Isidor Bush uncovered the fact that the mysterious Jacques, or Jacquez, was identical to the variety Black Spanish, also called Lenoir. Like Herbemont, Lenoir was banned in France in 1934. Thanks to its resistance to Pierce's disease, it lives on in Del Rio, Texas, where it is produced as a varietal wine. [NA/OV]

Magnolia. This popular, perfect-flowered Muscadine was introduced in 1961 by the North Carolina Agricultural Experiment Station and the USDA. The light bronze grapes are sweet and considered excellent for white wine. Magnolia is produced as a varietal by wineries in several southern states. [NA/M]

Merlot. Producing a softer, fruitier wine than its blending partner Cabernet Sauvignon, this Bordeaux native stands very well on its own. The few eastern Merlot wines marketed to date have been excellent examples. Unfortunately, lack of winter-hardiness will limit its culture to only the most climatically moderate sites. [V]

Millot (Léon Millot). This small-clustered, very early ripening variety is a good choice for short growing seasons. It is complementary to other varieties in a blend and produces a fine varietal. Currently overshadowed by its more notorious sibling, Foch, Millot has a solid place in future eastern reds. The two Millot "clones"

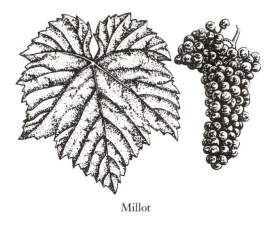

Millot

are, in fact, different varieties (see *Kuhlmann* above); for years they have been identified as the Foster Millot and the Boordy Millot. [EA/F]

Missouri Riesling. This Taylor (Labrusca × Riparia) seedling originated in Hermann, Missouri, circa 1870. It has not the slightest relation to the Johannisberg or any other Riesling in the world. Missouri Riesling is still grown for Labrusca-flavored white wine in Missouri and will probably continue there on a limited scale. [NA/L]

Muscat blanc

Munson. Texan Thomas V. Munson introduced several hundred grape varieties between 1890 and his death in 1913. A portion of these may be found at Denison in Grayson County, Texas, in the T. V. Munson Memorial Vineyard. At the present time, only a handful of his cultivars, including Neva Munson, Muench, and Ellen Scott are grown commercially to a very limited extent. [NA/OV, EA/US]

Muscat varieties. In refreshing, sweet, sparkling, or light dessert wines, a muscat aroma is nearly always greeted with delight. Italy's Asti Spumante contains muscat grapes. There are several grape varieties found in the East capable of producing muscat-flavored wines.

Three Vinifera varieties are Muscat Ottonel, Muscadelle (of Bordeaux), Muscat blanc (synonymous with Frontignan and Canelli). In 1961 the Geneva station released Canada Muscat, a white, and New York Muscat, a red, to provide more hardy vines with muscat character. There is a white Couderc cross, Muscat du Moulin, which produces muscat grapes that are, according to Philip Wagner, coarse-flavored in comparison with the muscat fruit of Seyve-Villard 14.287. All of these varieties are rare finds in the East. [V and EA/US]

New York 65.533.13. Just when this Johannes Seyve 23.416 (half Chancellor) × Gewürztraminer cross was about to be released by the Geneva station, the mother vines showed symptoms of virus infection, delaying its scheduled 1982 debut. Test wines of this variety have been promisingly fruity and spicy and should make a welcome addition to the European-American class. [EA/US]

Niagara. In the native American division, Niagara is unquestionably "the people's white." It is the greenish-white grape, alias "white Concord," that grows next to blue Concord in every backyard arbor. Since it does not ship well, it is best eaten straight off the vine. For inexpensive, sweet, uncomplicated Labrusca-flavored wine, Niagara has been the favorite since its introduction in the early 1870s and is likely to remain so in its class, however humble. [NA/L]

Noah.   Raised from seed by Otto Wasserzieher of Nauvoo, Illinois, in 1869, Noah bore its first greenish yellow fruit in 1873. While not considered an addition to the table-grape pool, it did show qualities for wine (high sugar and balanced acid). Eastern and western Europeans took a special liking to this hardy, rustic vine during the phylloxera siege and planted many thousands of acres of Noah despite its marked Labrusca flavor.

During Noah's apex in France there was sufficient acreage for 22 million gallons of *vin de table*. No wonder the government took steps in 1934 to ban this unfair competition to their more troublesome Vinifera vines. As popular as Noah was abroad, it never was warmly embraced back home. Curious enophiles might still find a few Noahs in southern New Jersey. [NA/L]

Noble.   Crossed in 1946 at the North Carolina Agricultural Experiment Station, Noble was introduced in 1971. Because of the relative stability of its pigments, it is to date the most popular black-berried Muscadine variety with southern wineries. The deep reds and rosés are often varietally labeled. [NA/M]

Norton (Virginia Seedling).   Although Norton's origin is still obscure, D. N. Norton of Richmond, Virginia, is credited with introducing the grape to general notice in the 1830s. Not until about 1845 when it was first planted in Hermann, Missouri, did Norton begin its commercial rise to international acclaim. According to George Husmann, "it caused a revolution in grape culture here [Missouri] as its merits as a uniformly reliable grape for red wine became fully known." Norton was enthusiastically planted in Virginia as well, where it was the base for renowned "clarets."

Norton wine was said to be deep-colored, full-bodied, astringent, and characteristically coffee-flavored. Its richness was such that blending was recommended to keep it from being too heavy.

Both Norton and Cynthiana have been kept alive commercially in Missouri and Arkansas, and interest is spreading to other states sufficiently warm to ripen them. In these varieties rests the best potential for cellar-aged wines made from pure native American grapes. [NA/OV]

Pinot noir.   This ancient Burgundian variety is grown on a small scale in many eastern states, both for champagne and red wine. It is low-yielding with small, compact clusters that are very susceptible to bunch rot as well as the other fungus diseases. Through trial and error, the French and the Californians have already discovered how few areas bring out the best qualities of this finicky grape—now eastern growers are beginning the process. Pinot blanc and Pinot gris are grown only experimentally in the East at this time. [V]

Ravat noir.   Ravat noir is half Seibel cross and half Pinot noir. Because of its low productivity and disease susceptibility, it is not destined for extensive planting. The wines it produces, however, are excellent with definite Burgundian character and are well worth trying when available. If you come across a white "Ravat," it is Ravat noir's sister Vignoles. [EA/F]

Rayon d'Or.   This Seibel cross with the glimmering name adds a spicy fruitiness to any blend and makes a pleasing still or sparkling varietal. Rayon d'Or enjoyed considerable popularity in France because of its early mid-season ripening and ability to reach high sugar in cool regions. A regular producer, its only cultural fault is the tightness of its golden clusters, which causes bunch rot unless they are picked very promptly. Rayon d'Or will endure on the eastern stage, but probably only as a member of the chorus. [EA/F]

Riesling.   Also known as White or Johannisberg Riesling, this is the variety that made the Mosel and Rhine rivers famous. In spite of its late fruit maturity, Riesling is a favorite of cooler climates. Riesling grapes develop their fruity aro-

Riesling

ma at relatively low sugar levels. In addition, the vines are among the most winter-hardy of the Viniferas. Late bud-break helps reduce the chances of spring frost damage.

The only real cultural difficulty with Riesling is its vulnerability to bunch rot, which in warm, humid climates can be decidedly unnoble. Because of its adaptability to many growing conditions, especially its winter-hardiness, Riesling is found in nearly every winegrowing state. With the use of German yeast strains and cold fermentation, some eastern Rieslings are ready to challenge Teutonic competition. As in Germany, the degree of sweetness is variable. [V]

Rosette. This early Seibel cross produces pleasant, neutral wines, usually light-bodied reds and rosés. Fruit set can be irregular and crops small, characteristics that reduce the popularity and future of Rosette. [EA/F]

Roucaneuf. This 1924 Seyve-Villard variety produces handsome clusters of ellipsoidal pink berries. Like its sister Villard blanc, Roucaneuf is late maturing and shows some tolerance to Pierce's disease. Whatever future there is for this vine lies in the South. [EA/F]

Rougeon. Several hundred acres planted in the 1970s probably represent the maximum acreage this Seibel cross will attain. The most notable feature of the wine, which can also be vinified as an attractive rosé, is its deep red color. Rougeon is an erratic producer—lots of fruit one year and nearly none the next. It has little future in the East. [EA/F]

St. Croix. Developed to stand up to temperatures as low as −40°F by Elmer Swenson, St. Croix has shown promise as a red-wine grape. Its low acid and neutral flavor are a welcome change from older cold-climate grapes like Beta. [EA/US]

Sauvignon blanc. Renowned both in Bordeaux and in the Loire Valley, Sauvignon blanc makes fine wine in the East, but only to a limited extent. Its vigorous vegetative growth is difficult to control, making it prone to winter injury. Wherever available, Sauvignon blanc is worth a try because those eastern wines produced to date have exhibited excellent varietal character. [V]

Scuppernong. In spite of the influx of new, perfect-flowered, bronze Muscadines (for example, Carlos, Magnolia), the female-flowered Scuppernong remains queen of the Rotundifolia clan. A North Carolina native selected from the wild at the beginning of the nineteenth century, Scuppernong has been preeminent in the South ever since. In 1982 this grape became the subject of a book: *Scuppernong* by Clarence Gohdes.

"Scuppernong" has become synonymous with white Muscadine. One must question the winemaker to discover just how much, if any, of the true Scuppernong is in a wine so labeled. It is still considered by many to make the superior product of its species. [NA/M]

*Seibel. The outstanding breeder of French-American crosses was unquestionably Albert Seibel (1844–1936). He began grape hybridizing in 1874. By the middle of the next

century, over 370,000 acres in France were planted with Seibel varieties such as Chancellor, Rayon d'Or, Aurore, Chelois, Verdelet, and De Chaunac. Most other breeders, including the Seyve brothers, Ravat, and Vidal, used Seibel crosses to make their own crosses. Nearly all plant breeders around the world today use Seibel progeny in developing superior wine grapes. [EA/F]

Sémillon. In Bordeaux, Sémillon is largely grown for Sauternes dessert wine. When used for dry table wine production there, it is generally blended with Sauvignon blanc and Muscadelle for additional complexity. A very few eastern wineries produce varietal Sémillon table wine, and their results have been worth trying. Sémillon is less winter hardy than either Chardonnay or Riesling. [V]

Seyval blanc. This was the first successful Seyve-Villard variety, dating from 1921. For the past two decades, Seyval has been the standard bearer of premium eastern whites. At first the wines were styled directly after French Chablis, that is, dry, flinty, somewhat oaky with subdued grape flavors. These wines were aim-

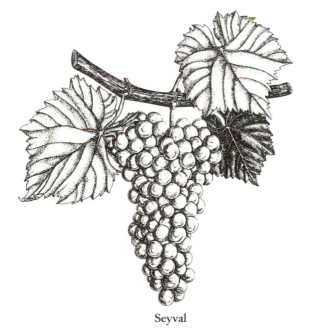

Seyval

ing for and achieving a European, specifically French, character. Wine consumers who had been equating the East with syrupy Labrusca wines were amazed and praised Seyval as "the Chardonnay of the East."

Today, as new wine styles and winemakers proliferate, Seyval is no longer necessarily a bone dry, austere dinner wine. Among the Seyval styles to be found are light, slightly spritzy; sweet, late harvest; fruity, dry, Sancerre-like; oaky, Chablis-like; semi-sweet, picnic; and sparkling.

With the rise of other varieties in the East such as Vignoles and Vidal blanc, Seyval no longer plays solo on center stage. It is, however, a grape of proven abilities both in the vineyard and cellar which will continue to be widely available. [EA/F]

*Seyve-Villard. Three members of the Seyve family were grape hydridizers. The crosses developed by the father, Bertille Seyve, are rarely found today. His two sons established competing nurseries. Joannes is most noted for Chambourcin. Bertille, Jr. married the daughter of early French hybridizer Victor Villard and chose to avoid confusion by marketing his crosses under the name Seyve-Villard. Several of his varieties, such as Seyval, Villard blanc and noir, and Roucaneuf, are of significance today in the East. [EA/F]

Siegfried (Siegfriedrebe). Produced at the Forschungsinstitut für Rebenzuechtung in Geilweilerhof, Germany, Siegfried is the result of a cross between Riesling and an Oberlin 595 seedling. In limited eastern trials, mostly in New York's Niagara district, Siegfried has proved itself to be a constant producer with good winterhardiness. According to grower Martin Schulze, Siegfried has high acidity and sugar levels that make a light, refreshing wine or champagne with a fruity aroma. Bunch rot and splitting of ripe fruit is a problem. Other "made in Germany" European-American crosses now under trial are thought to surpass Siegfried both in the vineyard and in the winery. [EA/G]

Steuben. Steuben was developed at New York's Geneva station and released in 1947 as a superior table/dessert grape. Recently, a few wineries around the East have found that the attractive blue-black grape also produces a well-received rosé. The wine has a light Labrusca flavor with a spicy, muscat-like fruitiness unique to this variety. [EA/US]

Stover. Stover, released in 1968, is the best wine grape to date from the Florida Agricultural Experiment Station. It is a Pierce's disease–tolerant cross between Mantey (thought to be one-half *V. Shuttleworthii*) by Roucaneuf. The fruit ripens in early July and produces a neutral, mildly fruity white wine. In Stover, the South has a neutral native grape to blend with the strong-flavored Muscadines. [NA/OV and EA/US]

Suwannee. Released in 1983 for commercial production by the University of Florida, this is a white, Pierce's disease–resistant bunch grape. The flavor is similar to Stover but with a hint of muscat. The wine has received scores superior to Stover in taste panels at the university. [NA/OV and EA/US]

*Swenson. Elmer Swenson began growing grapes on his farm in Star Prairie, Wisconsin, in the 1940s. He worked as a horticulturist for the University of Minnesota. Several hundred seedlings he has developed are now being evaluated for grape quality and, above all, cold-hardiness.

Swenson's goal has been to develop vines that will withstand −30° to −40°F after producing a commercial-size crop. Several of his named varieties have managed to do this in some years and are being used by Minnesota wineries. Edelweiss, Kay Gray, LaCrosse, and St. Croix are among his latest releases. [EA/US]

Veeblanc. This is a cross between Cascade and S-V.14-287 made at Ontario's Department of Agriculture Experimental Station at Vineland in 1953. Released in 1977, it is a white table wine variety that has not made an impact "south of the border." [EA/C]

Ventura. This Vineland cross between Chelois and Elvira was released in 1974. It is a white table wine grape of outstanding winter-hardiness in Canada which has not received much attention in the United States. [EA/C]

Verdelet. Verdelet is a delicate vine with delicate white clusters that make delicate wine. White-wine enthusiasts definitely should taste Verdelet if the opportunity arises. Chances will be somewhat limited, however, unless plantings of this Seibel cross are expanded. [EA/F]

Vidal blanc. Vidal is fast becoming one of the cornerstone varieties of the East. A favorite with growers, it is a productive, disease-resistant vine. Winemakers are finding that they have a great deal of flexibility when working with Vidal. It has a chameleonlike ability to change its character according to the environment. When grown in cool climates and fermented with German yeast and winemaking techniques, it resembles Riesling. Add some noble *botrytis* rot or very late-picked fruit and the similarity is even more pronounced.

Vidal blanc does have a pleasant vinous character similar to its mother, St. Emilion (known as Ugni Blanc in France and Trebbiano Toscano in Italy) and also some spiciness from its father,

Vidal

Villard blanc

Rayon d'Or. Excellent sparkling wines are being produced from it. Some wineries now have several styles of Vidal, both sweet and dry, with and without oak aging. Vidal may be found in almost all of the Eastern winegrowing states where bunch grapes are grown. [EA/F]

Vignoles.   Another of Ravat's Seibel by Pinot noir crosses, Vignoles is currently one of the finest eastern whites for cooler areas. This shy bearing, delicate vine has proven its quality in the Finger Lakes region both as a table and late harvest dessert wine. It is being tried in other regions and has a promising future in the premium class. [EA/F]

Villard blanc.   A late-ripening Seyve-Villard cross made in 1924, this variety is a grower's dream in warm climates but is not suited to cool regions. A tremendous hit in the south of France, its acreage actually increased there from 47,000 acres in 1958 to 53,000 in 1968. Villard blanc's popularity is due to its high yields of big healthy clusters. Winemakers tend to be less ecstatic than growers about this grape because it is uncooperative in the press and, due to a richness in iron, can be difficult to clarify.

For the French, Villard blanc provided a good, fruity, everyday table wine to be consumed young. It can do the same and more in the East, in the hands of an understanding winemaker. Look for Villard blanc in the warmer regions and areas subject to Pierce's disease—to which this variety has shown a degree of tolerance. [EA/F]

Villard noir.   Released around 1930, Villard noir increased in popularity in France from 1958 with 67,000 acres to 1968 with 75,000 acres. It overtook Chancellor, one of its parents, as the most popular French-American cross. This popularity has not extended across the Atlantic. Given the slow demand for red wines in general and competition from other varieties, Villard noir has never been widely planted. The wine is light-bodied, fruity, and low in tannin. It is a very suitable choice to fill a lunchtime carafe. In fact, that is probably where you will find it on your next trip to France. Villard noir is an easy-to-grow, productive grape suited to warm climates. [EA/F]

Part Three

Political Boundaries

8 WINE REGIONS AND STATE POLITICS: 1880s/1980s

Every wine is produced in a sociopolitical environment that is as critical for the producer as soil, climate, and grape variety are. Many wine-growing regions that share lake shores, river-banks, or valleys also traverse the borders of several states. Whereas states in these viticultural areas share very similar natural weather conditions, their political climates can be significantly different. Make-it-or-break-it regulations and taxation policies are formulated by U.S. state or Canadian provincial governments. Research, education, and extension programs depend on support from state agencies and institutions. Funds for marketing local wines are gathered by state-wide vineyard and winery organizations and sometimes by the state itself. The future success of winegrowers is thus dependent on the interest and vigor of state groups.

In the following chapters, the East has been subdivided into three main sections, and the states and provinces are listed alphabetically within each section. Personal accounts of grape-growing in 1880 introduce the discussion of near-ly every state. These accounts were first pub-lished in the USDA's Special Report No. 36, *Report upon Statistics of Grape Culture and Wine Production in the United States for 1880*. The com-ments of growers of the last century reflect the essential timelessness of viniculture, for these individual voices from the past resound with many of the same hopes and frustrations of mod-ern growers in the East and around the world. Although the insects and diseases that plagued vineyardists of the last century have largely been brought under control, the rigors and whims of nature and the marketplace have not. There is still much need for experimentation to match the right grape variety with a particular location. Striving to unite quality and profitability in a very competitive world market was as much a concern then as it is today.

Table wine is not booze, but it is often treated as such in the United States and Canada. There are low-cost wines whose sweet flavor and alco-holic content are the chief attraction, but these wines are *not* table wines (they do not comple-ment food) and they taint the image of fermented grape juice in the eyes of the American public. Just as some people should avoid salt or sugar, some should avoid alcohol altogether. Most peo-ple, however, can enjoy all three in moderation, and table wine certainly lends itself to moderate

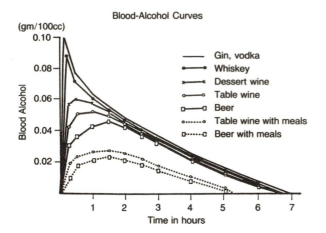

Blood-Alcohol Curves

(gm/100cc)

Blood Alcohol

- Gin, vodka
- Whiskey
- Dessert wine
- Table wine
- Beer
- Table wine with meals
- Beer with meals

Time in hours

Typical blood-alcohol curves resulting from ingestion of various spirits, wines, and beer, each at amounts equivalent to 0.6 gram of alcohol per kilogram of body weight.

consumption. Unfortunately, the law does not always make a distinction between table wine and other alcoholic beverages.

In Italy wine is a part of every family meal, and older children are permitted to drink a small amount diluted with water. At last count Italians were consuming ten times more wine each year than Americans (110 bottles versus 11 bottles per capita annually), yet the alcoholism rate in Italy is far lower than that of the United States. Medical studies have shown that the human body assimilates the alcohol in wine differently from the way it absorbs the same amount of alcohol in water, even on an empty stomach. But then wine rarely rests long on an empty stomach because, besides tasting much better with food, it stimulates the appetite.

A letter to the USDA Report in 1880 from P. A. Bonvallet of Kankakee County, Illinois, shows the frustration of being a winegrower in a nation with an ambivalent attitude toward wine—one that encourages wine grapes as an agricultural crop while at the same time adversely regulating the sale of wine.

> We have been very much deceived in engaging in the business of wine-making, having been induced to do so by the United States Government reports. And when on the eve of success the government put a bar in our way in forcing dealers of native wines to take wholesale liquor

dealers' licenses, so putting our products on the same footing with corn whiskey, as if it was not enough for us to work and experiment for 10 to 15 years and spend, like we did, some $12,000 before arriving at a satisfactory result. This is not just.

Bonvallet also complained about merchants' pricing practices.

> Besides, the licensed dealers act as a monopoly, cutting down the price of native wines to the lowest, while they go on the market and buy the poorest and cheapest grapes, making an adulterated article which they sell for imported wines, while the vintners are obliged to submit to their starvation prices. For if I put the average price of wine at $1 per gallon, it is being sold at that price in the neighborhood, but in Chicago it is sold for 40 to 50 cents per gallon wholesale, and the same wine being sold by the dealers at not less than $1 to $2 per gallon. Although by planting grapes we give value to a section of country 40 by 15 miles, we are also threatened by temperance advocates, who want to put wine on the same footing as whiskey.

The importance of politics cannot be underestimated when it comes to winegrowing. At Repeal, the Twenty-First Amendment gave control of all alcoholic beverages to the states. As a result each state has a different set of regulations governing the production, use, sale, and taxation of wine. In California, the state tax on table wine is $0.01 per gallon and there is no restriction on what type of establishment may sell wine at retail either on-sale or off-sale, that is, for consumption on the premises or elsewhere. At the other extreme is Kansas, which has a $0.30 per gallon tax plus a 4-percent "enforcement tax on retail sales to consumers." Only package stores may sell wine and only private clubs may serve wine or liquor by-the-drink.

Kansas recently passed a farm winery bill that permits sales to wholesalers and retailers at the winery but does not permit sales to consumers or tasting by anyone. The bill is an important first step, but farm wineries in Kansas as elsewhere need to sell directly to consumers (who expect to taste before they buy) in order to survive. Other states began with similarly weak legislation and

STATE OF RHODE ISLAND AND PROVIDENCE PLANTATIONS

Department of Business Regulation

LIQUOR CONTROL ADMINISTRATION

MANUFACTURER'S (FARMER-WINERY) LICENSE

Know all Men by These Presents: No. 5

That __DIAMOND HILL VINEYARDS__ of __CUMBERLAND__ has been granted this, a manufacturer's (winery) beverage license, under 3—6 of the General Laws of Rhode Island, 1956 as amended, authorizing the holder hereof to establish and operate a brewery at

__3145 DIAMOND HILL ROAD__   __CUMBERLAND__

Rhode Island, and to sell at wholesale at the above described place the product of the plant licensed hereby to other holders of licenses under said Title 3 as amended, and to deliver such product from the place of sale to another licensed place or a common carrier for such delivery.

This license expires on December 1, 1980 at midnight. It is issued and held subject to the condition that the holder hereof shall conform to and abide by all such rules and regulations as the Liquor Control Administration, (created by the Administrative act of 1939), has established or shall in the future establish, and all terms and provisions of Title 3 inclusive of the General Laws of Rhode Island, 1956 as amended.

IN WITNESS WHEREOF, the Liquor Control Administration has caused this license to be issued and authenticated by its seal and signature of the Administrator.

Date __December 1, 1979__ *1979-1980*

Liquor Control Administrator.

Post This License in a Conspicuous Place.

gradually improved it as the number of grape growers increased and they joined together to voice their needs.

In farm winery legislation during the past fifteen years, many states, as a means to encourage vineyard planting, included provisions lowering the state tax on wines made with locally grown fruit. However, the 1984 United States Supreme Court decision of *Bacchus Imports, Ltd. et al. v. Herbert H. Dias, Director of Taxation of the State of Hawaii*, appears to have rendered this practice unconstitutional. Grape growers and wineries in Virginia who had been exempted by their farm winery bill from paying state tax on Virginia-grown wines were shocked by the effect of the Supreme Court decision. The spirit of Thomas Jefferson notwithstanding, Virginia has the second highest tax on table wine in the nation, $0.40 per *liter*. As a result of the Bacchus decision, the wholesale cost of a bottle of Virginia wine increased by $0.30, the retail cost by $0.50 or more. Most farm wineries operate with such a small profit margin (if any) that excessive tax rates such as these are sufficient to kill their economic viability.

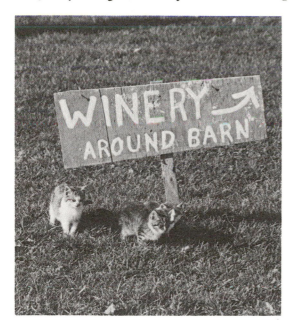

Bright, attractive tasting rooms staffed with family members eager to tell the story behind each wine are excellent forums for demonstrating that table wine is a social experience, something to be shared and discussed. The revival of wine-growing in the East presents an educational opportunity that should ultimately help give Americans a more intimate experience with all types of wine. The writers of the last century reveal how much home winemaking there was, for grapes grew in nearly every garden. Today, with the tremendous shift in population away from farms, many Americans have no "natural" wine experience. (How many of us have tasted milk straight from the cow?) Given that there is potential to grow grapes in all of the eastern states, certainly on a small scale, future development of new wine regions rests primarily on enlightened public attitudes and concerned political action.

KEY TO CHAPTERS 9, 10, AND 11

Historical Accounts of Eastern Grapegrowing. Preceding the discussion of the current situation in many states are comments on grape growing extracted from letters to the USDA's Special Report No. 36, *Report upon Statistics of Grape Culture and Wine Production in the United States for 1880.*

State Maps. The gray shaded areas of the state maps show which counties reported growing grapes in the 1880 report.
A single dot represents one modern (1984) winery.
A plus (+) sign represents more than one modern (1984) winery in a given location.

Per Capita Consumption. The state per capita consumption ratings are based on a table published in *Wines & Vines*, July 1983, 34. In 1982, the average per capita wine consumption in the United States was 2.21 gallons (up from 1.48 gallons in 1971).

9 NORTH AND MID-ATLANTIC STATES AND PROVINCES

Introduction

The Atlantic Ocean, the Great Lakes, and the Appalachian Mountains all influence climatic conditions in this region so that every state from Virginia to Maine has within its borders a wide variety of growing conditions. Growers in the North and Mid-Atlantic region are subject to the viticultural risks of very cold winter temperatures and false springs. Warm to hot and humid summers here necessitate a thorough understanding of rot and mildew control. Irrigation is not necessary, however, and spring frosts can generally be avoided by proper site selection. Each different climate zone planted to vineyards will eventually prove itself especially suited to foster a particular type of wine. Winegrowing is too new in this region for individual growing areas to have specialized yet in the production of only one or two wines as is the practice in Europe.

What is new about wine in New York, home of the oldest active U.S. winery? New York has long represented the Northeast in wine both in quantity and quality; the State Agricultural Experiment Station at Geneva has conducted grape

and wine research for more than a century. What is new is that New York no longer stands for sweet Labrusca-flavored wines produced by huge wineries. Riesling is becoming New York's most bemedaled wine. Vignoles, Cayuga White, Seyval, Chardonnay, Sauvignon blanc, Cabernet Sauvignon—these are the pride of New

York's estate winegrowers today. There are still some fine Niagaras and Catawbas to be found, but they are no longer the only show in town. And New York is no longer the only viticultural attraction in the Northeast.

Pennsylvania had the first commercial winery in the nation, but for more than thirty years after Prohibition, the thousands of acres of grapes grown along Lake Erie went to juice plants or out-of-state wineries. Then, in the 1960s, a group of Erie County growers led by Douglas and Marlene Moorhead battled with the State Liquor Control Board for the right to sell Pennsylvania-grown wine at the winery where it was produced. Passage of the Pennsylvania Limited Winery Act in 1968 is considered a landmark event in the modern history of eastern wines. Grape growers and amateur winemakers in other states were inspired to lobby their legislators for permission to open commercial wineries on their farms.

Winegrowing is flourishing in much of New England both on the mainland and out on such islands as Martha's Vineyard, Massachusetts, and Prudence Island, Rhode Island. New Jersey, finally freed from the iron grip of limited licensing, is blossoming with new vineyards. Virginia has burst on the scene with nearly thirty wineries in less than ten years: millions of dollars, including those of German, Italian, and French investors, are being used to plant Vinifera vines in the Old Dominion. After grappling with recalcitrant politicians, both Maryland and West Virginia are now able to host increased development of local wineries.

Across the border in Canada, where wine has been grown since the beginning of the last century, estate wineries are springing up where once only giant wineries existed. There are even wineries on Nova Scotia which use locally grown grapes.

Both Cornell and Penn State universities provide solid educational and extension support for winegrowers. The USDA has located a grape germ plasm repository in Geneva, New York, to preserve genetic stock that might prove useful in future breeding programs. The reference library of the American Society of Enology and Viticulture, Eastern Section, is also located in Geneva.

This is a region with a large cosmopolitan population. Per capita wine consumption is generally above average and it is likely to increase if legislation is passed in New York and Pennsylvania which permits the sale of wine in grocery stores.

Sherman Haight and Susan Adams in the deer park at Haight Vineyard in Connecticut

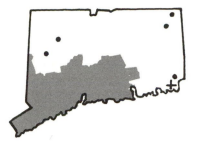

Connecticut

The state motto "Qui transtulit sustinet" (He who is transplanted endures) may have been true for human beings, but early vineyards transplanted in Connecticut were not able to endure the blow of Prohibition. Acreage here declined from 550 acres in 1920 to less than the number of grapes on the state seal in the 1970s. Today viticulture has revived and vineyards once again dot the state. New wineries appear yearly.

In his 1979 report to the Economic Development Administration on the potential for a wine industry in northeastern Connecticut, Haight Vineyard winemaker Shorn Mills noted:

> In Connecticut a widespread concern over rapid urbanization with its concomitant decline in the agricultural use of land has led to the recent passage of the Farmland Preservation Act which seeks to protect agriculture and calls for economic studies to identify viable agricultural operations. In May 1978, the State Legislature passed the Farm Winery Act (Public Act 294) which was primarily and ably advocated by Windham County grapegrowers and represen-

tatives. This Act recognizes the broad interrelationship of grape growing and wine-making and sharply reduces the selling constraints on a farm winery operation, thereby increasing its economic viability.

Within three years of the bill's passage, grape growers formed an association, five wineries appeared, state experiment stations planted grapes, and a tobacco company planted a vineyard in the Connecticut River Valley. By 1984 seven wineries had been established, one using native American varieties and the others using Vinifera or French-American grapes.

A careful choice of microclimate is essential here in order to prevent both winter cold injury and late spring frost damage. The growing season lasts generally from 150 to 180 days, longer near the coast. Average annual precipitation is 47 inches.

State regulations are restrictive from a consumer's standpoint. Retail sales are limited to package stores and drugstores. On-sale consumption is allowed by most towns, but local prohibition is an option. Farm wineries are limited to an annual production of 75,000 gallons, and at least 51 percent of the fruit used must be grown by the winery. Wineries may wholesale and retail, and tasting is permitted. Per capita consumption is above average.

Delaware

Ranking second in smallness only to Rhode Island, almost the entire state of Delaware lies within the Atlantic Coastal Plain and has the lowest mean elevation of any state. There is no commercial grape industry in the Blue Hen State today, but in 1880 two of Delaware's three counties had vineyards: 75 acres were reported in Kent and 50 acres in Sussex. The growing season lasts a long 210 days, and annual precipitation is about 47 inches. There is one winery in the state, but it does not have a vineyard and instead imports California juice. State regulations do not restrict the availability of wine to the consumer, and per capita consumption is near average.

Maine

Two Atlantic coastal counties, Lincoln and York, reported grape growing in 1880. There were 50 acres of grapes in Lincoln County with reported average yields of two-and-a-half tons per acre. York County had approximately 21 acres of vines with average yields of only one-and-a-half tons per acre. Only 5 or 6 percent of the grape crop was used for wine.

The weather in Maine demands a careful choice of varieties and micro-climate. Along the coast there is a 180-day growing season, but inland and northward the season shortens to fewer than the 120 frost-free days needed to ripen grapes. Annual precipitation varies from nearly 46 inches near the ocean to 40 inches inland. Some of the new cold-hardy, early-ripening Minnesota varieties might prove useful, but for

the moment wine drinkers must order out-of-state labels with their lobster—that is, if they want grape wine. The art of fermentation is currently being practiced at two new wineries that use local fruit and operate under a recently enacted state farm winery law. Perhaps a dry pear wine will become the perfect complement to steamed crustaceans.

The state government has a monopoly on liquor but grants private licenses for retail sales of table wine both on- and off-sale. Per capita consumption is below average, not a surprising fact given that Maine was the first state in the Union to ban alcohol (from 1851 to 1934).

Maryland

1880

According to the report from L. Giddings of Annapolis, table grapes were considered more profitable than wine grapes in Anne Arundel County.

Of late years there has not been a sufficient demand for native wines to induce our grape-growers to press the products of their vineyards. They prefer to sell the fruit at prices which, for the last two seasons, have ranged from 2 to 4 cents per pound. But few of our land owners have the capital to provide suitable cellars, casks, &c., for the business; nor are they willing to wait until a vintage matures for the profit of their labors. The light, warm, and naturally well-drained soils of this county are admirably suited for the vine and our climate is favorable for the full development of the fruit. It needs but the establishment of a thoroughly equipped and skillfully managed wine company to make grape-growing one of the most extensive industries of this section.

Winemaking was briefly successful for Col. James Wallace, Cambridge, Dorchester County, until fungi destroyed the vineyard.

The writer of this article has grown for a few years, very successfully, Catawba, Delaware, Clinton, and Concord. Made wine from Catawba and Delaware like unto and equal to pale sherry. Few, if any, connoisseurs could distinguish the difference. The wine was vastly superior to that produced in Western New York and on Lake Erie—being much richer in sugar, flavor, and coloring matter. The wine was made by the French and German methods, as described in the Report to Commissioner of Agriculture for the year 18—[sic]. The Catawba or light wine was readily sold for $3 per gallon. The red wine made from the Concord and Clinton grapes was sold for $1.25 to $1.50. The enterprise was profitable for a few years, but a series of damp, funky, hot summers, such as mildewed the wheat, gave the Catawba vine the leaf blight, destroyed the canes. The vineyard was abandoned. Still find the Concord profitable, but the fruit mostly sold for table use.

Given the impact the state has had on American viticulture, it is surprising that Maryland has never been one of the country's major wine producers. Thus far its contributions are best described as catalytic in nature. It was here that John Adlum discovered the Catawba, America's first internationally acclaimed varietal. The first varietal Seyval blanc (now one of the East's leading grapes) to attract connoisseur attention was produced in Maryland by Montbray Wine Cellars. Maryland also nurtured the winegrowing career of Philip Wagner, who is to the twentieth century what Adlum was to the nineteenth: influential author, American *Vitis* champion, new wine grape disseminator, vintner. Moreover, had the drys not thwarted it, a USDA enology research lab would have been located in Beltsville, Maryland. No matter what the future may bring in terms of gallonage, Maryland's vinicultural pundits will be the ones to watch when the next century comes around.

Very restrictive regulation was a primary fac-

In order to assure continuity of their winegrowing efforts, the Wagners sold their Boordy Winery (literally lock, stock, and barrel) to their longtime friends, growers, and nearby neighbors, the Defords.

tor in the relatively slow growth of winegrowing in Maryland even during the boom years of the 1970s. County by county, in a painfully slow process, vintners worked with their legislators for more favorable distribution policies. Laws like the one that restricted winery sales to one bottle of one label to one customer per year are becoming a thing of the past. Maryland grape growers are now organized and obtaining support from the state's department of agriculture. Both Vinifera and French-American varieties are being planted, and new wineries have opened to accommodate the new grapes.

Maryland is typical of many eastern states in having a wide range of heat summations. There are 2,000 growing degree-days in the mountainous western part of the state and 4,000 degree-days in the southern Eastern Shore. Maryland has growing seasons—measured as the number of days between killing frosts—as short as 120 days and as long as 240 days. Average precipitation varies annually from 38 to 46 inches in different areas.

Maryland laws, because they vary from county to county, are confusing for consumers. Grape growers, however, have finally achieved more uniform regulations for "Limited Wineries." All wine made under the limited winery law must be from Maryland fruit, although producers can receive exemptions from the agriculture department if they perceive a shortage of grapes for their needs. Retail sales may be limited in some counties. Per capita wine consumption is near (below) average.

Massachusetts

1880
Wine-grape growing was not considered a profitable venture, according to the reports.

E. S. Rogers, Salem, Essex County: The varieties which ripen pretty well here, as well as other standard sorts, like Catawba, that rarely mature in this county, are grown to so much greater perfection and of such superior quality on the lake shores of Western New York and Ohio, that grape culture or wine making would not be considered a profitable investment in this region.

William C. Strong, Newton Centre, Middlesex County: Grapes not raised for wine in this county, and there are not more than 10 acres of vines in the county. One man buys all the poor unsaleable grapes he can find and makes what he calls "native wine" for communion purposes, possibly 3,000 gallons, poor stuff. This is all I know of, except as made on a small scale for family use. But there are thousands of householders who have from one to ten vines for home table use. Delaware is best, and when old and well fed does pretty well. Worden is early and popular. Brighton is doing pretty well; but the Jefferson is most promising as a new grape. In quality it is unsurpassed, and it seems to be iron-clad. We have high expectations from it.

As far as modern Bay State winemakers are concerned, the town of Concord is best remembered for Emerson, Hawthorne, and Thoreau: numerous varieties of wine may be found here, but for Concord wine you will have to go elsewhere. Inspired by the water-moderated climate, George and Catherine Mathiesen planted fourteen Vinifera wine and table varieties on hitherto grape-barren Martha's Vineyard in 1971 and started the state's first modern winery. Romantic as life on this leisure island might seem, its sandy and rocky soil makes a very challenging job for grape farmers.

With Massachusetts's viticulture still in its infancy, one winemaker decided to use local fruit to produce dry table wine. Old-fashioned varieties of local apples, wild Maine blueberries, peaches, pears, and cranberries are aged in both American and European oak barrels just as if they were premium grape wines. The results are surprising and far superior to any Concord wine one might find.

Young vineyards are coming into bearing in Bristol, Plymouth, and Barnstable counties, and new wineries are opening around them at a modest rate. The Atlantic side of the state has a growing season ranging from 150 to 180 days and approximately 43 inches of precipitation annually.

Wine is readily available to consumers. Producers with "Farmer-Winery" licenses are free to use unlimited amounts of grapes and juice (but no wine) from out-of-state. Per capita consumption is above average.

New Hampshire

Owners of the state's only winery, John and Lucy Canepa, have proved that hardy, early ripening wine grapes such as Foch will grow and make fine wine in New Hampshire. The Canepas, however, have not been able to make their winery profitable using only New Hampshire grapes.

Along the coast there is a 180-day growing season, but the season shortens to an inadequate 90 frost-free days in the north. The Granite State has from 41 to 44 inches of precipitation annually.

New Hampshire has a state store system. License fees for local wineries are high. A domestic wine license is limited to a maximum of 50,000-gallon annual production. There is no restriction on the amount of grapes, juice, or wine from out of state which may be blended with New Hampshire–grown wine. Producers may wholesale, retail, and have tastings. Consumers will find retail sales in convenient outlets. Per capita consumption is well above average.

New Jersey

1880

Southern New Jersey has a strong viticultural history, as the town name of Vineland, in Cumberland County and Henry Brown's report from that area attest:

> The climate and soil of this county are peculiarly adapted to grape culture. The fruit is of excellent quality and makes good wine; our soil is not as well adapted to general farming as to grape and fruit culture. There seems to be considerable prejudice against the wine business, though it is the best of the branches of agriculture in our county and will likely improve, since insects are killing the vines of Europe. We have been troubled some with the rot, but it was not as bad last year as formerly and the farmers have had success in using paper bags to cover the clusters, so that the flavor and quality is much better than otherwise.

The climate and soils were favorable, but the economics were not: competition from foreign imports created financial difficulties.

> Julius Hincke, Egg Harbor City, Atlantic County: In 1878 this settlement had 615 acres planted in vineyards. Since that time small patches have been laid out, but I would estimate that the whole was now more than 700 acres. People are slow about taking up grape culture, since it pays so little and the public prefers the fashion of buying imported wine. I can assure you it is difficult to sell enough to meet my annual expenses.

While New Jersey's dense population somewhat limits the potential for vineyard expansion, at the same time it provides small farm wineries a large wine-drinking market from which to attract customers. Until 1981, however, when the state passed a farm winery law, grape farmers were constrained from establishing estate wineries by the fact that operating licenses were costly and limited in number.

New Jersey's oldest and largest vineyards are concentrated in the south, as are the large wineries that have in the past specialized in Labrusca wines blended with California wine. The older wineries are beginning to replant their vineyards with the French-American and Vinifera varieties that are the favorites of the new farm wineries being established in the central and northern parts of the state. Despite the risk of cold injury to Vinifera in the northern section of New Jersey, Riesling and Chardonnay are being planted together with French-American varieties such as Seyval, Vidal, and Foch.

New Jersey has a growing season that ranges from fewer than 150 days in the Piedmont Plateau to 210 days in the south, or from 2,500 to 4,000 degree-days. Annual precipitation is from 45 to 47 inches.

The farm winery law currently limits production to 50,000 gallons per year. Grapes must be grown in New Jersey, and the winery must be on at least three acres of land with a minimum of 1200 vines. Wineries may wholesale and retail. In theory, wine should be easily available both on- and off-sale, but in practice there are expensive and limited licensing requirements for merchants, and often restaurants that cannot afford wine licenses permit customers to bring their own wine. Per capita consumption is above average.

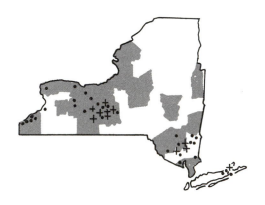

New York

1880

There are over thirty letters to the USDA from New York. Following are a few excerpts of viticultural and human interest:

G. W. Nichols, Hammondsport, Steuben County: In this region, including Yates and Steuben counties, it is estimated there are from 4,000 to 5,000 acres in grapes. . . . Two-thirds of amount grown here is in Catawba. We find the side-hill lands sloping to the east and south the best exposure, and with this exposure most all kinds of soil do well.

D. S. Martin, Watertown, Jefferson County: We lay down and cover vines for winter. . . . Our grapes have less sugar and more flavor than grapes grown farther south, and the foliage is less liable to be destroyed by sporadic diseases. Three-fourths of our seasons we ripen *Vitis vinifera* grapes in outdoor culture, and with no protection from glass, or artificial heat.

Grafting over unwanted varieties with new ones was suggested by J. Sagar of Naples, Ontario County:

The white grape is beginning to attract attention; and it has been proved that the tender sort of white grapes, like the Rebecca, do excellently well when grafted into the Isabella root, and but little is lost in making a change in this way. What has already been done has proved to be good, and the Isabella vines will no doubt all of them be got rid of in this way. . . .

Sagar continued his report with a tale of one grower's interesting way of fertilizing a new vineyard.

It is an interesting fact that the first grapes grown in the United States to be disposed of in market, occurred in the village of Naples, Ontario County, New York. Mr. E. A. McKay, a prominent lawyer of this place, conceived the idea of starting a regular vineyard, and early in the spring of 1854, purchased of a neighbor an acre of ground for that purpose; preparing the ground, as it has since proved, in an unusual and unnecessary way. It so happened at the time, that a number of cattle lately brought from the West, and were being pastured near by, a number of them died, and Mr. McKay getting possession of them, buried portions of them at intervals of 16 feet apart, in the row, the rows being 16 feet apart. Having got the ground thus prepared he went to Rochester and purchased of Elwanger & Barry, the necessary number of Isabella vines. The second year he purchased another acre, set it out, minus the animal manure. His first acre produced an enormous crop of grapes the fourth year. The question then was how to dispose of them.

The stress of marketing grapes proved to have unfortunate results.

Remembering that he had friends in Montreal, Canada, he purchased ten pound pasteboard boxes, sufficient to hold his crop, and started for Montreal. Mr. McKay had been subject to spells of insanity, so that the worry and flurry of getting to Montreal, and the excitement his grapes produced among the people, and the large amount of money he was evidently about to make, proved to be too much for him, and he became almost hopelessly insane. A person who had accompanied him, sent for Mrs. McKay, who sold the grapes and returned to Naples as soon as possible with her unfortunate husband.

Today the term "New York Wine" needs qualification. In the past decade, scores of new wineries have opened in the state's five main regions: Finger Lakes, Hudson River, Long Island, Chautauqua-Erie, and Niagara. Most of the new wineries are using European-American and Vinifera grapes instead of or in addition to the traditional Labrusca varieties. Stainless steel is replacing wood in most cellars for everything but oak ageing of red wines.

New York is subject to a crazy quilt of liquor laws pieced together after Prohibition by special interests. Currently, consumers may buy wine only in package stores or in wineries. "Farm Wineries" using all New York State grapes may wholesale, retail, and have tastings. Annual production is presently limited to 50,000 gallons.

Per capita consumption is somewhat above average and is predicted to increase dramatically when wine is permitted to join dinner in Empire State grocery bags.

Finger Lakes

The Finger Lakes region has all the requisite components of a fairy-tale wine region: natural beauty, historic charm, and wonderful wines. The area is now undergoing a difficult period of transition. Because of earlier miscalculations of market trends, many growers have relatively young vineyards of overplanted varieties, notably De Chaunac, for which there is very little demand. Taylor Wine Company, the region's largest winery and once the bedrock of the grape industry, has changed ownership three times in the past decade. The historic Gold Seal Winery was closed in 1984. Faced with a depressed market and an uncertain future, more and more growers are establishing estate wineries. Vintners are banding together to promote their products and to push for a less restrictive distribution system for wines in the state.

The east side of Seneca Lake with its favorable microclimates is being transformed with new Vinifera plantings. Finger Lakes Chardonnays and Rieslings are winning international contests. Vignoles, Seyval, and Cayuga White are becoming increasingly popular varieties for white wines. The trend in reds is to produce fresh, fruity wines called "nouveau" which are meant to be consumed very young, as early as mid-November following harvest.

A congenial place to discover the changing world of New York wines and to compare Finger Lakes wines with those from other New York regions is Turback's Restaurant in Ithaca, which serves an extensive list of exclusively Empire State wines. To visit all the Finger Lakes wineries requires several weeks. For those with limited time upstate, a trip to the Corning Wine Center, with its impressive regional wine museum, tasting room, and retail outlet, is in order.

The growing season in the Finger Lakes region ranges from 135 to 150 days with a heat summa-

Four Chimneys Winery
in New York

tion of approximately 2,300 degree-days. Beyond the warming influence of the deep lakes, only very hardy vines can survive. There is no shortage of viticultural expertise here, though—growers, some of whom are fourth-generation grape farmers, have access to a full-time extension viticulturist, an extension enologist, numerous support groups, the Geneva research station, and Cornell University.

Hudson River Region

Easily accessible to the New York metropolitan area are several very large wineries and numerous small ones dotting both sides of the Hudson River and situated in a long viticultural

Hudson River Region, Benmarl Winery cork

area that encompasses all of three and part of five counties. Winemaking has been carried on here for over three hundred years beginning with French Huguenots in 1677. The Brotherhood Winery in Washingtonville, founded in 1839, is the oldest continuously active winery in the United States. By far the largest operation here is the Royal Wine Corporation, a two-million-gallon kosher winery that uses a large portion of local grapes. In contrast, Northeast Vineyard, the region's smallest winery, produces less than 750 gallons.

The Hudson River is the source of microclimates that favor fruit growing. Chardonnay and Riesling are being planted in the warmest spots, and Seyval and Foch are becoming something of a regional specialty. Annual precipitation is about 43 inches, and the growing season lasts between 150 and 180 days.

The Hudson has also been the source of inspiration for two books about tending vineyards on its banks. In *The Vintage Years: The Story of High Tor Vineyards* (1973), Everett Crosby describes the fun and frustrations of being a winegrower during the pre–wine boom decades of the fifties and sixties. Benmarl Vineyards proprietor Mark Miller continues the story through the volatile 1970s and early 1980s in *Wine—A Gentleman's Game: The Adventures of an Amateur Winemaker Turned Professional* published in 1984. Anyone considering the winery business in the East should read both books *before* making a start.

Long Island

In the early 1970s Alexander and Louisa Hargrave planted a vineyard on the North Fork of Long Island and proved that New York State has within its boundaries a prime area for growing premium Vinifera grapes. Today the eastern end of the island is one of the fastest expanding wine regions in the East: in 1984, there were five wineries and nearly a thousand acres of grapes planted (over half of which were less than four years old). New wineries, including several large ones, and more vineyards are anticipated in the region, and, in addition, Long Island is providing fruit for other northeastern wineries as well.

The growing season is a generous 210 days long, and annual precipitation about 45 inches. Risk of winter injury is greatly reduced by the island's water-moderated climate. Temperatures rarely drop to 0°F--fortunately, since many vineyards occupy sites of former potato fields, whose soils make for very vigorous growth and therefore increased susceptibility to cold damage. Vigorous vegetative growth does not always

mean large yields, however. Rain during bloom, for example, can substantially reduce fruit set by decreasing the number of berries per cluster. Alex Hargrave reported to *Wines & Vines*, February 1985, that in 1984 the average yield of the island's 250 acres of four-year and older Vinifera vines was three tons per acre.

Chautauqua-Erie

New York's Chautauqua-Erie grape belt shares the "Lake Erie" viticultural appellation with Pennsylvania, Ohio, and Canada's Pelee Island. Because in the past it was a center of Prohibitionist zeal, this region, which has the largest vineyard acreage in the state, has been planted mostly with Concord for the last hundred years. A group started in 1873 by Esther McNeil in Fredonia became the nucleus of the Woman's Christian Temperance Union. Native wine grapes originally planted in the area were replaced with Concords for Welch's juice. After Repeal much of the area's harvest was used for Mogen David wine.

Recently, the demand for the Lake Erie Concord grapes has declined. Estate wineries here are planting European-American and Vinifera vines for the most part to make table wines and champagnes. In 1984 a seventy-five-acre research project was established by Woodbury Vineyards to

Valley Vineyards Winery
in New York

discover the best varieties, clones of varieties, rootstocks, and training systems for Vinifera culture in the region. History has come full circle, and wine grapes are now replacing juice grapes. Annual precipitation is approximately 35 inches, and the growing season near the lake lasts up to 180 days.

Niagara

Birthplace in 1868 of the Niagara grape, this peninsula gets its relatively mild (for New York) climate from its location between the Niagara River (home of honeymooners' favorite falls) and Lake Ontario. Although several thousand acres of vines, including some wine varieties, are planted here, this region has not yet seen the proliferation of local wineries which New York's other regions have experienced. Climatic conditions in the Niagara district are similar to those of Ontario, Canada, where there is currently much greater winegrowing activity.

Nova Scotia, Canada

Visitors to this far northern outpost of eastern American viticulture will delight in the unusual collection of grape varieties now under trial. In addition to some of Germany's modern releases such as Domfelder, Bacchus, and Kerner, there is an assortment of European-American crosses, including unnamed varieties from Ontario's Vineland research station. The most unusual varieties under commercial cultivation are Eurasian grapes, crosses made in Russia with the Asian species *Vitis amurensis* which are supposed to be extra winter-hardy. Severnyi and Michurnitz are two such grapes being used to a limited degree for red wine. More familiar varieties such as Seyval and Foch are also available.

The heat summation necessary for ripening fruit is minimal here, where the climate is said to resemble that of Germany's Mosel region. Site selection is extremely critical. Growers, like those in England and Northern Europe, must follow cultural practices that promote efficient photosynthesis of limited sunshine. It is the bodies of water surrounding this 380-mile-long peninsula that moderate winter temperatures sufficiently to permit grape growing at all.

Given the peninsula's nearly one million residents and the large seasonal influx of tourists, there is certainly a market for local wine. The ultimate profitability of winegrowing here will depend on the regulations and taxes imposed by

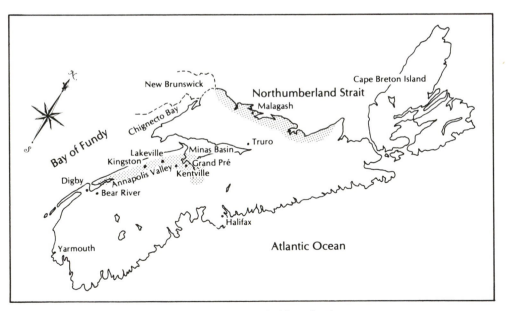

Grape-growing areas in Nova Scotia

the Liquor Commission; in 1984 they were untenable if any real growth of this fledgling industry is hoped for.

Ontario, Canada

The history and development of grape production here is similar to that of the rest of the eastern region: early winemaking with native American varieties; provincial dry laws and prohibition; new plantings in the 1970s of European-American and Vinifera grapes; and the struggle of grape farmers for the freedom to produce and sell their own wine.

The fruit-growing regions of southwestern Ontario share Lake Ontario and the Niagara River with New York and Lake Erie with New York, Pennsylvania, Ohio, and Michigan. Currently, vineyard acreage is concentrated in the Niagara Peninsula near Buffalo, New York, where over half of the 40,000 acres planted in fruit is devoted to grapes. There is a much smaller but growing vineyard area about two hundred miles to the east in Essex and Kent counties, neighbors of Detroit, Michigan. Canada's Pelee Island, which now boasts a large Vinifera vineyard, is a short boat ride across the international border from the grape-growing Bass Islands in Ohio.

The Great Lakes moderate the climate to provide growers in this northerly latitude with a growing season of 170-plus days and more than 2,500 degree-days to ripen the fruit. Humid summers increase the risk of mildews and rots, and cold winters necessitate careful management of Vinifera and other cold-tender varieties.

Labrusca varieties and dessert (port/sherry) wines were the stock-in-trade of Canadian winegrowing until after World War II, when Adhemar De Chaunac, winemaker for T. G. Bright and Co., began importing French-American and Vinifera vines to Canada to produce grapes suitable for dry table wines. Working with De Chaunac was viticulturist George W. B. Hostetter, who directed Bright's extensive grape variety research program. This research led to the planting of new vineyards with wine-grape varieties that replaced Concords and others unsuitable for wine. The Experimental Station at Vineland also developed a sizable research vineyard with an international collection of *Vitis* species and varieties used in the breeding program.

Using data produced by aerial infrared photography and strategic temperature readings, Vineland researchers created a map of the microclimates between Lake Ontario and the 350-foot-high Niagara escarpment that bounds the fruit-growing zone of the Niagara Peninsula. They

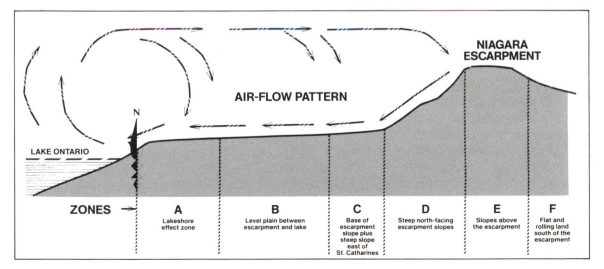

The influence of Lake Ontario on frosty conditions in the Niagara Peninsula

interpreted the data and identified cold spots and frost pockets. Using the map as a guide, growers can tell which locations require hardy vines and which should be avoided altogether. Would that such maps were available for every winegrowing region!

Canada's political climate for wine is even more problematic than America's. National prohibition lasted from 1917 to 1927 in all the provinces except French-influenced Quebec, where liquor was banned in 1919 while wine and beer remained legal. Ontario did make a concession to its grape growers by permitting the production of wine for export. Wineries were allowed to sell wine from their premises (and nowhere else) in five-gallon containers or case lots only. This restriction dampened domestic sales, but the illicit export trade to the United States boomed and made the fortunes of many Ontario wine producers.

After Prohibition each province set its own regulations and taxes for wine. Sales restrictions and limited licensing made the establishment of estate wineries an impossible option for grape farmers, and as a result the course of Canadian viniculture has rested with a few giant wine producers. As recently as 1984, Ontario had only four wineries that produced less than 200,000 gallons, only two of which produced less than 100,000 gallons.

Despite an unfavorable political atmosphere, Canadian wines have greatly improved in recent decades and are much decorated at international competitions. Viticulture and enology research conducted in the province is relevant to conditions faced by other eastern growers, who would be well-advised to make a vinicultural excursion across the border.

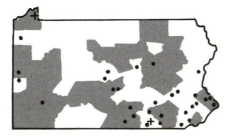

Pennsylvania

1880

A. W. Butt, North East, Erie County: The leading varieties are Concord, Ives Seedling, Delaware, and Hartford, either of which makes a good wine. I have been in the grape business to a considerable extent for the past eighteen years, and I find that the Concord and Ives Seedling pay best, both for table use and wine. Grapes grown on gravel make a finer wine than those grown on lighter soils. I have raised as high as five tons per acre of Concord and Ives, and seldom less than three tons. The Ives are the most productive and make the best red wine.

In Pennsylvania, there are basically two grape-growing areas: the Lake Erie region, in the northwestern corner, and the rest of the state. The Lake Erie region has the largest acreage with a predominance of Concords grown for juice and a smaller portion devoted to wine grapes. Led by Douglas Moorhead, who has been experimenting successfully with European-American and Vinifera varieties since the 1950s, Erie County growers obtained passage of the landmark Pennsylvania Limited Winery Act in 1968, 175 years after the first commercial American winery, the Pennsylvania Wine Company, was started outside of Philadelphia. Without this legislation there would have been no future in growing wine grapes in Pennsylvania.

Most of the Keystone State's forty-plus wineries are now located in the populous southeast quadrant of the state, many in picturesque, enologically adapted old barns. The majority of these operations are very small and use grapes from their own vineyards or those from local growers. In the southeast the growing season is warmer (by 500 or more degree-days) and more late-ripening varieties are planted than along Lake Erie. Fungus diseases though are more troublesome in the warm, humid southern and eastern sectors. Annual precipitation varies from approximately 40 inches in the northwest to 45 inches in the southeast.

Adapted barn at Nissley Vineyard in Pennsylvania

Penn State University provides active support in both viticulture and enology through extension, research, and teaching activities, and hosts an annual technical conference on the State College campus. Penn State viticulturist Carl Haeseler, who has conducted grape variety research for over a decade at the North East Agricultural Station, confirms that two French-American varieties, Vidal blanc and Chambourcin, are gaining popularity for varietal table wines. In Pennsylvania, however, one can find as wide a selection of wine grape varieties as in any eastern state.

Pennsylvania is currently a monopoly state—that is, a state liquor control board handles sales of all alcoholic beverages. Wine may be purchased only at state stores or wineries and winery outlets. There is a strong movement to abolish the present system and return sales of wine and spirits to private enterprise. Winery production is limited to 100,000 gallons annually, and all grapes must come from Pennsylvania. Tastings are permitted in addition to retail sales, and wineries may operate up to three "extensions of premise" or retail outlets.

Rhode Island

1880

B. H. Lawton, Wickford, Washington County: A great many kinds of grapes do well in this county, such as Delaware, Isabella, Catawba, Concord, Hartford Prolific, Black and White Hamburg, &c. I grow the Delaware and Concord with much satisfaction, more especially the former, which I consider the most delicious grape produced in this section.

One grower found that rose bugs devastate the grape flowers and thus the crop.

Bill Bacon and Don Siebert enjoy a glass of RI wine aboard ship.

James Nisbet, Pawtucket, Providence County: This season has been very poor, owing to the ravages of the rose bug, at the time the grapes are in flower; in some localities, near waters, salt, unless protected by netting or hand picking, the crop has been a total loss. Only varieties suited to this locality, 1st, Concord; 2d, Hartford Prolific; 3d, Delaware; 4th, Clinton. The Brighton promises well; the Clinton is a good wine grape, perhaps the best here.

Water, water everywhere, and who cares if it's potable when there's wine? The coastline and waterways surrounding the Ocean State provide excellent microclimates for Vinifera and French-American grapes in this "microstate" that would otherwise be quite inhospitable viticulturally. The growing season on the coast lasts 180 days or more, but winters get sufficiently cold to necessitate careful Vinifera vine management even in the most favorable spots. Precipitation averages 43 inches per year.

A sailboat is the recommended conveyance to Prudence Island Vineyards, but the proprietors, members of the Bacon family, will meet visitors at the ferry. Sailing enthusiasts on the mainland can drive to Little Compton for some Spinnaker White or Compass Rosé from Sakonnet Vineyards, which, with its 30,000-gallon capacity, is the state's largest winery. The smallest wine-growing estate, Diamond Hill, consists of five acres of Pinot noir; its owners are hoping to emulate the great Burgundies of France.

A farmer-winery license allows production of up to 50,000 gallons per year. Out-of-state fruit is permitted from the first year in decreasing amounts to no more than 1,000 gallons' worth from the fourth year on. Some grapes (but no juice or wine) may be imported in the event of crop failure. Wholesale and retail sales are permitted, as are tastings. Wine is conveniently available to consumers. Per capita wine consumption is well above the national average.

Vermont

Vermont is too far inland to receive climatic benefit from the Atlantic Ocean. The growing season is very short, generally less than 120 days, and the cold winters would necessitate burying most varieties of vines. In Vermont, per capita consumption of wine is above average, making this a promising market for New England wine from other states. Wine may be purchased in package and food stores.

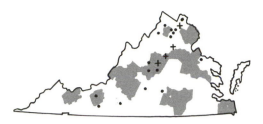

Virginia

1880

Grape acreage and related statistics were reported by J. Ran. Bryan of Charlottesville, Albemarle County:

> Having been for some time secretary and treasurer of our wine company, and being also a grape-grower, I think my estimate approximately correct; it is only made for vines in bearing now. There are probably 25 to 30 percent more acres planted not yet in bearing; making a total of, say, 480 acres in the county. The yield in pounds per acre varies very much. The strong growers (Nortons, Concord &c.) yield from 6 to 10 pounds per vine, and often over (my vineyard average 13 pounds one year), whereas Delaware, Alvey, and other weak vines vary from 2 to 6 pounds per vine.

Bryan surveyed the grape market, too.

> Now about 80 percent goes to wine, formerly not one-half. The table grapes are too uncertain to sell, prices dropping often below cost of production and freight, &c. It usually takes about 14 pounds of grapes to make 1 gallon of wine, varying from 13 to 16 pounds. The wine value of the grapes depends on the kind, ripeness, &c., and varies from $1\frac{1}{2}$ cents per pound to $5\frac{1}{2}$ cents. The prime cost of grapes for a large cellar this year was about 45 cents per gallon. The wine sells wholesale at from 60 cents to $1.25. Thus you perceive an average is hard to arrive at, as one year there will be more high grade, and another more low grade, wine made.

Bryan showed an active interest in experimenting to develop the viniculture of his day.

> I am testing a good many new varieties: most of them disappoint our expectations. For wine Norton's is still pre-eminent, though Delaware (could we raise enough pounds per acre) makes a number one wine. Concords still continue the "grape for the millions" and for growers, who are careless about their vineyards are as profitable as any, as they stand abuse and bear anyhow. We now "hope great things" from the "Cunningham" as we did from the Lady and Elvira, and with better prospect, as it is an Aestivalis. The Prentiss, Lady Washington, and Ricketts last I have not tried. You [at the USDA] have the good wishes and thanks of all good men in your endeavor to promote new and diversified subjects for our agriculture. The old ruts are worn down, so if longer followed we would soon be all bankrupt.

Another grower reported that Muscadines flourish in southeastern Virginia.

> J. E. Baker, Bowen's Hill, Norfolk County:
> The varieties mostly cultivated for wine are grapes of Southern origin, such as Norton's Vir-

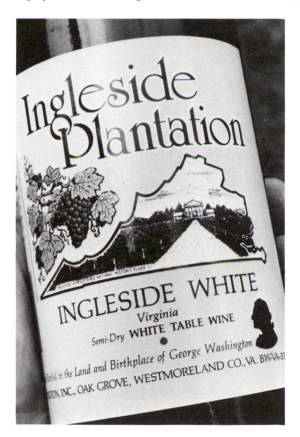

Several Virginia wineries, including Ingleside Plantation, are located on historic property.

ginia seedling, Scuppernong, Mish, and Flowers. The sorts shipped away in green state are mostly Hartford, Ives, Telegraph, and others, of Northern origin, and which ripen early.

Although it enjoys freedom from the Pierce's disease that plagues the deeper South and from the extreme cold that grips much of the North, Virginia is still a challenging home for Vinifera vines. Periods of warm weather from December to March followed by a sudden drop in temperature have caused damage to the buds and trunks of Vinifera varieties (with some varieties sustaining more damage than others), as have the occasional winters when temperatures have fallen below −10°F. Warm, humid, and often rainy summers make rots and mildews a constant concern. Annual precipitation averages from 40 to 45 inches. The length of the growing season varies from 150 days in the mountains to as long as 240 days on Virginia's Eastern Shore.

Many of the Vinifera vines planted on favor-able sites in the mid-seventies are alive, well, and furnishing grapes to the nearly thirty local wineries that have cropped up since 1976. Wine grape acreage is dominated by premium whites such as Chardonnay, Riesling, and Seyval. Cabernet Sauvignon and Chambourcin are popular reds. Before 1976 there was one giant (two-million-gallon) winery in Virginia, and it used nary an Old Dominion grape: Richard's Cellars in Petersburg still uses Muscadines from the Carolinas for its Mother Vineyard Scuppernong and multistate fruit for its best-selling Richard's Wild Irish Rose. Virginia Dare, now a Canandaigua brand, has moved to New York.

The majority of Virginia wineries today are local family operations, but there has also been an impressive amount of foreign investment in the state. The Zonin Wine Company of Italy has a vineyard and winery on the historic Barboursville estate. Physician Gerhard Guth of Germany planted a largely Riesling vineyard for his Rapidan River Vineyards near Culpeper.

Pliska family vineyard in the hills of West Virginia

Also outside of Culpeper is Virginia's largest wine estate, Prince Michel Vineyards, a joint state-French venture. In addition, Seagram Wine Company of Canada (which also owns Taylor Wine Company and the Gold Seal brand of New York, Paul Masson, The Monterey Vineyards, Taylor California Cellars, and Sterling Vineyards of California, and many wineries abroad) is considering a winery for its Ivy Creek Vineyard outside of Charlottesville.

Virginians enjoy the cooperation of their departments of agriculture and tourism, and of their state legislators, all of whom appreciate the economic benefits of the state's new "wine country." State ABC stores, the only outlets for liquor in the state, carry only Virginia wines. All types of wine are available in grocery, drug, and specialty stores. The farm winery law requires use of a minimum of 75 percent Virginia grapes or juice and special permission from the department of agriculture to lower that amount in the event of crop loss. There are no production limits. Wineries may wholesale, retail, and have tastings.

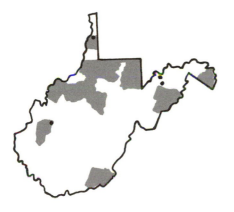

West Virginia

1880

J. Linders, Winefield, Putnam County: The Concord and Ives' Seedling grapes are the only varieties that will adapt themselves to this climate and yield a paying crop, the former having the preference in regard to quantity, the latter for a good keeper and quality.

In 1981 persistent West Virginia grape growers triumphantly won passage of a farm winery bill in spite of opposition by Governor Jay Rockefeller, who vetoed the bill for three consecutive years but was overridden the third time by the legislature. Now there are four wineries fermenting local grapes into Mountain State wine, and more are planned. Grape growers have an active association through which they provide technical assistance and share their experiences in growing various wine grape varieties.

There are many microclimates where vineyards can prosper, although late spring frosts, cold winters, humid summers, and the predations of deer and birds are sources of risk to viticulture here. The frost-free season increases from 150 to 180 to 210 days as one moves westward from the Allegheny Mountains toward the Allegheny Plateau. Precipitation averages from 36 to 50 inches annually.

West Virginia has recently released wines from state monopoly stores into licensed grocery stores and specialty shops. Except when there is a crop shortage, farm wineries must use 75 percent West Virginia fruit, 25 percent of which must be grown on the premises. Wholesaling, retailing, and tastings at the winery are permitted.

10 GULF AND SOUTH ATLANTIC STATES

Introduction

In all of Florida and large sections (from the coast inward) of states from Texas to North Carolina, a bacterial infection known as Pierce's disease has seriously limited the culture of bunch (non-Muscadine) grapes. Sharpshooter-type leaf hoppers and spittle insects infect the xylem tissue causing leaf scalding, irregular mottling along the cane, withering of the fruit, and ultimately death of the vine. Breeding programs in the South are producing multispecies varieties such as Stover which resist Pierce's disease and make good table wine.

Pierce's disease (P.D.) has been found on grapes in California and northern Mexico, but it is thought to be indigenous to the South because there are native southern species that are resistant to it. The problem is far less devastating in California than in the Gulf States, probably because

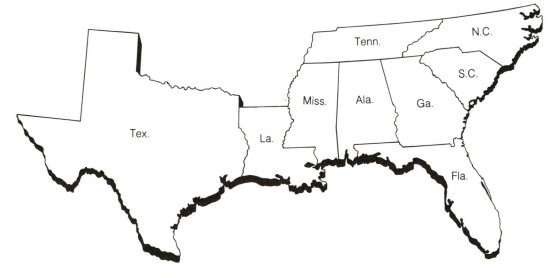

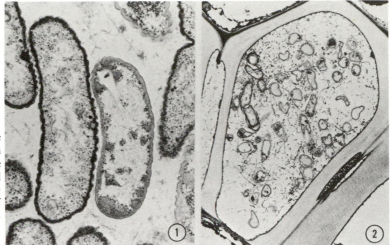

(1) The bacteria in Arkansas 1019 grape have the same size, form, distribution pattern, and general appearance as those previously suggested to be the causal agent of Pierce's disease. (30,000 ×)
(2) Transverse section through xylem of a Catawba leaf vein showing typical low-density distribution pattern of bacteria. (700 ×)

dry summers limit the growth of host weeds and carrier insect populations. It is serious enough in California, however, to attract funding for research to seek a remedy. If an effective, affordable cure for P.D. were found, Vinifera culture would increase dramatically in the Deep South.

Most of the farm wineries in P.D. areas are making a virtue of necessity, that is, making Muscadine wines that are unique to their region. Most widely planted are the new improved varieties that have been released in the past two decades from a North Carolina breeding pro-

gram. Even better Muscadines, with fruit characteristics more suited to wine, are on the horizon.

Great improvements in vinification techniques have been made in recent years as a result of both university research and experimentation by individual winemakers. Enology research and education in the South takes place at the A. B. McKay Food and Enology Laboratory at Mississippi State University in Starkville, where the results of viticultural experiments are vinified and evaluated. Students are trained in the art of winemak-

Pierce's disease on Chambourcin leaves

Grapevine root borer

ing while learning the specifics of southern wine-growing in particular.

Not all of the South is caught in the grip of P.D. As we move away from the Coastal Plain toward the Appalachians, the possibility of successfully growing Vinifera and European-American wine grapes increases. Truluck Vineyards, in Lake City, South Carolina, is something of a test case: located on the Coastal Plain, they have planted European and European-American varieties for the most part, only two of which, Villard blanc and Roucaneuf, have shown some tolerance to P.D. Heat and high humidity in the South brings with it the constant menace of fungus disease. "Heading for the hills" can be the best way to minimize this problem.

In addition to the ubiquitous phylloxera root louse, which can be defeated by growing resistant varieties or by grafting, the grapevine root borer plagues vineyards in the South and contiguous states to the north. This thick white worm (alone or with others) digs a tunnel up a root and around the base of the vine cutting off vital supply lines of water and nutriments. Whether or not root borers kill a vine depends on the vine's ability to put out new roots fast enough to compensate for the damage. Various strategies, such as preventing pupation by hilling up soil at the base of the vines in mid-summer, have been developed to enable vines to coexist with these pests.

Winegrowing is beginning to flourish in the South, although strong religious disapproval has

created an inhibiting cultural climate. Eight of the nine states in this region have substantially below-average per capita rates of consumption; Florida is marginally above average. Passage of farm winery legislation is critical if these states are to realize their vinicultural potential.

Alabama

1880

Reports came in from two climatically different parts of the state. Henry County is in the low-lying southeastern corner.

D. W. Merritt, Abbeville, Henry County: The Scuppernong grape is about the only grape that will live for any length of time. It has no disease or insect to attack it. The fruitage is enormous. It rarely fails. Heavy rainstorms, when in bloom, will greatly injure the yield. It makes a very fine wine. There is or would be no limit to the wine production from this grape if attention was given to it. Wild vines are found at times. Lands are very cheap here and timber in abundance for arboring. White oak in the swamps for staves. Many have one or two vines for eating purposes.

If wastage could be made cheaply into brandy much more attention would be given to it and also to fruit raising.

Cullman County is located in the mountainous northcentral section.

Charles Blato, Cullman, Cullman County: The high situation of this settlement is a great drawback on the successful cultivation of grape vines. Herbemont and Agawam grape vines suffer principally by frost, and Catawba will not succeed here. The most reliable grape vines are Concord, Clinton, Virginia Seedling, Missouri Riesling, Elvira, Merrimac, while some other white grape vines grow very well here. There has been made a trial with some imported German grape vines, but it proved unsuccessful.

The production of Muscadine wine in 1980 by Alabama's first modern farm winery signaled a new start for commercial winemaking in the state. It was made possible by passage of the Alabama Farm Winery Bill the previous year, the fruition of efforts by Jim and Marianne Eddins to ensure a better fate for their Perdido Vineyards than had befallen two other post-Repeal wineries in Baldwin County (bounded on the south by the Gulf of Mexico). A visit to Perdido is a must for any Alabaman considering becoming a winegrower and, of course, for the wine-minded tourist.

Although Muscadines and other vines resistant to P.D. belong in the southern half of the state, potential exists in the Appalachian and Piedmont areas of the north for Vinifera and European-American varieties. In fact, Alabama's second winery, Chateau La Caia in Madison County (which borders Tennessee), specializes in estate-bottled Chambourcin and Seyval blanc. Annual precipitation ranges from 50-plus inches throughout most of the state to 65 inches in the Gulf area. There are between 180 (in the north) and 300 (in the south) frost-free days.

Per capita consumption is far below average. Regulation by county determines availability of wine in other than state (monopoly) stores. In wet counties table wine may be purchased in privately licensed package stores. "Native Farm Wineries" must use 75 percent grapes grown in-state on land owned or leased by and in the vicinity of the winery. In case of natural disaster causing crop failure, a petition can be made to the state. Wholesale, retail, and tastings are permitted at the winery.

Florida

1880

A newcomer to the State saw a future only in Scuppernong.

Joseph G. Knapp, Simona, Hillsborough County: Five years' residence on the Rio Grande, at Messilla, N. Mex., and a like period at this place, have convinced me that grapes will not thrive here as there. Whether we are in a region of too great rains, too far south, or by reason of the root louse destroying the vines, or the sandy character of the soil, I will not pretend to decide, but I am convinced that grape culture is out of the question here, except with the Scuppernong varieties. Tropical fruits, or nearly such, are more profitable and better fitted to our climate and soil, and more easy of culture.

When 1979 farm winery legislation removed the very high state tax from wines produced with 100 percent Florida fruit (including citrus) there were not enough Florida grapes to meet the demand.* Several hundred acres of both Muscadines and new P.D.-resistant bunch grapes have been planted, and between 1981 and 1984 five wineries were established.

Active enological and viticultural research is being conducted at the University of Florida at Gainesville and by the Center for Viticultural Science at Florida A & M in Tallahassee. Mus-

*In 1984 the legality of preferential taxes for local wines was called into question by a Supreme Court decision involving Hawaiian legislation that favored Hawaiian-grown wine.

cadine varieties with nearly neutral fruit flavor have been identified and vinified by researchers. Scientists at the Leesburg Agricultural Research Center are breeding complex hybrids that produce commercial yields and good table wines. Recently released bunch-grape varieties include Stover, Suwannee, and Conquistador. It will take some years to discover the full potential of these new grapes for wines, but tourists to the Sunshine State should plan on omitting a few grapefruit in order to have space for a less perishable souvenir of their next spring vacation.

Annual rainfall in Florida averages about 52 inches, except in the northwestern section, which sees an average of 58 inches. The growing season ranges from 240 to 365 frost-free days.

Wine is readily available to consumers. Retailing and tastings are permitted at the winery. Per capita consumption is slightly above average.

Georgia

1880

One grower reported from the Fall Line Hills.

David Milne, Macon, Bibb County: In this county the Norton's Virginia is the standard, and is the variety most esteemed for wine. The Concord is grown for the most part for the marketing of the fruit. About one-fourth of the area is in the Scuppernong, which makes a very delicious light wine, but by many not relished.

Another report came in from the Atlantic coast.

Geo. T. Harrison, Savannah, Chatham County: The soil in this county being sandy loam, is well adapted to the healthy and vigorous growth of the Scuppernong. This grape is planted well-nigh to the exclusion of other varieties, it being a steady bearer and free from disease.

And a third from the Blue Ridge.

O. S. Bentley, Gainesville, Hall County: This is a fine grape county and might be made very profitable. The best varieties are Concord, Martha, Norton's Virginia, Hartford Prolific, Delaware, and Scuppernong.

If Georgia's founder, James Oglethorpe, had realized his dream, the Peach State would have become the Silk and Wine State. He and other early settlers tried to establish vineyards, but the vines they imported were short-lived, and the colonists had to rely on wild vines for grapes. By the late 1880s, Georgia had developed a local wine industry based on native American varieties (largely Muscadines), only to have it curtailed by state prohibition, enacted in 1907.

From 1936 until 1979 the Monarch Winery (founded as a final resting place for the state's surplus peaches) was Georgia's only winery. Then in 1979 the Happy "B" Farm began producing wine from surplus tomatoes. Most of the Muscadines grown in the state (now circa 1,000 acres) are sold to a large out-of-state winery. When Georgia passed its farm winery law in 1983, French-American and Vinifera pioneers who had been planting in the higher elevations began to build wineries with the hope of producing premium wine. The largest Vinifera vineyard belongs to Chateau Elan in Braselton, Jackson County.

The Blue Ridge Mountains melt into the Piedmont Plateau, which leads to the Fall Line Hills, which flatten into the Coastal Plain. Vinifera and European-American varieties will be the choice for the higher elevations, native American and P.D.-resistant vines for the lowlands. Average precipitation varies throughout the state from 46 to 53 inches. The growing season lasts fewer than

Several thousand vines ready to plant at Chateau Elan, Braselton, Georgia

180 days in the extreme north, about 240 days in the central section, and over 270 days in the southeast.

Wine is widely available in wet counties. "Domestic Wineries" must use a minimum of 40 percent Georgia fruit. Production is limited to 3,780 hectoliters (approximately 100,000 gallons). Producers may wholesale only if a licensed wholesaler does not want to carry the wine. Retailing is permitted at the winery. Per capita consumption is below average.

Louisiana

1880

John T. Munsch, Covington, Saint Tammany County: Grape culture is only in its infancy in this locality; several vineyards have been started. Ives, Concord, Norton's Virginia, and Herbemont are the leading sorts.

Louisiana has never been remarkable for its commercial wine production. Because a good deal of the Bayou State lies below sea level, Muscadines and P.D.-resistant varieties will be the basis of Louisiana winegrowing when it is developed. The growing season ranges from 210 to over 300 days. Annual rainfall averages from 49 inches in the north to 62 inches in the south.

State law allows convenient consumer access to wine, but local prohibition may be enforced by parish, ward, town, or city. Per capital consumption is below average.

Mississippi

1880

As did many of the reports, this one called for European immigrants to develop the area's vinicultural potential.

J. M. D. Miller, Iuka, Tishomingo County: Vines do well generally—the soil is porous—a few have tried, but have no home market—not profitable without more capital. The Scuppernong is the most profitable. There is one vine about twenty years old that produces annually

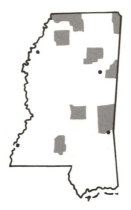

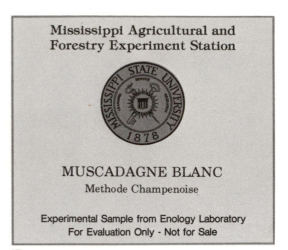

50 gallons. It is three miles south of Iuka. The Hartford Prolific being early is used for table grapes. The Catawba is the next most profitable. The Clinton is a hardy wine grape but not fit for table use. There are other good varieties. If Italians or Germans would locate in this vicinity they could buy lands at $1 per acre that would yield handsomely in grapes and small fruits generally. The location is unsurpassed for health.

1980: Louis D. Wise, vice-president of Mississippi State University reports: "We're putting more effort and class into everything connected with the project than would normally be done in a research program of this sort, the rationale being the nature of the products and the fact this is all happening in Mississippi! Who'd believe it?" The project is the million-dollar, Swiss chalet–style A. B. McKay Food and Enology Laboratory in Starkville. Fruit from four research vineyards is vinified under the direction of microbiologist Boris Stojanovic and enologist/author Richard Vine. The potential of grape varieties for use in table, dessert, and sparkling wines is evaluated. There are degree programs in viticulture and enology.

Within four years of the 1976 Native Wine Act, four wineries were established in the Magnolia State and a fifth was started in 1984. Vintners are emphasizing the regionally distinct Muscadines. French-American varieties that survive for several years in the humid, P.D.-ridden conditions are also vinified. There are even a few Vinifera wines made in Mississippi from young experimental vineyards.

Boris Stojanovic, Ruth Ellen Church, Leon Adams, and Louis Wise celebrate the opening of the A. B. McKay Laboratory during a visit to the Thousand Oaks Winery, Starkville, Mississippi.

This wine was made and bottled under authorization of the Code of Federal Regulations, 240.545 approved by the U. S. Bureau of Achohol, Tobacco, and Firearms.

This sample exemplifies both grape and wine research which is conducted by the Mississippi Agricultural and Forestry Experiment Station at **Mississippi State University.**

Variety		
Vintage	Lot	Serial

The Hartford Prolific grape mentioned in the 1880 report by J. M. D. Miller is a Labrusca variety, as is Catawba. The fact that these vines survived P.D. may be due to the fact that Tishomingo County has the highest altitudes in Mississippi—Woodall Mountain is 806 feet. Most of the state from the Mississippi Delta to the Gulf of Mexico is flat or nearly so. The frost-free season ranges from 210 to 300 days, with annual rainfall averaging from 50 to 60 inches. Given the serious interest in and state support of winegrowing, more microclimates may be identified where non-Muscadines may be grown profitably.

The Magnolia State is not the easiest place to market wine. Mississippi has the lowest per-capita consumption in the country, and, in 1966, was the last state to repeal Prohibition. The state monopolizes wholesaling, a situation that always drastically restricts selection. Retail sales are limited to package stores. There is local prohibition by county. "Native Wineries" that use at least 51 percent Mississippi-grown fruit may wholesale (to the state), retail, and have tastings. There is no limit on production. Native wineries are the only producers of alcoholic beverages in the state allowed to advertise.

North Carolina

1880

The report from North Carolina's westernmost county tells of hard work and mixed results.

William Beal, Murphy, Cherokee County: Scuppernong does not do well here: the hardiest and most productive is Concord. Catawba does well generally and is of first-class flavor, but rots sometimes; Iona does well but is rather acid. A grape was sold here from Cumberland nurseries as Iona which is a round black grape, rather earlier than Concord, hangs well on the vines, and bids fair to be quite an acquisition. Cherokee does well where sheltered. Eumelan does not yield well, and we have but few other varieties.

I have labored hard to introduce grape culture here, but have found it hard work. The people are becoming interested in eating grapes, and are beginning to cultivate them for eating. The climate is well adapted to them, and they have not failed but once in twenty-five years.

The picture seemed a bit brighter on the Coastal Plain.

J. P. McLean, Fayetteville, Cumberland County: The largest vineyard in our county, and is now perhaps the largest in the State, is owned by Col. W. J. Green; it embraces 140 acres in vines of the best varieties. The Scuppernong grape has heretofore been the leading variety in our county, but it is now being superseded by better varieties. The Scuppernong is the most hardy and prolific grape in our State. Our state legislature is about to pass a "Maine liquor law": this, I think, will give a new impulse to our

Sparkling Moselle label from a nineteenth-century North Carolina winery near Asheville

vineyards and orchards, as wine and cider will be all the stimulating drinks we can then get.

The ranging topography of North Carolina enables the state to host the full range of grape families, from Vinifera in the mountainous west (Mount Mitchell at 6,684 feet is the highest point east of the Mississippi River) to Muscadines on the Coastal Plain. The state's two largest wineries illustrate the topographical picture. At Biltmore Estate in Asheville, the opulent French-American chateau built by the Vanderbilt family in the 1890s, more than a hundred acres of Vinifera and French-American varieties are planted,

and a showplace winery/visitor center has been built. In contrast, at the opposite end of the state is Duplin Cellars, a grape farmers' cooperative winery that uses exclusively Muscadine grapes to make many types of wine and brandy.

Most of the state's several thousand vineyard acres are planted in Muscadines. An active breeding program has produced such popular Rotundifolia varieties as Magnolia, Carlos, and Noble. The state also has an active enological research program to help solve some of the special vinification problems posed by Muscadine fruit.

Biltmore Estate

Table wines are generally available and, unlike dessert wines, are not subject to local prohibition. Wholesaling, retailing, and tastings are permitted at the winery. There are no restrictions on production. Per capita consumption is below average.

South Carolina

1880

Land was inexpensive and viticulturally suitable in the Piedmont area of the state.

M. L. Donaldson, Greenville, Greenville County: Viticulture for profit in Greenville County is of recent date, though from the earliest settlement of the country a few grape vines were planted about every household for the use of the family. . . . The climate and soil of this portion of the State is peculiarly adapted to the growth and maturity of the vine and its fruit. I would further state that this county, more especially the upper, or northern half, abounds in small mountains of gradual ascent, upon the sides of which the grape grows to perfection. These lands can be bought from $5 to $10 per acre, and all that is now necessary to produce thousands of gallons of the finest of wines is immigrants from the wine-growing districts of Europe.

Most of South Carolina's grape acreage is devoted to Muscadines and some Concords for sale to large wineries. The historic native American vines that originated here—Isabella, Lenoir, and Herbemont—are no longer cultivated commercially. The hilly section of the state should be able to accommodate Vinifera and European-American varieties, but the flat "low country" probably hosts the dreaded Pierce's disease.

James Truluck began testing that topographical risk in the mid 1970s, when he brought "a touch of France to the Old South" by planting Vinifera and Vinifera crosses to supply his winery near Lake City in the heart of the Coastal Plain. Truluck is the area's pioneer in table wines, instead of sweet "sippin'" types. There has not as yet been a strong push from the state or

Truluck Winery

from growers' groups to develop local winegrowing as there has been in other southern states.

As we move east from the northwestern corner of the state, the Blue Ridge Mountains (whose highest point is Sassafras Mountain at 3,560 feet) and the Piedmont Plateau give way to the Sand Hills and Coastal Plain. Except for the northern tip, the state has a growing season of from 210 to 300 days. Average annual precipitation is 45 inches, except in the northwest mountain area, where it reaches over 70 inches per year.

South Carolina is one of the few states in the nation that do not have local prohibition. Table and sparkling wines may be purchased at grocery and other stores, whereas sale of dessert wines, vermouth, and other alcoholic beverages is restricted to package stores. Wine producers may wholesale, retail, and give tastings. Per capita consumption is below average.

Tennessee

1880

In days before refrigeration, summer heat was a major obstacle to viniculture.

M. Crass, Murfreesborough, Rutherford County: Grapes are the most certain of our fruits here. They never miss, and sometimes bear remarkably large crops. Many people have from 10 to 100 vines; the fruit is used in the family, making very good preserves, and some will be sold at Murfreesborough from 3 to 6 cents a pound. The great obstacle in the way of making wine is in keeping it. There is not a vaulted cellar in the county, and to be sure no wine can be made, or kept, in temperature ranging from zero to 100. Another obstacle is the ripening of the fruit in the heat of the summer. We have no variety here that could be kept until anything like temperate weather. Some of the newer sorts were recommended to ripen the latter part of September, like the Goethe and Hermann, and others, but have not done so this far. The best

varieties are Concord, Brighton, Goethe, Iona, Martha, and, in my opinion, the Herbemont Madeira, of which there is a vine in Murfreesborough, brought there by Mr. Wendell, 40 years ago, and been bearing fruit for 3 generations. The flavor is equal to the best foreign. This State will be a great wine country in time.

The hills of Tennessee are full of active enophiles dedicated to the cause of Tennessee table wine. There is an active growers' network that conducts varietal evaluations and lobbies for increased state and Tennessee Valley Authority (TVA) support. As a result, new wineries will continue to be established to accommodate the harvests of the new vineyards.

Spring frost and fluctuating warm and very cold spells make Vinifera growing difficult in many areas. Matching variety with microclimate is of utmost importance. It is not unusual to find single vineyards in Tennessee with a mix of European-American, Labrusca, and Vinifera varieties.

The western section, bordered by the Mississippi River, is the lowest-lying part of the state. Rolling hills appear eastward toward the Cumberland Plateau and the Appalachian range (where the highest peak is Clingmans Dome at 6,642 feet). The length of the growing season varies from 240 days in the east to as few as 150 in the mountains. Average precipitation ranges from 48 to 54 inches annually.

The state's political climate is not favorable for wine consumers. Local prohibition is still in force by county. Wine sales are limited to package stores, although farm winery legislation permits a restricted amount of retailing at the winery. Producers must use 85 percent Tennessee grapes unless crop loss from natural disaster can be claimed. Per capita consumption is very low.

Texas

1880

Winegrowing was a wild affair in the Lone Star State.

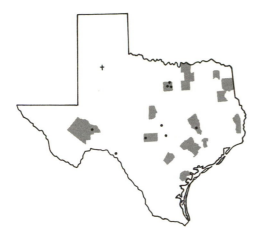

E. B. Johnson, Hallettsville, Lavaca County: The Mustang grape of different varieties and flavor grows along our creeks, and nearly all the wine made in this county is made therefrom. About every other year there is an abundant crop, but the birds and the hogs get the most of it; the former from the branches of the vines that climb to the tops of the trees, and the hogs get the benefit of the fallen grapes, for which they as regularly make their rounds as a soldier on guard duty.

Winemaking seems to have been a simpler process then:

I am under the impression that four gallons of grapes make one of wine. The process of wine making here from the Mustang is as follows: The grapes are first washed in a tub or water-tight flour-barrel, and allowed to stand three days, about which time the pulp and skins rise to the top and must then be skimmed off, and the juice put into casks or barrels. Water is sometimes added, and also sugar, both of different quantities to suit taste or whim of makers. A strong Mustang wine is sometimes thick and will intoxicate quickly. The German population, constantly on the increase, use the Mustang grapes for wine, buying them at from 25 to 50 cents per bushel and selling the wine at from 25 to 50 cents per gallon, generally not less than 50 cents and sometimes as high as $1 per gallon.

Fear of taxes endangered the accuracy of survey data.

This soil varies so much in different parts of the county that a grape that will flourish in one locality may die in another. The Black Spanish yields well. The revenue laws are detrimental to grape growing and wine making in this section. No one can afford to pay the large income tax, and you will readily perceive the difficulty in getting information from those who make wine, as no man will willingly expose himself to a penalty for wine making.

Vinifera culture was threatened by false springs then as now:

Dr. D. W. Fentress, San Saba, Saba County: Grape growing is yet an experiment in this county. The ones which promise best are Black Spanish and Herbemont, both seedlings of the summer grape of the South. The varieties of Vinifera stand our winters well, but we very often have sufficient warm weather in January or first February to start the sap, which is frozen by cold snaps which are apt to visit us the last of February to 10th March. I am mulching this year to prevent this as well as weaving cedar brush through the trellis. I make an excellent wine from the Mustang grape, which readily brings $1 per bottle at retail—has most resemblance to Port wine.

Texas is a veritable organic encyclopedia of viticulture. The variety of grape species both cultivated and wild found in this vast state are unrivaled anywhere. The dividing line between East and West runs through Texas, and the spectrum of climates, soils, indigenous pests and diseases, and natural disasters here is phenomenal. Western Texas has a Mediterranean-California environment, and hosts a burgeoning acreage of Vinifera vines in its alkaline soils. This western section encompasses the Great Plains, the High Plains (Llano Estacado), and the Trans Pecos region (which includes the Stockton Plateau and the Davis Mountains, the state's highest, coolest area). In the center of the state is the Edwards Plateau or "Hill Country." The altitude gradually decreases as we move east to the Coastal Plain.

Hail is a more serious problem for growers here than in any other state. Both cotton root rot and Pierce's disease are also limiting factors to viticulture in Texas. Growing seasons extend from fewer than 180 days in the far north to more

Chateau Montgolfier's balloon, Texas

than 330 days in the deep south. Average annual precipitation is 11 ½ inches in the westernmost region and 45 inches in the east.

There are many areas in the southern, central, and eastern sections of the state where only vines with Aestivalis, Candicans (the "Mustang" grape), or Rotundifolia heritage can survive. Viticulture historians can visit the T. V. Munson Memorial Vineyard in Denison, which houses a unique collection of the hybridist's interspecific crosses. Herbemont and Lenoir, two old native American varieties once popular in France, are still under commercial cultivation in Del Rio.

For the past decade, Texans have been actively searching their 267,338 square miles for the proper microclimates and soil conditions suitable for planting the Vinifera and Vinifera crosses necessary for premium Lone Star wine. Undaunted by the wide geographic expanse and diverse growing conditions, Texas winegrowers are banding together to promote their rapidly expanding new industry. Both Texas A & M and the University of Texas have active programs in enology and viticulture. U.T. has also planted several experimental vineyards in west Texas and developed a commercial Vinifera vineyard of more than a thousand acres near Bakersfield, where investors from France and Texas built the giant state-of-the-art Ste. Genevieve winery in 1984.

The state permits sales of wine in food stores and other outlets, but local prohibition is still in force in many parts of Texas. There are no restrictions on farm winery production. Wineries may wholesale, retail, and have tastings, although sales at the winery are not permitted in dry areas. Per capita consumption is below average.

 **I I** CENTRAL STATES

Introduction

The central United States is etched by major waterways—the Mississippi, Missouri, Ohio, Red, and Arkansas rivers—and crowned by the Great Lakes. America's earliest large-scale winegrowing began before the Civil War along the riverbanks in the heart of this region. Within a few decades, however, fungus diseases became an increasingly serious problem in the warmer

Low winter temperatures are a prime concern of Central States growers.

areas, and the major grape growing efforts were moved to the cooler northern section, around the Great Lakes.

Because these central states experience some of the coldest winters of any in the country, vines must be covered with soil or snow to ensure reliable crops from tender varieties such as Vinifera. Native American or European-American vines that can withstand frigid temperatures are most often the choice of local winegrowers. High winds, hail, drought, and icy spring blasts are all part of the climate here. Black rot and the mildews that devastated nineteenth-century vineyards have, however, been brought under control. Today, state extension services in several central states provide growers with comprehensive guides for both insect and disease control.

Concord used to be king here, but stiff competition from Washington State and other regions has made Concord farming increasingly less profitable in recent years. Vineyards without firm contracts from processors are being pulled, and researchers are looking into the feasibility of grafting Concords over to varieties that are more in demand. In some states variety-evaluation trials are being conducted by viticulturists in conjunction with state enologists to determine which wine grapes can be recommended to growers. States that support grape and wine research have seen a dramatic increase in the number of new wineries over the past decade. Conversely, there has been very little vineyard and winery development in states with no viticultural experts in their employ.

The old-fashioned exteriors of the historic midwestern wine cellars can be deceiving; behind them may be the most modern winemaking equipment. In Missouri and Ohio, especially, we find a rich winegrowing history combined with progressive enological methods. Although old-style sweet Labrusca wines remain popular in the region, there is an increasing demand for drier dinner wines and brut champagnes made with European-American and Vinifera grapes. In addition, two historic grape varieties, Cynthiana and Norton, are enjoying a renaissance of popularity because of the rich red wine they produce and their hardiness in the vineyard.

Per capita wine consumption remains low to very low here relative to the rest of the nation. Religious prohibition restricts much of the population. The situation is exacerbated by a political climate dominated in the nation's "bread basket" by grain interests. Grapegrowers' complaints about injury to their vines from the 2,4-D herbicide sprayed on grain fields often fall on deaf ears. On the brighter side, there is a strong regional pride that can be rallied in support of local products—including home-town wine.

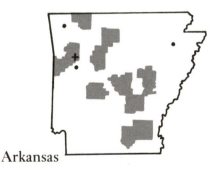

Arkansas

1880

Cynthiana makes a world-class wine in the opinion of D. D. Forman, Hackett City, Sebastian County:

The true Aestivalis does remarkably well here, among which the Cynthiana (supposed to be a native of this State) grows luxuriantly, and produces a wine which will rank among the best *red* wines of this *or any other country*. Foreign varieties have not been tried here. We plant our vines 9 by 18 feet apart, and trellis the long way with three to four slats.

Muscadines are best in the state's southernmost county.

J. F. Shuler, El Dorado, Union County: The grapes raised in this county are the Scuppernong, and a continuous rain in the month of May (when in bloom) is very ruinous to them.

This Ouachita Mountain grower felt that Arkansas is the best place on the continent for grapes.

Dr. Geo. W. Laurence, Hot Springs, Garland County: I have the largest acreage in vineyard, with the greatest variety of vines in culture in the county. Our standard vines are of the *Vitis aestivalis*, belonging to our State, together with Norton's Virginia seedling. Concord, Delaware, and Martha are a success with us. Ives seedling is one of our hardiest vines; grapes good for table and wine; flavor very fine. Scuppernong is a choice wine grape in this re-

gion. Catawba is a failure with me. . . . I have twenty-one acres in grapevines, and over one hundred and thirty varieties of grapes. I feel sure that we are in the best belt or zone of latitudes, embracing the whole State, for the culture of grapes, in productiveness and flavor, on the continent. My vineyard is from four to seven years old.

Visitors to Arkansas can add wine touring to the roster of vacation pleasures found in the state. The two largest producers are Wiederkehr Wine Cellars (1,750,000-gallon storage capacity) and Post (500,000-gallon storage capacity). Both are family-owned wineries that date to circa 1880 when the families' Swiss and Bavarian forebears settled in Altus. In the past, native wines were appreciated more for their stimulative properties than their finesse. Times have changed. The leading wineries are now producing table, aperitif, and sparkling wines for the more sophisticated palate in addition to sweet native American wines. There is also a substantial juice industry that currently absorbs about half the grape production.

A full repertoire of grape families finds a home today in Arkansas: Vinifera, European-American, Labrusca, Aestivalis, and Muscadines are all represented by varietal wines. The Ozark

Wiederkehr Gift Shop, Altus, Arkansas

Plateau, and the Boston and Ouachita Mountains in the northwestern half of the state provide microclimates suitable for European and European-American wine grapes. Native American varieties are better suited to the flat, humid southern and eastern sections of the state. Annual precipitation ranges from 43 to 51 inches. The growing season varies from under 180 days in the Boston Mountains to more than 240 days in the southeastern corner.

A state breeding program has released several new seedless table varieties, including Venus and Reliance, that promise to broaden the viticultural picture in Arkansas and in other states as well. Justin Morris, a viticulturist at the University of Arkansas, is optimistic about Arkansas's wine-growing future: "The most encouraging factor is the utilization by our industry of our recent research findings. It is rewarding to see the new plantings going in with drip irrigation and improved trellis systems."

Spring frost, hail, fungus diseases, grape scale, and the grapevine root borer are the principal obstacles faced by growers. Drought has also been a severe problem in recent years—the reason that irrigation lines are going in with many new plantings.

"Drought" can also be a problem for wine consumers living or traveling in the state. The per capita consumption is one of the very lowest in the nation. There is local prohibition, and state law permits wine sales only at package stores or local wineries. Availability in restaurants is determined by local option electives. Retail sales and tastings are permitted at those "Native Wineries" that use at least 50 percent in-state fruit.

Illinois

1880

According to one grower, most Americans lack winemaking skills and prefer to sell fresh fruit.

> John Balsiger, Highland, Madison County: There are some vineyards in which the rot caused some loss, more or less, particularly on the Concord. One of the best yielders last year proved to be the Norton's Virginia seedling.

> With me it yielded rather over one gallon per vine, and was perfectly healthy. But it must be said that the previous season it yielded nothing at all, the buds being killed by the cold of the preceding winter. In the part of the county where I live, the largest part of the crop is used for wine-making. In the western part, near Saint Louis or other markets, nearly the whole crop is sold for eating or shipping to other places, particularly north. Generally (but with many exceptions) the vine-growers of American birth prefer selling their fruit, as they do not understand the manufacture of wine: German or French growers, particularly those at a distance from a market as they are here, think it more advantageous to press their grapes.

Strong thoughts on native varieties from L. L. Lake, M.D., Belvidere, Boone County:

> Have experimented with over 100 varieties in the last twenty-five years. I have discarded almost all the pure natives, such as Concord, Hartford, Tallman, and Clinton. I consider them as abominations. There are a few pure natives, such as Delaware and Prentice and Wyoming, that I can tolerate. . . .

With 60 percent of its population concentrated around Chicago, there is plenty of open space left for vineyards beside the cornfields in Illinois. Indeed, grape growing was widespread throughout the state before Prohibition. Many former wine cellars are now used for aging cheese. These days, large-scale grain farming brings with it the use of 2,4-D, a herbicide which is deadly to grapevines. A vine can be damaged by drifts of 2,4-D originating from as far as twenty miles away. Illinois winegrowers are joining with neighboring states in the Upper Mississippi Valley to help resolve this and other regional problems.

Annual precipitation ranges from 34 inches in the north to 43 inches in the south. The growing season ranges from north to south between 150 and 210 days. Vines in the northern sector can be subjected to winters of −20°F. The southern half of the state is warmer and more hospitable to viticulture as long as there is no 2,4-D in the air.

Wine may be purchased in convenient locations. There is a need for farm winery legislation to improve the economic viability of winegrowing in Illinois. Per capita consumption is near (below) average.

Indiana

1880

Once again the sentiment was expressed that European immigrants possessed winegrowing skills that other Americans lacked.

> Calvin Fletcher, Spencer, Owen County: While I have no commercial data for any of the above [survey questions about grape and wine production], I give, as you request, my studious estimate, based on my own experience, knowledge, and conference with my neighbors. The depredations of insects, the exigencies of seasons, the semi-paralysis pervading horticulturists and vine-growers arising therefrom causes me to wonder at any attempt to overcome the above-named casualties. "The hope that springs eternal," &c., is the only explanation. Skilled

> Germans accomplish more than others, but their children fail as we natives do. Nature affords us the wild grape two years out of five, and man has only equaled that proportion by use of such second-quality grapes as Concord, Clinton, and Ives seedling. I have 50 most approved varieties, and indorse [sic] only the above.

Winegrowing preceded statehood in Indiana. Switzerland County and the town of Vevay were founded in 1804 by Swiss vinedresser J. J. Dufour. Dufour succeeded in producing wine with native American varieties as did other Indiana winegrowers throughout the nineteenth century. But problems first with vine pests, then with the forces of temperance, plagued Hoosier viticulture almost to extinction. While grape growing is still a challenge, modern viticulture and farm winery legislation (passed in 1971) have brought winegrowing back to life here.

From the sand dunes of Lake Michigan to the banks of the Ohio River, wine-grape vineyards are appearing. The region's warm summers and average 180-day growing season allow good ripening of the fruit. Cold winters (except in favorable sites along the Ohio in the south) tend to limit the choice to the hardier varieties. The majority of the state's circa five hundred acres are planted in French-American wine grapes; Labrusca accounts for almost all the rest. There is a very small acreage of Vinifera. Annual precipitation ranges from 37 inches in the north to 43 ½ inches in the south.

One of the handful of states with no local prohibition, Indiana permits wine sales in package, drug, and food stores. "Small Wineries" must use 100 percent Indiana fruit unless there is a demonstrable crop failure. Production is limited to 100,000 gallons. Wholesaling, retailing, and tastings are permitted at the winery. Per capita consumption is well below average.

Iowa

1880

C. N. Eggert of Iowa City, Johnson County complained that fruit sold by small home vineyardists brought down market value.

The greatest drawback to viniculture hereabouts is the excessive cheapness of grapes and wine. In my estimate of 100 to 150 acres I am not at all certain whether the many small patches are accounted for that one finds on nearly every farm and village property. From these smaller plots a large quantity of grapes is thrown on the market and sold at any price. Hence, no more than 1 cent per pound could be realized for the best ripe Concord grapes.

One winemaker reported a preference for wild Riparia grapes over the cultivated varieties.

J. Gregory, Ames, Story County: I am a wine manufacturer, but do not cultivate any grapes, as I find the native grapes (in which the woods of Central and Western Iowa abound, and from which they can be obtained as cheap as they could be harvested from a vineyard, the price ranging from 1¼ to 2 cents per pound) to be far superior for the purpose of wine-making to any cultivated grapes in Iowa, making a wine of higher alcoholic content per cent., richer in color, more delicious in flavor, and maturing quicker than any other kind. Wine made in September is ready for the market in January, thus enabling the manufacturer to get quick returns from his investment. The average amount of wine produced from a bushel of grapes is about 5 gallons. The variety of grapes from which I manufacture my wine is known as *Vitis cordifolia* and *Vitis riparia*, or common blue grape. The color of the wine is a brilliant dark red, and is in quality considered by those who use it equal to the imported article, and finds ready sale when placed upon the market; as an evidence of its worth, all the wine I manufactured last season is already disposed of.

Annual precipitation ranges from 28 to 33 inches (less in the west). The growing season averages from 150 (or fewer) to 180 days between

Little boy holding grapes in Amana Colony

frosts. Winter temperatures can plummet to −35°F and necessitate burying of Vinifera and other tender vines. The region is a good one for some of the new, very cold-hardy varieties being developed in Minnesota.

The grapevine's vulnerability to 2,4-D herbicide severely limits commercial vineyard potential in Iowa, the source of one tenth of the nation's food supply. Despite the lack of viticulture, however, there are nearly a score of wineries in Iowa, most of which are located in the historic Amana community, where grapevines traditionally grew up the sides of houses and in communal gardens. In his *Story of an Amana Winemaker*, George Kraus observes that "the grapes visitors see growing in Amana today on the trellis supports on the side of some homes end up being spread on hot biscuits as jam or jelly. I doubt that any villagers bother to make even a gallon of wine from Amana grapevines any more" (p. 133).

Kraus makes six kinds of grape wine using Michigan-grown Concord, Fredonia, Ontario,

Niagara, Delaware, and Catawba. In addition, he ferments his home-grown rhubarb (a plant that requires the ground to freeze several inches deep each winter—no problem in Iowa!), and recommends the Sutton Seedless variety for wine because "its sugar and acid levels are more uniform than old-fashioned rhubarb and that makes it easier to balance the wine formula." For people who live far from vineyards, Kraus gives tips on making wild grape, dandelion, cherry, red clover, wild blackberry, beet, tomato, blueberry, cranberry, grapefruit, and orange wines.

Iowa has a monopoly on the sale of alcoholic beverages. Wine must be purchased from a state monopoly store or from local wineries, an inauspicious situation for wine lovers. Per capita consumption is extremely low.

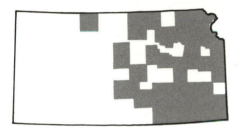

Kansas

1880

Western Kansas was too beset by natural disasters for vineyards to be successful.

J. A. Poff, Russell, Russell County: There is not a bearing grapevine in this county. Every effort has been made to raise grapes, but grasshoppers, drought, or some calamity overtook us and the vines destroyed. Vines of all kinds are a poor experiment here in Western Kansas.

The eastern part of the state seemed a better bet.

J. N. Insley, Oskaloosa, Jefferson County: The Concord, Hartford Prolific, Clinton, and Delaware succeed admirably in the eastern half of Kansas, the limestone hillsides producing a luxuriant growth of wine and fruit. About the only enemy to the grape in this locality is mildew, caused by excessive rain in August and fore part of September.

Just as the vineyards came into bearing, Prohibition went into effect.

George W. Ashby, Chanute, Neosho County: Our country is comparatively new; nearly all grapes have been planted in the last eight years. Little wine is yet made, but of good quality, and eagerly sought for. The prohibition law now going into force in the State of Kansas, will destroy the traffic in wine here. Its manufacture in a domestic way may possibly continue for household purposes. Grape planting does not appear to be affected in anticipation of the law, as our people are largely increasing the number of their vines. Owners of vineyards will be likely to make a little wine for sacramental purposes.

A recent vintage of grand champion jelly at the Harvey County State Fair was made with the wine grape Baco noir, a clear sign of viticultural progress in the Sunshine State. For the most part, Labrusca destined for nonwine markets still dominates the very small acreage in Kansas. A few individuals now planting European-American varieties are planning wineries, now that Kansas, too, has passed (in 1983) farm winery legislation.

The climate is suitable for most types of vines in the central southeast, where the growing season ranges from 180 to 200-plus days and winter temperatures are not unduly low. Annual precipitation increases from fewer than 20 inches to 25 to 37 inches as we move eastward from the western edge of the state. High winds are reported to be an inconvenience that causes shoot breakage.

The unfavorable political situation in Kansas has already been mentioned. Wine sales are limited to package stores, and statewide on-sale prohibition outlaws consumption everywhere but in private clubs. The current "Domestic Winery" bill permits sales only to wholesalers and retailers and does not permit tasting. Per capita consumption is, needless to say, among the lowest in the nation.

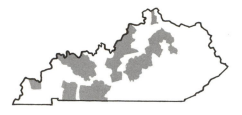

Kentucky

1880

Problems with rot kept one grower on a continual search for new varieties.

Thomas S. Kennedy, Louisville, Jefferson County: The kinds of grapes tried previous to 1860 in vineyard culture in this vicinity, such as the Isabella, Catawba, and Alexander, became so subject to the rot that the annual crops could not be relied on; and the vineyards, which embraced hundreds of acres, were totally abandoned. During the past twenty years such grapes as the Concord, Ives, Perkins, Venango, and other Labrusca kinds, have been cultivated with partial success, and are still relied on with other kinds of the other classes, such as Delaware, Norton's Virginia, &c. for both table use and marketing and for domestic wine. The large majority of vines however, . . . are of the newer varieties, being seedlings and hybrids, which are being tested . . . either for table or for wine.

A Kentucky vine was sent to France to fight phylloxera.

It has been found that a variety, originating in Shelby County, Kentucky, and known as Taylor's Bullitt, has dry, wiry roots, that resist the attacks of the *Phylloxera vastatrix*. In consequence, a large demand has sprung up for cuttings for shipment to France, where these cuttings are used to make roots upon which to graft the European vine. The Taylor's Bullitt belongs to the Riparia class, and from it some seedlings have been obtained, such as Elvira, Black Taylor, and others, which promise to prove themselves to be our best and hardiest wine and table grapes.

Founded by Jean Jacques Dufour in 1798, the original Kentucky Vineyard Society lasted little more than a decade because Dufour relocated his vineyard in Indiana. With hopes of catalyzing a

The author examines a vine trunk for injury at the Colcord Vineyard, Bourbon County, Kentucky, in 1975.

lasting viticultural revival in the state, a group of growers reestablished the Kentucky Vineyard Society in 1981. Many vineyards and several wineries have sprung up in recent years, but restrictive state regulations currently inhibit the economic viability of local wineries. Kentucky is renowned for home-grown horses, tobacco, whiskey, and music. Why not Kentucky wine to age in Blue Grass barrels?

The potential of wine-grape varieties has already been proved in many parts of Kentucky. Average precipitation is 45 inches, and the growing season lasts 180 days, plus or minus (minus in the Cumberland Mountains and Plateau). Winter lows are rarely less than −5°F.

Wine may be sold only in package stores, drug stores, and to a very limited extent in local wineries. On-sale consumption is permitted in wet jurisdictions. At this writing, the Kentucky legislature limits retail sales by local wineries to 12 bottles per year. Only when more favorable legislation is enacted for winegrowers will there be a true revival of viniculture here. Kentucky has the second lowest per capita rate of wine consumption in the country.

Michigan

1880
Rose-bugs plagued the grape crops in this lake-shore county.

> W. T. Withey, Benton Harbor, Berrien County: The grape crop was rather light for 1880 in our section, on account of the rose-bug. When the grape blossoms, and just as they are going out of blossom, the air seems filled with rose-bugs, who alight and eat all, and sometimes only a few berries out of a bunch, which makes imperfect bunches. Whatever damage they do is done in a few days. There are very few grapes made into wine in my section, and that mostly for private use. But people are talking of going into wine-making, as the prices for grapes have ruled low of late years.

Any state, no matter how northerly, with the motto "Si Quaeris Peninsulam Amoenan, Circumspice" (If you seek a pleasant peninsula, look around you), is bound to have vineyard potential. Michigan touches four of the five Great Lakes and indeed has prosperous fruit acreage along the Lake Michigan shore.

Concords for Welch's juice have been the mainstay of the grape industry since the turn of the century and continue so today. During Prohibition, Michigan Concords were used not only by Welch but also by nearby Canadian wineries that made wine for export (often no farther away than the bootleg market across the border). Today the market for Concords is very depressed. The white Labrusca variety Niagara remains more in demand as a base for champagnes and cream sherries as well as white grape juice.

The leading white French-American variety in Michigan is Vidal blanc. Research conducted by Michigan State University's department of horticulture demonstrated the potential for Vidal both in the vineyard, in areas with a sufficiently long growing season, and in the winery. Vidal champagnes, dry table, and late-harvest dessert wines have brought critical acclaim to Michigan wines. Seyval, Vignoles, Riesling, and Chardonnay all appear to have a future for white wine here. Red wine is currently in much less demand, but its leading varieties are Baco noir, Maréchal Foch, and Chancellor.

Wine-grape growing is expanding beyond the southwestern counties; there is now a high concentration of new plantings around Traverse City in Leelanau and Grand Traverse counties. The eastern shores of the state are also the site of new vineyards. Proximity to a lake shore can add 30 days to the growing season and increase winter temperature lows by as much as 10°F. Frost-free days in Michigan number as few as 60 in the north and as many as 180 in the south. Annual precipitation varies from 28.5 to 35 inches.

Wine is conveniently available to consumers in Michigan. When they use at least 75 percent Michigan fruit, winemakers qualify for reductions in state license fees and excise taxes. Annual per capita consumption is below average.

Minnesota

1880
Temperature and economics limited grape raising to table varieties, according to one report.

> Truman M. Smith, St. Paul, Ramsey County: Grapes raised here have to all have

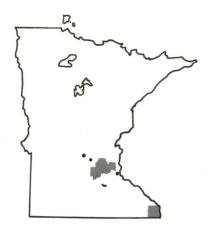

winter protection; that is, pruned in the fall, laid down, and covered with earth. The expense is so much and labor so great that no one will undertake to grow grapes in this northern latitude for wine-making in competition with more favored climes; but grapes are raised and sold for table use and preserving, and before railroads came here paid very well; but now transportation is so cheap, they come so quickly, and in pretty good shape, that grape-growing here will not pay any profit. I have grown grapes for twenty-one years, and have had but two entire failures. I have raised as high as 4 tons per acre, but here not over 2 tons per acre should be left on the vines. The vines should be planted 8 to 10 feet apart each way, to let in sun and air, and give the fruit a chance to ripen before early frosts in fall; and hence the plan not to let the vines overbear pays in earlier ripening, and better and larger bunches of fruit, which is very desirable for table grapes.

L. M. Ford of Saint Paul, Ramsey County, had a more positive outlook:

One important feature of grape culture here is the fact that our climate appears to suit the Delaware remarkably well, while in many localities farther south they succeed, but very poorly. Of course vines are covered here in the autumn, which adds to the expense of the crop. Our climate in many respects is very good for grapes, as we have very little mildew or other diseases peculiar to southern localities.

In Minnesota, there are growing seasons similar to those of the cooler regions of Europe and California. Winter temperature lows of −20° to −40°F, however, are more than most vines can take standing up. Foch, Millot, Seyval, and other early French-American varieties grown in Minnesota's Mississippi Valley have produced prize-winning wines, but only after their owners have literally lain them down for their winter sleep. Covered with a blanket of earth or mulch, vines will not be subjected to subzero temperatures, nor will they be as susceptible to damage from sudden temperature fluctuations occurring in open air.

Flexible though they are, grapevines are not entirely amenable to seasonal yo-yoing, and the process of burying vines is costly for growers. The future of Minnesota viniculture rests with grape breeders who have already made impressive progress in producing "polar-guarded" wine grapes. Varieties such as Edelweiss and St. Croix have withstood temperatures to −30°F when they had good conditions and care the previous summer. Newer crosses are able to withstand temperatures as low as −40°F and still produce a crop. Experimental wines produced from these new crosses have already won awards in national home-wine competitions. For the small winegrowing community to maintain its regional identity and obviate the necessity of importing grapes from out-of-state, skilled vine management and specially adapted varieties are essential.

Extra-cold-hardy wine grapes are also needed in other states, in Canada, and abroad; hardy

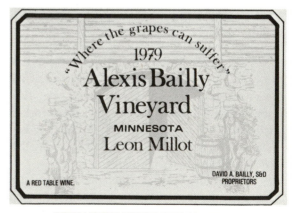

"Where the grapes can suffer"

1979

Alexis Bailly Vineyard

MINNESOTA

Leon Millot

A RED TABLE WINE.

DAVID A. BAILLY, S&D PROPRIETORS

PRODUCED & BOTTLED BY ALEXIS BAILLY VINEYARD, INC. HASTINGS, MN.

Minnesota wine label tells all.

native American vines such as Isabella are now growing in some Soviet provinces (the twenty-first century may see a vinicultural détente—Siberian wine made with Minnesota-bred grapes or, conversely, North Dakota wine made with Russian-bred varieties). The growing season in Minnesota ranges from fewer than 90 to about 150 days. Annual precipitation averages from 21 to 29 inches.

Wine is readily available to consumers. Farm winery legislation allows a maximum 50,000-gallon yearly production. The operator of the winery must own the farm and use a majority of Minnesota-grown grapes unless there is a crop shortage. Wineries have wholesale, retail, and tasting privileges. Minnesotans consume below-average quantities of wine per year.

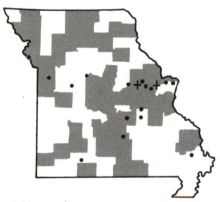

Missouri

1880

One grower was also an innovative winemaker.

> Frederick Muench, Dutzow, Warren County: The cheapest wine is that made of Concord grapes; the most precious wine is the so-called Missouri Black Rose made from Norton and Cynthiana grapes by a method first introduced by me. Highly promising wines are made from the Neosho and Far West grapes, both of them quite new varieties of the Aestivalis class, found growing wild in the primitive forests in Newton County in Southwest Missouri, and first cultivated by me.

Riparia was deemed a good parent for wine grapes.

> Of the best grape vines belonging to the Cordifolia [Riparia] class the Taylor seedlings seem to do best, some of them, such as Noah, Missouri Riesling, Beauty, Amber, &c., yielding a most delicious light wine; but experiments with these and other new varieties have only just begun. Vintners of this country (except myself) have too long depended on the Concord and Clinton, and as these varieties latterly failed from year to year, no progress was made. And yet this county, extending about 60 miles on the northern bank of the lower Missouri River, contains a large number of most favored situations for vineyards which will be sought after and properly used in, perhaps, no distant future.

Aestivalis varieties received praise from other parts of the state as well.

> Gottlieb Segessemann, Amazonia, Andrew County: . . . It is commonly between June 15 and the ripening of the grapes, when the damp weather following rains occurs, that the rot sets in and damages almost all of the Labrusca class, and to some extent those of the Riparia, but leaves the Aestivalis uninjured. It would therefore be desirable to have the latter, represented by Norton, Cynthiana, and others, propagated more extensively, not only because of the sure crop, but also for the superior quality, which enables them to compete with the best foreign wine. . . .

Of course, there's a nay-sayer in every crowd.

> A. H. Tamter, Booneville, Cooper County: Wine-growing is not considered profitable, and is being discontinued by a number of our wine-growers. Reason: 1. Uncertainty of crops—too much rot; 2. Low price, and no demand even at the low price; no regular market.

Formerly one of the East's preeminent wine-producing states, Missouri has hopes today of reliving past glories. Two historic areas have already been designated U.S. viticultural areas: Augusta, the first viticultural area to be recognized by the federal government, and Hermann, the historic center of Missouri winegrowing. Current studies show that the demand for wine

Visitors to Stone Hill enjoy sparkling Catawba.

days. Average annual precipitation increases as we move southward, from 36 to 45 inches. Many areas in southern Missouri have a problem with midsummer drought stress caused not only by lack of rain but by shallow soils resulting from a root-stopping impervious layer of acid soil and rock. Drip irrigation systems have been established in an effort to relieve the vines of the stress and maintain commercial yields. Winter temperature lows in recent years have ranged from $-16°$ to $-26°F$ and have caused damage to cold-tender varieties.

Concord and Catawba still dominate Missouri vineyards because there is a juice industry that demands them. For Vinifera or other tender varieties to succeed here, microclimates must be carefully researched and special cultural practices implemented. Winegrowers greatly prefer Vidal and Seyval for white wine; Norton is the prize red wine variety. There is an abundance of Catawba in the state, and it is being used to produce an impressive variety of styles of wine, including dry or nearly dry table wines and champagnes.

Active state support of both enological and viticultural research and extension work are paying off both in improved wine quality and better

grapes will exceed the supply at least through the mid-1980s because new wineries are coming into being and old ones are expanding production.

Almost all of Missouri's grape acreage is in counties contiguous to and south of the Missouri River. The growing season is plus or minus 180 days with an average of nearly 4,000 degree-

Stainless steel tanks at Stone Hill

vineyard management. The state extension service has produced a model harvest contract to establish guidelines for grape quality and issued numerous special publications on enological and viticultural subjects which are useful to wine-growers in other eastern states as well.

Wine may be sold in "package, drug, cigar, confectionary, delicatessen, general merchandising and food stores." A "Domestic Winery" is limited to 500,000 gallons annual production and must use 85 percent Missouri grapes. A petition to the state can be made to increase allowance for out-of-state grapes in case of crop failure. Wineries may wholesale, retail, and give tastings. Per capita wine consumption is below average.

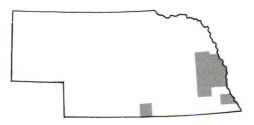

Nebraska

1880

James T. Allen, Omaha, Douglas County: Vineyards, comparatively new; success, good: variety, mostly Concord; no trouble with mildew; price per pound, 4 cents, at wholesale. Our bluff lands well adapted to grape growing. Worden, Elvira, Lady, Cottage, Hartford, Goethe, Delaware do well.

Wine growing was new to young Saunders County, but some early experiments, if reported correctly, show enormous yields.

S. G. Chaney, Wahoo, Saunders County: I referred this subject to Hon. Peter Lancing of this county, who has had some experience in the matter, and he answers as follows: "You have requested of me a very difficult service. Saunders County, Nebraska, has only been organized 14 years, and grape culture is a new industry and the acreage is small, as no one in the county has made it a specialty, and grapes here as yet are not of sufficient quantity to make them

an article of commerce. Nor has wine-making attained to the dignity of one of the industries of the county, although some excellent wine has been made by individuals for their own use. I interviewed one farmer who has given some attention to grapes, and he reported the result of his experiment on Concords on given number of rods, which, reduced to acres, showed the product in pounds to be 19,200 pounds [sic] per acre; and Clintons about the same. Other varieties not sufficiently tested to warrant a correct judgement on their adaptation to the climate, or their commercial value."

There is still not much to report about the viticultural situation in Nebraska, although the passage of new farm winery legislation aimed at encouraging grape growing shows that there is some interest. The eastern part of the state receives from 25 to 29 inches of precipitation annually. The southeastern corner has a growing season of 150 to 180 days; by burying vines during the winter or using very cold-hardy, early-ripening varieties, one could no doubt produce a crop of grapes here for wine.

Wine is sold in package, drug-, and food stores. Legislation provides for wholesale, retail, and tasting privileges for wineries that produce up to 50,000 gallons and use at least 75 percent Nebraska fruit (except in emergencies). Per capita wine consumption here is below average.

North Dakota

No 1880 data were returned from North Dakota, and there is still nothing to report. Only a tiny corner in the southeast has enough rain to qualify the area as eastern. North Dakotans should look to Minnesota and South Dakota for wine grapes and vine-management techniques.

Per capita wine consumption is less than half the national average, close to that of Oklahoma.

Ohio

1880

Thirty-year-old Catawba vineyards were still going strong.

Richard Crawford, Bridgeport, Belmont County: . . . The Catawbas are alone made into wine and the grapes mostly bought by Cincinnati wine makers, except some 15,000 to 18,000 gallons made from out side of the river in Wheeling [West Virginia]. The soil and exposure of the section reported has been the most reliable for the Catawba of any section on the Ohio. Some of our vineyards have been continuously in bearing for thirty years without any evidence of exhaustion, most probably sustained from a soft limestone or marl lying above them.

Another grower found that Catawba requires good soil, but that Concord is not particular.

J. W. Doane, Collamer, Cuyahoga County: But a small percent. of the best grapes are made into wine. Probably not more than 50 tons of the best grapes are used for wine. The most wine is made from grapes of an inferior grade, not fit for table use. . . . Grapes in this section are best on a soil of clay and shale, with soapstone a few feet below the surface. In fact Catawbas will ripen on no other kind of soil, unless it is an exceedingly favorable season. Concords, however, will ripen on almost any soil, and for several years past have been set out very freely and extensively here. So many have been putting out Concords for two or three years that there is beginning to be an over production of this vari-

ety, and Concords do not sell for enough to pay for cultivating and marketing. Last season they did not average over 2½ cents per pound.

East of Cleveland, a mile from the lake, was considered a choice site for Catawbas.

There is a strip of land about one and a half miles wide just east of Cleveland, and from six to eight miles long, back a little over a mile from the lake, that seems to be best adapted for grapes of anything in the county; in fact, it is where nine-tenths of all the Catawba grapes in the county are raised. It is in the townships of East Cleveland and Euclid. The two towns have over 500 acres in bearing.

Nearly three-quarters of the island was covered with grapevines that brought a handsome return.

George M. High, Middle Bass, Ottawa County: This township (Put-in-Bay) has nearly 1,600 acres of the 2,200, and this year received for the crop grown very close to $300,000. Three-fourths of grapes are Catawbas; the other one-fourth made up of Concord, Delaware, Ives seedling, Norton's Virginia, Clinton, and Schraidts seedling in order named. Prices paid by wine companies last fall, 4 cents, 2 cents, 6, 3, 8, 5, and 5, in order as above, per pound; 450,000 gallons wine made last fall by Wehrle Werk & Son at their cellar on this island. Probably 600,000 gallons in the county. Gallizing [adding sugar] is done to considerable extent.

Ohio, the nation's leading wine producer before the Civil War, is one of the East's most active winegrowing states today. Beginning in the late 1960s, the wine industry—both the viticultural and the enological sectors—in Ohio has received the strong support of state legislators. Public dollars invested over the last fifteen years have paid off in growth and development, and the industry now supports much of its own research and promotional efforts.

In 1984 there were nearly 3,000 acres of vines in Ohio divided among 242 individual vineyards. Three counties contain over 70 percent of the acreage: Ashtabula (46 percent), Lake (13 percent), and Ottawa (12 percent). Concord ac-

View of Lonz Winery from offshore, Middle Bass, Ohio

counts for slightly more than two-thirds of the acreage. There are two main grape-growing areas, the one on (and in) Lake Erie and the one comprised of the rest of the state with its scattered microclimates, including the Ohio River Valley viticultural area.

The Lake Erié Islands, and the peninsula called Catawba Island, have all held vineyards for many years. Being surrounded by water that moderates temperatures, these vines bud out later in the spring, thereby escaping late frosts, and have an extended period of maturity since the warm water fends off early frosts. As a result, the islands have a 180-day growing season, as does the southern section of the state, although their summer temperatures are cooler and humidity levels lower than in the south. This is not a perfect haven for Vinifera varieties, however, because Lake Erie is shallow enough to freeze over and winter temperatures can drop substantially below zero. Vinifera vines on North Bass Island (Isle St. George viticultural area) owned by Meier's Wine Company are trained low to the ground so that canes can be buried in the winter.

There are also limited plantings of Vinifera vines along the lake shore in the Ohio section of the Lake Erie viticultural area. It is a struggle to keep the tender buds alive during bitter winters, but some people feel that the wine produced makes the effort worthwhile. Others are happier with the European-Vinifera crosses both in the vineyard and in the winery. Labrusca is still the traditional flavor of the region and is represented at all but the smallest wineries.

The success of grape growing beyond the influence of Lake Erie depends largely on microclimate. Growing seasons range from more than 180 days long to less than 150. Spring frost is a serious hazard in some areas. Summer heat and humidity and low winter temperatures are both factors in the southern part of the state. Precipitation averages from 34 to 41 inches with more in the southern section. The Ohio Agricultural Research and Development Center in Wooster has identified many potential grape-growing regions and makes recommendations of grape varieties for those areas. Small farm wineries have been proliferating steadily in Ohio, and state viticulturist Garth Cahoon predicts that the trend of replacing Concord grapes with European-American varieties will continue.

Wine is conveniently available to consumers. Wineries are permitted to sell to wholesalers and to retail. Visitors are required to pay for tastings at the winery.

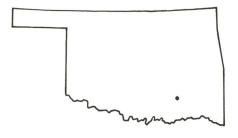

Oklahoma

There were no grape or wine reports from Oklahoma in the USDA survey, and there is still not much to report on Oklahoma viniculture. One notable exception exists: a commercial vineyard in Caney which was originally planted to provide work for welfare families and has undergone several changes in ownership since then. I visited this vineyard in 1976, and at that time all the vines, including Vinifera, French-American, and Labrusca varieties, appeared to be healthy and productive. With a growing season of over 200 days and annual precipitation ranging from 25 inches in the west to 46 inches in the east, there is no climatological reason that commercial grape growing could not be established in areas of Oklahoma. For sociopolitical reasons, however, winegrowing will develop later in the Sooner State than elsewhere in the East.

Sales are strictly limited to package stores. State on-sale prohibition outlaws wine in restaurants and in any public place. Annual per capita consumption—five bottles—is far below average (it exceeds Mississippi by two bottles and Kansas by one).

South Dakota

1880
Out on the prairie, winegrowing was introduced by "Russians."

A. Zienert, Bon Homme, Bon Homme County: Three years ago a party of Russians (German Russians, called the *Hutterische Society*) planted on a hill facing to the south about 1½ acres of grapes. This is the first experience in this county; a few in gardens have been planted since. The Russians, as we call them, say they are satisfied with their grapes; they raised about 800 pounds last summer, but think on the prairie, or even on a hill facing to the north, they would do better, as our overheated south winds are as injurious to grapes as they are to nearly all our other crops. On the bottom of our Missouri are wild grapes in plenty, with a very good grape some years; two years ago I tested some which were nearly as sweet as cultivated. I think that in this county 100 barrels of wine are produced every year from wild grapes. Mixed with water and sugar it makes a very good drink.

There is not much vinicultural news to report from South Dakota. The state university has recently released a new grape variety called Valiant. It is a cross between Fredonia and a wild Riparia seedling gathered from northeastern Montana, which is said to be the northeastern limit for wild vines on the Great Plains. Valiant is an early maturing, small-clustered blue grape with the flavor of Fredonia (Labrusca) and might be more successful than Beta in very cold areas. South Dakota has 22½ inches of rain annually in the southeast and at its very southeastern corner has a 150-day growing season.

Wine is sold in food, drug-, and package stores. Per capita wine consumption in South Dakota is very low.

Wisconsin

1880

Good air drainage and alkaline soil were recommended by J. C. Plumb of Milton, Rock County.

Wine-making is hardly a business here, and not any vineyards set apart for the industry. Fresh grapes of good quality bring 5 to 10 cents per pound for eating and canning. The Delaware is our most popular variety, next the Concord, Rogers, 3, 4, 9, 15, are all very well liked by careful growers. In close-sheltered locations mildew is common; on the oak hills it is hardly known, and there are our best vines. High lands, limestone soil, and plenty of air are requisite to success in the Northwest.

Fresh grapes brought such high prices that they were too costly for winemaking.

Geo. J. Kellogg, Janeville, Rock County: We do not raise enough grapes to supply the home demand, and cannot afford to make them into wine. We wholesale at 5 cents per pound for Concord; other varieties according to quality; Delaware, Rogers, &c., at about double. There are a great many California grapes sold here at exorbitant prices. The past season mildew and the *Phylloxera* have injured the thin-leaf varieties, so that the Concord, Worden, and that class of grapes, have done much the best and the only ones to tie to. We have to protect our vines, and protected by a slight covering of marsh hay any kinds will winter.

Wisconsin today produces fruit wines for the most part. Notable exceptions are the products of the historic Wollersheim Winery in Prairie de Sac. In addition to fruit wines, the Wollersheims produce French-American and a small amount of Vinifera wine from their own twenty acres of vines located on the site of a historic vineyard first planted by the famous (in the annals of California viticulture) Hungarian, Count Agoston Haraszthy. Haraszthy was correct in believing that Vinifera grapes would ripen well during the Wisconsin summer, but he was wrong about their chances of surviving the region's winters without some protection. Before leaving for sunny California in 1849, Haraszthy built a cellar in the hillside of the vineyard which is now part of the Wollersheim tour.

The growing season lasts as few as 60 days in the coldest areas to as many as 180 days in the

Vines buried in Wisconsin for protection against bitter sub-zero temperatures

warmest. Annual precipitation averages 29 to 32 inches. New vineyards are being planted in Wisconsin and wineries established with them. The scale of wine-grape growing here, however, is likely to remain very small.

Wine is available in food, package, and drugstores. There is no special small winery legislation. Wholesaling, retailing (with an additional license), and tasting at the winery are permitted. Per capita consumption is below average.

Part Four

A Closer Look

I2  INSIDE THE VINEYARD

Eastern vineyards and wineries tend to be smaller and more scattered than those in other wine regions throughout the world. Many growers have had to struggle with outdated information about grape growing in their area and conflicting opinions among the books and experts they consult. These handicaps are due partly to the newness of wine grapes as a commercial crop in many states and partly to the innumerable ways one can treat a vine and still get fruit.

As have other types of farming and food production, viticulture has been changed by modern science and technology. Machines are available to do almost every vineyard task from planting rooted cuttings to harvesting ripe fruit to pruning the vines in winter. Scientifically developed vine-training systems have led to higher and more consistent yields. The guesswork has been taken out of fertilization requirements through sophisticated (yet inexpensive) tissue analysis.

Nelson Shaulis (*right*) and Cornell University President Frank H. T. Rhodes at the Geneva station

Advances in monitoring and controlling insects, diseases, and even birds have greatly reduced some of the problems in grape growing.

Working mostly with the Concord grape, New York viticulturists under the leadership of Nelson Shaulis at the Geneva Agricultural Experiment Station have developed an internationally acclaimed vine training and pruning method, the Geneva Double Curtain. Mechanical grape-harvesting machines, now used around the world, were originally developed in New York with the help of Cornell University scientists. Mechanical harvesting and pruning are common today in those areas—for example, the Lake Erie region, Ontario, and the Carolinas—where there are large plantings of Labrusca or Muscadine varieties. Mechanical harvesting is rare in regions comprised of small, dispersed Vinifera and French-American vineyards—for example, Virginia, New England, and Nova Scotia.

Before enjoying the first harvest, a grower first makes many decisions regarding the vineyard: the location, varieties, training method, weed control strategy, spray schedule for disease control, and desired crop size and quality. Following are some of the questions a winegrower must consider prior to having the satisfaction of tasting the first grapes.

Site

Site selection is primarily a question of common sense. Temperature is a principal consideration. Frost pockets must always be avoided. Good air drainage can prevent cold air accumulation in winter and thus reduce damage caused by low winter temperatures. Many growers have observed significant differences (as much as six or more degrees) in temperature at various locations in their vineyards, the lowest spots being coldest.

Never mind those picturesque vineyards along the Rhinegau—steep slopes are not desirable; they are subject to erosion and can be hazardous for the tractor driver. Layout of the vineyard should allow for long straight rows. Curved rows along a contour can be used for erosion control, but maintaining wire tension on the trellis and mechanical cultivation are both more difficult on curved rows.

Breezy sites facilitate quick dryup of moisture and discourage fungi. A grower in Pennsylvania wondered for some time why an odd-shaped area in his Gewürztraminer was plagued by black rot when the rest of the vineyard was clean. Early one morning he discovered that the shadow cast by several tall trees at the edge of the vineyard corresponded exactly to the trouble spot. Watch-

Prototype of a mechanical harvester at Bully Hill Wine Museum, Hammondsport, New York

Mechanical harvester at work

ing the sun rise, he realized that the lingering shadow was sheltering the dew from the sun and giving black rot spores the extra moisture they needed to proliferate. Remembering that the same trees also provided the birds with a convenient dive-bombing station during harvest, he went back to the barn for his chain saw. Trees are best kept at least thirty feet from the edge of a vineyard. In addition to harboring birds and casting shadows, they compete with the vines for food and water.

Soil

Most grapes will grow in a wide range of soil conditions, although they prefer deep, well-drained soils of moderate fertility. Shallow, compacted, or water-logged soils will not foster healthy vines. Most native American species and their hybrids prefer acid to alkaline soils. The relationship between soil and wine quality is an oft-disputed topic. At this time there are so many other more compelling factors influencing grape and wine quality in the East that it would be difficult to single out soil as a conclusive variable. One region to watch in this regard, however, is West Texas, where the chalky soils have an exceptionally high pH that may one day be shown to have an effect on wine character.

Grapes spew from machine to gondola.

Howard and Betty Bryan with "Man Plow" in their Stonewall Vineyards. Most Easterners (now including the Bryans!) use a hydraulic grape hoe that requires only one operator.

Labor

Grapes are a labor-intensive crop in both qualitative and quantitative terms. Each vine requires some individual care each year. A certain amount of informed judgment is involved in training, pruning, cluster and shoot thinning, and even picking (to avoid second-crop fruit). There are those who claim that female is the sex of choice for many vineyard chores such as training, tying, and cluster thinning. A study made in 1928 in Chautauqua County, New York, and Erie County, Pennsylvania, yielded the results shown in Table 1.

The women above would still have been a bargain if they had received the same pay, because they worked faster at this particular task demanding manual dexterity. One large vineyard owner in Michigan found an excellent crew in the girls' track team of the local high school. The key element in choosing vineyard workers of either sex is that they enjoy working with vines in spite of summer heat, winter cold, and an occasional bee sting.

Enemies in the Vineyard

Eastern growers can and must control several common fungi and pests with an effective spray and integrated pest management program: black rot, powdery mildew, downy mildew, bitter rot, *Botrytis cinerea* (bunch rot), anthracnose, phomopsis cane and leaf spot, eutypa dieback, Japanese beetles, flea beetles, grape berry moths, mites, leafhoppers, aerial phylloxera, and weeds all plague vineyards to some degree.

For a normal crop the bloom period of the

TABLE 1.

Cost of labor to dry-tie grapevines when all work was done by hired women, by family labor, or when one-half or more was done by operator or by hired men

Labor performed by	Vineyards (number)	Labor per acre (hours)	Cost per hour (cents)	Cost per acre (dollars)
Hired women	100	9.0	29.7	2.67
Family labor	46	9.4	32.9	3.09
One-half or more by operator or hired man	27	10.5	45.3	4.76

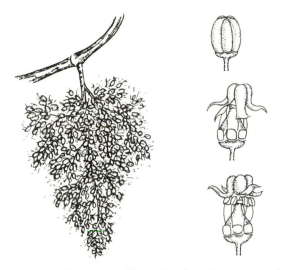

Bloom, or flowering, which takes place about 6–8 weeks after bud break, is a pivotal point in the spray program and also determines the season's crop level.

vegetative cycle is critical. Growers must be especially alert to the vulnerability of their fruit to both insects and diseases at this time. The most common form of bunch rot, *Botrytis cinerea*, often infects the fruit during and just after bloom; the spores remain dormant within the cluster until the grapes begin to ripen and wet weather transforms the spores into a destructive gray mold (in rare cases during dry autumns botrytis mold can produce "noble" results by concentrating the grape sugars through dehydration, such as happens in good years in Sauternes). Unfortunately, there is no way to protect flowering clusters from prolonged rain, which causes the cap to stick to the anthers and thereby prevents pollination.

No two spray schedules are exactly alike. Each grower is working with a particular set of conditions: location, grape varieties, past pest-control performance, spray material availability, and time schedule. Weather conditions will determine the number of sprays required in a season, which generally ranges from six to eighteen. Local extension agents in most states can provide information on which materials to use for which problem. The Finger Lakes Grape Coop in Penn Yan, New York, annually issues a *Grape Pest Control* guide which provides current information on insect and disease management in a con-

cise format that is useful for growers in other regions as well.

Weeds are perhaps the greatest problem faced by eastern growers, especially in young vineyards. These bountiful plants must be dealt with from the start because they have the power to rule the vineyard. Diligent mechanical cultivation with or without the aid of herbicides is the usual method. The need for erosion control combined with the fact that most eastern regions have goodly amounts of rain during the summer often leads growers to clean cultivate only under the trellis and to maintain mown-grass strips in the vineyard aisles.

Training and Pruning

While not the most aesthetically pleasing part of the vegetative cycle, the leafless period of vine dormancy is a revealing one for growers. Evidence of powdery mildew, phomopsis, eutypa, mechanical injury, hail and some forms of insect damage remain on the canes after leaf fall. Growth and development during the previous season can also be assessed at this time by observing the increase in trunk diameter and by weighing the wood.

Training and pruning is one of the most intellectually challenging jobs for vineyardists. The variables of climate, soil, topography, variety, rootstock, degree of mechanization, and labor all come into play, as well as the availability of trellis materials. Around the world, the choice of a training system used to be a matter of local tradition. More and more, however, old methods are being replaced with new ones developed by modern research.

In choosing a training system it is very important that the grower consider the grape variety. American, European-American, and Vinifera varieties all have different requirements, as do individual varieties within each group. An indiscriminate training and pruning policy will lead to problems with winter hardiness, disease control, and fruit quality.

Pruning is concerned with how *many* buds, training with *where* they are located. Simply de-

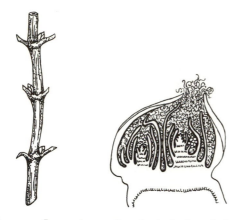

Baby grape flower clusters form in the buds at the base of each leaf stem the summer before their vintage. They hibernate during the winter in a well-insulated nest until spring, when they are pushed out on the new green shoot that will carry them through to harvest.

fined by John McGrew in the American Wine Society's *Basic Guide to Pruning* (1978), "pruning controls the size of the crop; training puts the crop in an economical and convenient position."

An experience during a vine anatomy class forever changed my attitude toward pruning. We were disrobing a single dormant bud beneath a binocular microscope. The professor had given each student a piece of vine wood (cane) and told us to find in it a bunch of grapes (actually the grape flower primordium). It is a painstaking job to peel away the necessary layers without obliterating the prized life form; only two of us achieved our goal because we were willing to miss lunch.

From the outside a grape bud is uninspiring. There is a plain brown bud scale lined with an impressive amount of downlike insulation to shelter the embryonic shoot from the elements. It is this protective hairy down that makes exposing the baby leaves and grape primordia such an exercise in patience. Cradled in the furry nest we found not one but three prenatal shoots. Some had remarkably mature-looking leaves complete with veins. On the central shoot there were two tiny "clusters." The sight of those four glowing green leaves and two mini-bunches carefully arranged with tweezers under the microscope, imperceptible to the naked eye, left a lasting impression on me. I realized then that pruning was not a

matter of wrestling with a lot of dead wood on the trellis; it was in truth handling a multitude of little green plants in tiny brown cones. Admittedly, this poetic perspective can be lost rapidly when one is fending off frostbite on a gray day in February and wondering if the row really does have an end.

The All-Important Leaf

When spring arrives and warms the earth, the roots awaken and send nutrient-enriched water through the plant. Tiny grape shoots push through their winter cover and begin their summer-long journey in the open air bearing leaves, tendrils, and grapes. Leaves are solar-powered generators of plant food and sugar. The idea behind trellises (other than to make cultivation easier) is to position the leaves for maximum reception of sunlight. One measure of the relative importance of foliar exposure was made by Muntz in his book *Les Vignes*, written in 1895. He estimated that 1,200 square meters of leaf area were needed to produce a hectoliter (26.4 gallons) of wine in the cool Champagne district, whereas only 320 square meters were needed in the hot Midi (Mediterranean) region.

Natural selection and evolution seem to corroborate Muntz's observations. Cool-region varieties such as Pinot noir, Chardonnay, Riesling, Gewürztraminer, Baco noir, Foch, and Concord have small clusters relative to their leaf output. In hot climates huge-clustered raisin, table, and wine grapes are fed by a modest number of leaves. In eastern America the northern species, Riparia and Labrusca, have very large leaves compared with the small leaves of Rotundifolia, Shuttleworthii, and other species of the deep South.

The important differences among native American varieties, European, and European-American wine grapes are sometimes ignored, with ill-effect, by growers. When the French-American varieties were first planted by the large New York wineries, few growers treated them differently from their Labruscas. As a result the French-Americans were grossly overcropped;

Energy for the entire food manufacturing process of the vine is solar-powered through the leaves. If the grapes are to ripen properly, the foliage must be kept free of insect and fungi damage and well exposed to sunlight. Leaves are also the chief means of varietal identification.

fruit quality was poor; the vines were severely weakened and therefore short-lived.

Pruning formulas developed for native varieties, which called for thirty buds for the first pound of pruned wood and ten more for each additional pound, have proved disastrous to premium-wine-grape growers. Seyval blanc with two or more pounds of wood can be pruned to fifteen buds in the winter, cluster-thinned in spring to one cluster per shoot, and still easily produce four to five tons per acre. One reason for this is Seyval's tendency to push two fruitful shoots from one bud position and to push non-count or blind buds from old wood. Pruning weights are a good measure of vegetative vigor, but pruning equations must be carefully custom-tailored.

Because labor costs have become increasingly burdensome, mechanical pruning is the object of much research around the world. In Australia it

Scales are used to measure wood when implementing balanced pruning formulas.

is already a widely used commercial practice. Pruning may one day be no more complicated than mowing the lawn, and training young vines the only person-to-vine task left. Before calling in the engineers, however, eastern growers must first decide which of numerous training and pruning systems will provide the most consistent and best quality grapes.

Whatever the choice of training system, high quality trellis materials should be used to avoid costly maintenance problems in the future. Midsummer failures of trellises with loaded vines not only are a nuisance but can cause serious damage by bending trunks and breaking shoots. A general rule is: Do not plant unless you can afford to install the trellis with at least the lowest wire in the first year. Good weed control and sufficient moisture together with regular tying often result in vines reaching beyond the low wire the first year.

Low-Wire Training Systems

On a standard six-foot trellis (which calls for eight-foot-tall, 3- to 4-inch-thick posts), the lower wire is approximately 42 inches from the ground with from three to five foliage-support wires. All vegetation is trained upward. Excessive shoot growth is often "hedged" or summer-pruned. Either cane-and-spur or cordon pruning may be used. When the leaves fall off a shoot, it becomes a *cane*, which when pruned very short (usually 1 to 4 buds) becomes a *spur*. If a cane is not pruned away after one season, it becomes a *cordon* or arm on which fruiting spurs are left each

Low-wire cordon

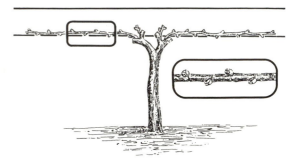

Low-wire cane-and-spur

year. Most vineyards that train to the low wire have regular vertical trellises, sometimes with parallel movable "catch wires," but a horizontal cross arm may also be used to contain the foliage. The common factor is that the shoots are trained upward from the lowest wire.

This system works well for most of the upright- or semi-upright-growing European-American varieties (such as Seyval, Rayon d'Or, Chancellor, Chambourcin, Vidal, and Villard blanc). It is also suitable for most Vinifera varieties (including Chardonnay, Riesling, Cabernet Sauvignon, Merlot, and Pinot noir). Catawba is a native American vine with a semi-upright growth habit that is sometimes trained low.

Advantages of a low-wire system are: good cross-ventilation beneath the trellis throughout the season; good fruit exposure for quick drying and good spray coverage; well-placed grapes for easy picking; a comfortable height for pruning. In addition, it is possible to establish a cordon in the first year. In those places where winter conditions necessitate burying trunks or maintaining multiple trunks, a low-wire system is a virtual necessity.

Disadvantages include: the expense for more wire; the need for some tying during the growing season (more if catch wires are not used); and, in highly vigorous vineyards, the need for summer pruning.

Top-Wire Training Systems on a Vertical Trellis

On a standard six-foot trellis (with eight-foot posts), the lower wire is 48 inches to 60 inches from the ground with the top wire at six feet. The vines may be cordon or cane-and-spur pruned. All vegetation is directed downward, and is not tied to the trellis during the growing season. Shoot positioning or "combing" the shoots like hair is necessary to prevent shade-producing horizontal growth. One vigorous or "bull" cane running along the top wire can shade the tops of as many as four neighboring vines.

Top-wire training, especially the "single curtain" cordon system, lends itself to a high degree of mechanization: prepruning, brush removal from the wires, suckering (removing unwanted growth from the trunk), and even combing—with huge nylon bristle brushes—may be done mechnically. European-American varieties with a "trailing" or nonupright growing habit, such as Foch, Millot, and Baco, and most native American varieties do well when trained to the top wire. Although not perfectly suited to top-wire training, many Vinifera and European-American varieties will adapt unless high winds cause too much shoot breakage.

Advantages of a top-wire system are: no need for shoot tying during the season once the cor-

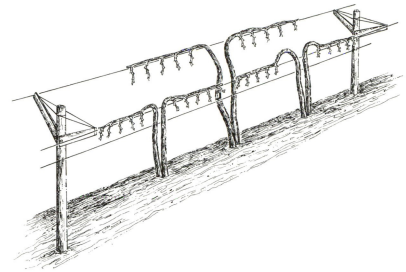

Geneva Double Curtain

dons are established; easy pruning, (although it can be tiring for short people); early spring growth that is higher and slightly less susceptible to frost; need for less wire; a foliage curtain that shades out midsummer weeds.

Disadvantages include: the need for young shoots to be positioned or "combed" twice during the season; a foliage curtain that blocks fruit from salubrious breezes and creates a more favorable climate for fungi; increased difficulty of multiple trunk management in cold climates.

Vinifera growers in much of the East usually choose a low-wire system. It is risky to rely on a single- or even a double-trunked permanent cordon that requires two years to reestablish in the event of trunk injury. For native American varieties—Labrusca, Riparia, Aestivalis, and Rotundifolia—however, a single upper wire cordon or Geneva Double Curtain is ideal.

Geneva Double Curtain or GDC

The value of applied research in training and pruning methods can be seen in the result of work done on Concord grapes by Nelson Shaulis at the Geneva station. The big leaves, long internodes, and small bunches of Labrusca vines were well adapted for survival in the wild, but only in parts of Italy are domesticated vines treated to exceptionally tall trellises of uncut tree proportions. In the East the old standard was a two-wire trellis that supported weak vines adequately and produced less than two tons to the acre. Modern vineyard practices— such as improved soil management and pest control—led to increased vine growth but did not immediately result in correspondingly larger yields of Labrusca grapes. When a vigorous Labrusca vine is confined to a small trellis, there is excessive shading, especially of buds near the base (trunk) of the vine, and for years growers assumed that the basal buds of a Labrusca were sterile. Shaulis determined that in order for Labrusca buds to be fruitful, they needed to be exposed to sunshine during the floral initiation period (July) of their development.

Shaulis and his coworkers developed the Geneva Double Curtain trellis, which uses horizontal as well as vertical supports and is similar to a structure used at the turn of the century by Texan T. V. Munson. Unlike Munson's "clothesline" T, the cross arms atop each post of GDC trellises are movable—because they were made to complement the first mechanical harvesters that worked by agitating the wires up and down, causing the fruit to drop from the stem onto conveyor belts (today's machines do not work on this principle and can harvest many different training systems and trellis configurations). By placing on the top wire cordons that have several four- to six-bud spurs and combing vegetative growth downward, two curtains of foliage are possible rather than one within the same row. The basal buds become fruitful, being in an upper position exposed to sunlight, and thus the need for long canes is eliminated. Where the soil is sufficiently fertile, yields can increase dramatically with no loss in fruit quality.

Must Vines Suffer to Make Good Wine?

Before going to France, I had assumed that grapevines were like other plants and animals that one fed and cared for with the hope that they would grow healthy and strong. But after I tasted wines produced by tortured-looking ancient grapevines growing in distinctly hostile-looking ground, my ideas began to change. This new perception was reinforced by the professor's frown when we arrived at a beautiful valley floor covered with luxuriant rows of vines and the smile that lit up his face when he gazed into the hills at old vines whose grasp on life seemed tenuous at best. It was apparent that he preferred faded, seemingly dying vines to vibrant living ones. Thus evolved what I call my dying vine theory: those vineyard characteristics that make an uncompromising French traditionalist smile probably contribute to quality wine; or, any factor that contributes to increased vine vigor beyond what is necessary to keep the plant alive will result in decreased wine quality.

The dying vine theory is thus a distillation of what I heard, saw, and drank as a student in the Cours International Supérieur de Viticulture, a traveling graduate course in viticulture for eigh-

teen students from five countries. We visited hundreds of vineyards in western Europe and questioned growers about soil profiles, rootstock and fruiting varieties, training and pruning methods, climatic conditions, disease and insect problems, methods of cultivation, and so on. These sessions were followed by wine tastings. After we had been through this procedure many times in several languages, some basic principles about the relationship between vineyard practices and wine character began to emerge.

Unquestionably, we students were influenced by our professors, especially by Jean Branas of Montpellier, who is uncompromising in his views about what viticultural practices produce the best wine in a given region. We were taught to see certain vineyard characteristics as suspect, including flat land, clay soils, irrigation, over-generous nitrogen fertilization, wide vine spacing, the use of high trellises and tall trunks, the practice of leaving more than one cane and one spur at pruning, and the planting of vigorous rootstocks, nontraditional grape varieties, and high-yielding clonal selections.

It is rare in America to find someone smiling at a vineyard that suffers from viruses. But as we students stared at an irregular yellowish-green hillside in Clos de Vougeot, Branas asked which of us thought that that vineyard, with its obviously mixed population of old, virus-ridden Pinot noir, should be pulled and replanted with heat-treated superclone X. I thought that the replanting would be an interesting experiment but could see that from a traditionalist's point of view such a change would be for the worse. No matter what the improvements in yield and even soluble solids (sugar content) might be, the wine would be different.

In a measure to reduce labor costs, some French vineyardists are pulling every other row of their closely spaced vines and building two-meter trellises for the remaining vines. The trellises give the more widely spaced vines additional space for foliage exposure so there need be no overall loss of yield. In fact, by increasing the vigor of the vines and leaving extra buds, a grape farmer often increases yields. Needless to say, our professor did not take kindly to this modern trend. He was a firm believer in high density plantings where each vine bears only a small amount of fruit.

We were taught that our duty is to make wine in the vineyard. At the same time, however, we were given a crash course in enology and made aware of different enological practices. Like good institutions of higher education, wineries exist to provide a place for the grapes to achieve their own maximum potential. On the other hand, wineries can also serve as reform schools for wayward grapes (but as we were not studying enology that year, we did not go into the specific details of *cum laude* or remedial vinification programs).

It was five years after returning home from my European studies before I felt able publicly to express my thoughts on the dying vine theory. At that time I was growing grapes in Tidewater Virginia, and enjoying the resulting wine. If my former professors had found out about our rich clay loam, abundant rainfall, nine-foot spacing, six-foot trellises, and, worst of all, youthful happy-looking grapevines, I feared that they would get the impression I had learned nothing from them. But I do believe in the dying-vine theory, although I know that it cannot always be put into practice in the French manner.

Every year nature provides us with situations that can illustrate our theories about optimal conditions in the vineyard. Too much water, be it from irrigation or wet soils, was on my professors' list of impediments to wine quality. In 1977 we had a summer drought in Virginia, whereas in 1978 it rained heavily right up to harvest. The '77 wines were definitely richer (more body and complexity) and had a better sugar-acid balance than the '78s, and, of course, there was less fruit rot during the dry season. Even growers with the best intentions suffer from unfavorable weather conditions.

As a viticulturist I am concerned primarily with the health and well-being of grapevines, caring for grape clusters from floral initiation through maturity. Harvest brings a kind of death to grapes, and destruction as they pass through the crusher-stemmer. But there is no doubt about the afterlife of grapes—they are reborn into wine—and there is a direct correlation between their life on a vine and their reincarnation on the palate. Wine can be heavenly, hellish, or somewhere in between. It is the job of all winegrowers to place at least some wines in the company of angels.

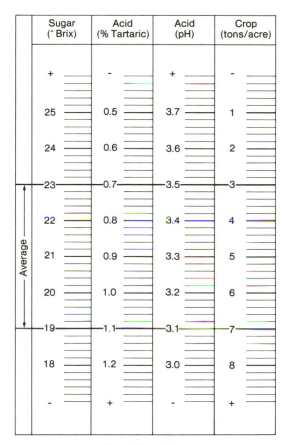

Sugar (°Brix)	Acid (% Tartaric)	Acid (pH)	Crop (tons/acre)
+	-	+	-
25	0.5	3.7	1
24	0.6	3.6	2
23	0.7	3.5	3
22	0.8	3.4	4
21	0.9	3.3	5
20	1.0	3.2	6
19	1.1	3.1	7
18	1.2	3.0	8
-	+	-	+

Chart Your Must

13  INSIDE THE WINERY

Birds were probably the world's first winemakers and they continue this work every year. We do not need to go to a winery at harvest time to experience the scent of fermenting grapes as long as there is a grapevine with a single berry on it nearby. Once a grape's skin is pierced by any means, natural yeasts enter the berry and convert the grape sugars to alcohol, carbon dioxide, and heat. At the level of a single berry with a bird in charge, things happen very fast. Juice becomes wine which in turn becomes vinegar.

Temperature control is one of the single most important factors in winemaking. It has been possible to produce the fresh, fruity wines of Germany and Alsace for centuries because of the cool climate there during harvest. The same is true in upstate New York. But in southern climates where vines ripen well before autumn, warm temperatures during harvest make it much more difficult to control oxidation and acidification (vinegar spoilage). George Washington observed that his chances for making sound wine from wild grapes were much better with late-ripening *Vitis aestivalis* than with early-maturing *Vitis riparia*. Without refrigeration, it was almost impossible for Washington to keep his wine from turning to vinegar during a hot August in Virginia. Today's technology, however, is freeing winemakers from such climatic limitations so that with a properly equipped winery, they can produce any style of wine they wish.

"Grandpa's recipe" for wine is becoming largely a thing of the past as winemakers, even at the smallest wineries, are becoming better educated. In the East, children of farm winery owners (many of whom started with only home-winemaking experience) are now commonly taking degrees in viticulture and enology. More and

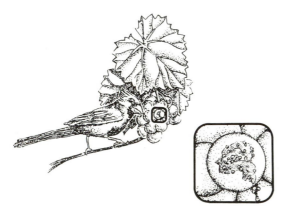

Bird and fermenting berry

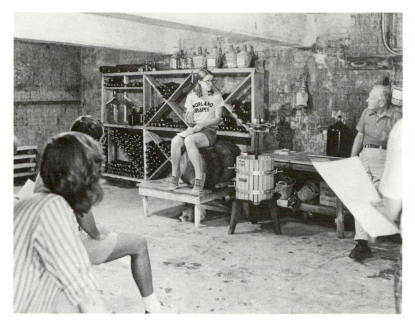

Home-winemaking class given in the author's former basement

more eastern universities are offering wine courses; eastern students are also studying in California and abroad.

Individual eastern wineries produce from as little as five hundred gallons to more than ten million gallons annually. Part of the fun of visiting wineries is to see all the various ways people do exactly the same thing. The elements of scale and degree of sophistication make much of the difference. Some small wineries are extremely sophisticated with well-outfitted laboratories, insulated stainless steel tanks, sterile filtration, and mini-bottling lines. Modern equipment does not guarantee good wine, but it certainly makes the job easier. These days it is not very practical to round up enough legs to foot stomp grapes-by-the-ton. Sometimes a wine that tasted delicious at the winery will taste and even look different (oxidized color, heavy sediment deposit, or tartrate crystals) at home several months later. This could be the result of mishandling in the winery or the consequence of riding in the trunk of a car during the hot summer or frigid winter.

Home winemakers who are not concerned with the ability of their wines to withstand the rigors of travel and life on a store shelf have much more latitude in the ultimate sugar, acid, and alcohol content of their wine than do professional winemakers, who must make a consistent wine from year to year for a demanding public.

Whether the wine is being made in a basement at home or in a large commercial winery, there are four basic, unavoidable tasks the winemaker must perform to produce a bottle of wine, once the grapes have arrived at the door: testing, extracting juice, storing, and bottling.

Testing

The handiest and least accurate way to assess the grapes' sugar and acid content, by *mouth*, is not sufficiently precise for making wine. However, there are some very inexpensive instruments that are widely available which will give the necessary accurate readings.

The least expensive way to test the sweetness of grape juice is with a *hydrometer*. To measure the soluble solids or sugar content one floats the hydrometer (similar to those used by mechanics to measure antifreeze or battery acid) in a tube of grape juice. Hydrometers made for winemakers have scales calibrated in degrees Brix; this figure is then multiplied by a factor of from .55 (in

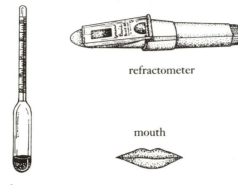

refractometer

mouth

hydrometer

warmer climates) to .60 (in cooler climates) to give the approximate amount of alcohol that the grape juice will contain when fermentation is complete. Readings of from 19° Brix to 24° Brix are desirable for winemaking.

A *refractometer* is a much more expensive tool for measuring degrees Brix or the sugar content of grapes. It requires, however, only one drop of juice to obtain a reading, and the hand-held, temperature-compensated models are easily carried right into the vineyard during the harvest season. A refractometer is also a handy companion on fall winery visits for the traveling connoisseur who wants to find out first-hand just how ripe the grapes at Chateau X really were at harvest.

An inexpensive way to measure the total acidity of grape juice is with an *acid titration kit* (which includes a 0.1 ml.–graduated burette with stand, a 5-ml. pipette, phenolphthalein indicator solution in a dropper bottle, and 0.1 normal sodium hydroxide reagent). A reasonable range for total acid content measured as a percentage of tartaric is 0.7 to 1.0.

Titration measures the amount of acid in a wine but it does not measure the degree or strength of the various acids. To measure the active or effective acidity in a wine, a *pH meter* is used. In his bulletins issued to Missouri wine-growers, enologist Bruce Zoecklein observes: "pH is perhaps the most important wine production parameter. It affects just about everything in a wine ranging from color, stability, body, to flavor, and complexities. . . . For example, we know that Chelois often takes on a bitter stemmy aftertaste when it is produced from grapes with a pH higher than 3.5. Foch and Baco, on the other hand, may turn orange and tawny very badly at pHs above 3.5." Even the smallest commercial winery should have a pH meter. For the best quality, wine grapes should have pH readings in the 3.1 to 3.4 range.

According to law, commercial winemakers must know the exact alcoholic content of their wines although the federal regulations allow for a 1.5 percent margin of error. The most common instrument for measuring alcohol is an *ebulliometer*. Table wines generally contain from 9 percent to a maximum of 14 percent alcohol, depending on the ripeness of the grapes and the style of wine.

titration kit

pH meter

ebulliometer

automated/computerized analyzer

crusher-stemmer

Today the largest wineries have extremely so-phisticated laboratory setups that look more like the control panels of a spaceship. Every possible constituent of a wine can be analyzed with *automated computerized equipment*. Large wineries also abound with Ph.D.s to interpret the data re-vealed by these machines. It should be noted here that none of this advanced technology is required to produce fine wine. Scientific understanding, however, has drastically reduced the quantity of poor wine in the world.

Juice Extraction

Without a doubt, the most famous meth-od of extracting juice from ripe grapes is *foot stomping*. A pair of willing legs can express a surprising quantity of juice in a short time; for small quantities even an active pair of *hands* will do. *Loose-woven cloth* may be used to wring the last drops from crushed or fermented skins.

Anyone with more than a few vines, however, soon graduates to a small hand-powered or elec-tric *crusher-stemmer*. These handy machines are usually adequate to make the transition from advanced amateur to small professional wine-maker, together with a hand or hydraulic *basket press*.

As vineyard and winery expand, the tons of grapes that arrive at the receiving station become too voluminous for the original small equipment. Some wineries install giant augurs to crush grapes arriving in one-ton bins. Others use a *field crusher-stemmer* (some models come complete with pressing units) to bring grape must (grape juice and skins) back to the winery ready to put into the fermenting tanks.

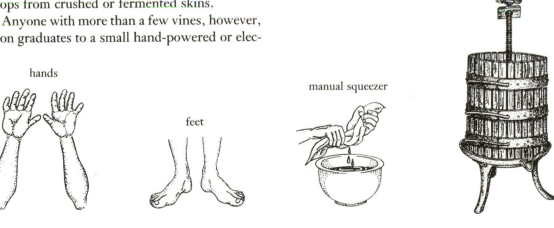

hands

feet

manual squeezer

basket press

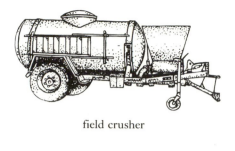

field crusher

glass carboy

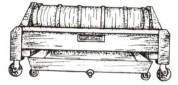

horizontal screw press

the goal is fruity, slightly sweet white wines, few enologists would eschew the aid of a centrifuge to quickly clarify the must and stop a fermentation before all the residual sugar has been converted to alcohol.

The *horizontal press* is one type commonly used to handle fresh must for white wine or the limp skins of fermented red musts. These presses have either augur-driven plates or an inflatable rubber bladder to force the juice through slats in the side of the press into a receiving tray. A hose and pump attached to the tray send the juice to the fermenters. Horizontal presses are available in many sizes and are often programmable to automatic cycles of mild or more forceful pressing, depending on the quality of wine desired.

Many small winemakers can only dream of the control over juice composition obtainable with a *centrifuge*. These powerful machines are prohibitively expensive for most small operations. A favorite debate among aficionados is whether centrifuges make excellent wine possible or whether it is impossible to make excellent wine with a centrifuge. Of course, as with many things, it depends: on the type of wine desired and on the skill of the operator. Certainly when

Fermentation and Storage Vessels

The five-gallon glass jug, known as a *carboy*, has been the ideal vessel for home winemakers for some time. It is easy to clean and stoppers with water seals are easily available. Being transparent, the carboy affords an immediate view of what is going on inside. Is it time to rack (siphon) the wine off its lees (fermentation sediment including dead yeast cells)? Has someone been sampling the new wine without topping up (filling the carboy with more wine to minimize air space)? And, although heavy when full (about 45 pounds), carboys are not unmanageable.

The only drawback to carboys as fermentation vessels applies to making red wines: the opening

hand siphoning

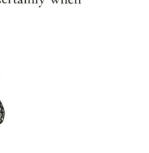

centrifuge

wooden barrel

stainless drum

oak tank

is too narrow to get the skins in and out easily. Home winemakers use ceramic crocks or food-grade plastic buckets and cans to ferment reds and transfer to the carboys (taking the skins back to the vineyard for fertilizer). Commercial wineries use carboys for making experimental lots and storing tag-end leftovers for use in topping up later.

The ubiquitous *wooden barrel*, for many the symbol of winemaking, renders far less service to the profession than one might think. They are usually found abundantly in the cellars of the very rich or the very poor winemakers. The former pay premium prices for new American or European oak barrels in which to age their premium reds and sometimes their whites. The latter have gotten a "good deal" on used whiskey barrels, the cheapest source of an aging vessel. Cheap in purchase price but expensive in time and labor to recondition and maintain, used 55-gallon barrels are often not the bargain they seem. Another inexpensive vessel, the blue plastic concentrate container, is not very attractive but is definitely easier to maintain and less potentially injurious to the wine. In this league of used containers the vessel of choice is probably the *stainless steel drum*, a castoff of the soft-drink industry. It is sanitary and sightly, although not easy to clean.

Larger wineries of course need larger containers for wine storage. A common sight fifty years ago was the *redwood tank*, which could hold tens of thousands of gallons. These huge containers are now for the most part being converted into tasting rooms and replaced by the far easier to maintain *stainless steel tank*. Enologists must have as much control over the environment of their wines as possible. A stainless steel tank with a glycol jacket allows for individual temperature control which can be monitored by computer.

stainless tank

insulated outdoor tank

redwood tank

The romantic Brotherhood
Winery cellar

Should a winemaker want to store large quantities of wine in oak, *oak tanks* of quite large dimensions are made to order in the United States, and there are also some elegant models available in Europe.

At the top of the big league of wine-storage containers are *outdoor insulated tanks*, often made of epoxy-lined steel and sprayed with foam insulation. In California such tanks exist with capacities of a million gallons! That's more wine in one tank than in the total output of dozens of estate wineries! Outdoor tanks, while utilitarian, lend a certain "oil refinery" look to a winery and

six spout filler

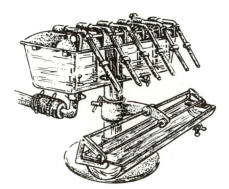

hand corker

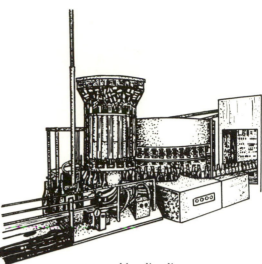
automated bottling line

strain the romantic image that wooden barrels have given to the profession for so many years.

Bottling

By the time the bottling stage has been reached, one would think 99 percent of the job was done, but that, unfortunately, is not the case. Simply obtaining bottles of the proper shape and color can be a major headache for wineries in remote areas unless they are willing to buy an entire train-car load of one type. Then there is the dust in the new bottles to be rinsed or blown out. Finally, once the sterile bottle is ready, how is a small producer going to be sure everything else is sterile until the cork is in place?

Hazards abound at the bottling stage. There are millions of micro-organisms just waiting to contaminate a valve in the bottle filler. It is possible for ever-present oxygen to be introduced during filling and compressed into the bottle during corking unless one has a vacuum corker or CO_2 injector. Oxygen introduced at bottling and unwanted bacteria can cause spoilage in an otherwise sound wine.

In no other area of the winemaking process are the leaps from one level of equipment to the next so quick or so extreme as in bottling.

floor corker

semi-automatic corker

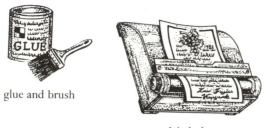

glue and brush

label gluer

One can fill a few carboys *by hand* and use a *hand corker*. A floor-stand-model corker is fairly inexpensive and may be practical for up to a few thousand gallons in a family operation. Automatic *spout fillers* (of two to six spouts) are useful in small to medium-sized operations and relatively modestly priced. A *semiautomatic corker* represents a sizable jump in cost over the old reliable floor models, but eventual savings in labor costs will in time justify its purchase.

If you want to hear a grown wine producer cry with frustration, visit the winery during the inaugural labeling run. First of all just any old *glue* will not do for a wine label. Wine labels are a very personal item to the producer, who does not like to see them wrinkled, torn, or half-fallen-off ten days after they were lovingly applied to the bottle. There are various *label gluing machines* in table and floor models, but getting them to work smoothly takes a great deal of trial and error. In the end, each winemaker finds a workable solution to labeling, such as resorting to expensive self-stick labels or adapting a second hand Rube Goldberg machine.

Bottling is a necessary evil. At present, only large producers can afford their own *automated bottling line*, which cleans the bottles, vacuum seals the corks, and puts a front and back label on perfectly each time. For the smaller operations in California, there are specially outfitted trucks that bottle wine door-to-door and guarantee the

Norton wines aging in the bottle

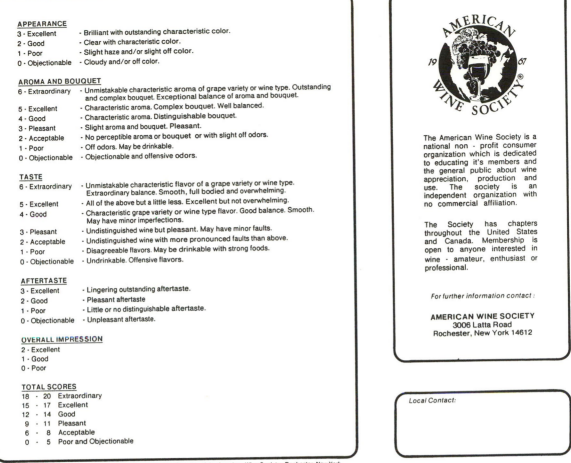

American Wine Society tasting chart

sterility of the process. Unfortunately no such services exist for the widely-scattered eastern industry, but they would surely be welcome.

While touring a winery, one should always keep in mind that one of the quickest ways a wine producer can go broke is to overinvest in expensive equipment. Modest outfitting need not be a reflection on the quality of wine as long as the cellar is clean (no smell of wine or vinegar). If you purchase a case of wine at a "low-tech" winery, it is often advisable to drink it at regular intervals rather than hoarding it for six months or a year before trying it again. That way, if some oxygen was introduced at bottling, it will not have time to do any damage. A basically sound "low-tech" wine can be more enjoyable, than a "high-tech" counterpart that is ultra-clean but has less character.

One way to judge whether a wine has withstood the test of time is to evaluate it, first, in the winery tasting room, second, at home a few nights later with dinner and, third, at one-to-two-month intervals for whites and two-to-six-month intervals for reds. All wines are bound to gradually improve or gradually decline with age. A dramatic shift in quality accompanied by fizziness, cloudiness, or change in color, however, usually indicates a defect somewhere in the

NAME : _____

PLACE : _____

DATE : _____

THEME : _____

	WINE	PRICE	APPEARANCE 3 MAX	AROMA/ BOUQUET 6 MAX	TASTE 6 MAX	AFTERTASTE 3 MAX	OVERALL IMPRESSION 2 MAX	TOTAL SCORE 20 MAX
1								
2								
3								
4								
5								
6								
7								
8								
9								

COMMENTS :

ROCHESTER AWS 7/79

American Wine Society blank tasting notes

grapes and/or in the cellar practices. If you have left the wines to bake on a hot summer day, or kept them next to the stove, or allowed them to freeze in your garage, you of course are more responsible for their demise than the winery is.

14  VINICULTURAL ECONOMICS PAST AND PRESENT

A brief examination of the financial side of grape growing in the East reveals some sobering facts for anyone who is considering getting into the wine-grape business for the money alone. As does most farming, vine culture demands the total involvement of the proprietor and family. Unlike the office or factory where one works to afford a nice home and fun vacations, the vineyard *is* one's home and vacation spot. The work must be so thoroughly enjoyed that each day in the vineyard is its own reward. Often a multi-generational family operation, a farm winery requires outdoor-oriented, scientifically talented, and business-inclined individuals. It is a constantly evolving, intellectually challenging workplace—but it is no gold mine.

Bottom Lines from the Past

Even the extremely successful Nicholas Longworth, who propelled eastern wine into national preeminence during the mid-1800s, was realistic about the limits of profitability in the vineyard. His thoughts on the topic are quoted by Robert Buchanan in *Culture of the Grape and Wine Making* (1850):

> I would not recommend any individual to hire hands, and cultivate the grape extensively for wine, with a view to profit. But I would recommend landlords to rent from fifteen to twenty acres to Germans, for vineyards and orchard, on shares. We have more to learn in the manufacture of the wine, than in the cultivation of the grape. And I would recommend our German vine-dressing emigrants, to purchase or lease a few acres of rough, cheap land on the Ohio, or near it, with a view to the cultivation of the grape. Land will be suitable for it, that is too rough for the plow, and eight or ten acres will give employment to a whole family. [2d ed., p. 44]

Buchanan reckoned the cash costs of a six-acre vineyard with 14,400 vines or 2,400 vines per acre spaced at 3 feet by 6 feet:

Trenching two feet deep, $65 per acre	$390 00
Sodding avenues	60 00
Cost of 30,000 cuttings, at $2.50 per thousand	75 00

Planting	70 00
Fourteen thousand five hundred locust stakes, at $3 per hundred	435 00
Setting 14,500 stakes	55 00
	$1,085 00
Cost of attending the first year—vine-dresser, $216, and a hand for one month, $15 (and board themselves)	$231 00
Second year—vine-dresser, $216, a hand for two months, at $15 per month	256 00
Cuttings, after first year, to replace failures, say,	20 00
Hauling, carting, etc.	68 00
Contingencies, etc.	150 00
Average cost, say $300 per acre,	1,800 00

The vineyard being on a gentle declivity did not require *benching*, which would have been more expensive than the draining by sodded avenues—nor did the ground contain stone enough to add to the expense of trenching, which, in some positions, is a very serious item. [Pp. 44–45]

In his book *American Grape Growing and Wine Making* (1885), George Husmann discusses the cost of establishing a vineyard:

This must of course, vary greatly with the locality, price of labor, manner of preparing the soil, variety planted, manner of training, etc. I give below the cost of an acre in our locality, (Boone Co., Mo.) on ordinary soil with no unusual obstructions, such as stones, stumps, etc.:

Plowing and sub-soiling, three teams	$ 7 00
650 Elvira (or Goethe) plants, $5 per 100	32 50
Planting	5 00
Cultivating 2 years	30 00
300 Trellis Posts, 8 cts.	24 00
500 lbs No. 12 Wire, 7 cts. per lb.	35 00
Setting Posts and stretching wire	5 00
Total	$138 50

This cost will vary with the varieties.—If Concord are taken, they can be had for $1.50 per 100; Norton's Virginia or Cynthiana will cost from $8 to $15 per 100. Thus, the cost may vary from $120 to $200 per acre.

The above is for a trellis of three wires; for two it will be about $11 to $12 less. The distance is for vines set 6 × 10 or 8 × 8, with a row in the center left out for a road.

The returns will vary so much with the locality, and with the season, that it would be useless to speculate upon them here. Every planter can form his own estimate. It will depend upon the price that can be obtained for the grapes or the wine, and many other circumstances which cannot be foreseen in a work like this, which is merely intended to give an outline of the necessary operations. [Pp. 191–92]

We note that trellis posts cost $3.00 per hundred in 1852 and $8.00 per hundred in 1885. Today, a century later, trellis posts cost around $300.00 per hundred, but the posts are larger and fewer are required per acre.

The effect of the Great Depression was naturally extremely deflationary on both income and expenses for grape farmers. Many of the circumstances such as state of indebtedness, availability of family labor, outside income, and efficiency of production are as crucial to economic survival today as they were during the Depression era. A comparison of costs between 1928 and 1932 was made in *An Economic Study of Grape Farms in Eastern United States* by G. P. Scoville (published in 1934).

In the Chautauqua-Erie belt in 1932, grapes sold for only $14, compared with $35 in 1928. In 1932, the cash income on these farms from the sale of grapes, other crops, milk, eggs, and outside labor was less than one-half what it was in 1928.

In 1928, there was left for the farmer and his family $349 after paying the cash farm expenses, such as hired labor, groceries, clothing, etc.

In 1932, only one family had a net cash income from farming, equal to $1000. This family had a large farm, were out of debt and spent practically nothing for labor, as the work was done by the father and two grown sons. Four other families of the 84 [growers] had cash income of $1000 or more, made possible by an income earned away from the farm. One farmer had a full-time government job, another dealt in

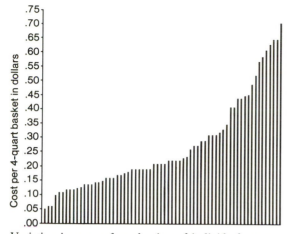

Variation in costs of production of individual growers (includes those within two standard deviations), in Missouri, 1928

cattle, another peddled fruit and vegetables, and another took in $1900 from trucking. In 1928, 19 families had incomes of $1000 or more, compared with 5 in 1932. . . .

With the same production, an average of 1.6 tons per acre, grape costs were 50 per cent less in 1932 than in 1928. Growers who have succeeded in lowering costs 50 per cent or more without impairing the productiveness of the vineyard will be in the best position to make money when grape prices advance. [Pp. 46–48]

The Modern Day

Studying economic reports past and present can lead only to the conclusion that grape growing for the average person is marginally profitable at best. It is clearly financially imprudent to borrow the capital necessary to start from scratch, even when tax laws currently in effect might enable an investor to benefit from a negative income from a "tax shelter" loss in the future. Partly because they are relatively new operations, many eastern vineyards are not self-sustaining. They are in fact supported with incomes from the primary professions of their owners, whose involvement with vines stems more from enthusiasm than from expectations of wealth. The ranks of eastern winegrowers contain a high proportion of doctors, engineers, professors, and airline pilots. For many, a vineyard is the means to a winery where the profit margins are somewhat more generous.

The cost of establishing and maintaining a vineyard varies tremendously with individual circumstances. Estimates in 1984 ranged from $5,000 to $10,000 for the first three years, with annual maintenance expenses of from $1,000 to $1,600 per year. Much of the variation depends on whether or not the family owns the land, buildings, and equipment and does most of the labor.

Other variables include grape variety (some are much more prolific than others), climate, and soil conditions. Grafted Vinifera vines cost more to buy and maintain than do European-American crosses, especially if it is necessary to cover the graft unions each winter. The additional expense, however, is sometimes repaid by the better price that Vinifera grapes can bring. On the other hand, higher yields and lower maintenance costs of non-Vinifera varieties can compensate for lower prices per ton.

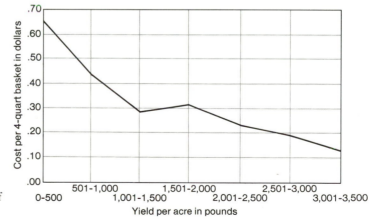

Relation between yield per acre and cost of production in Missouri, 1928

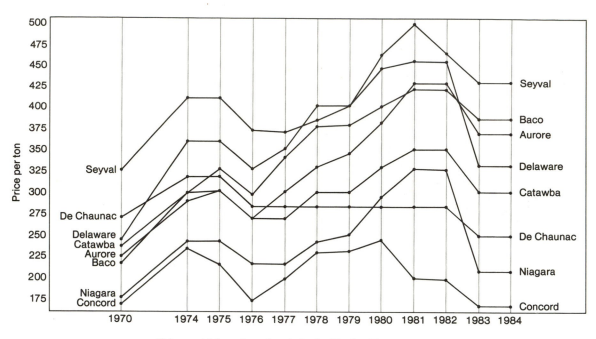

Prices paid for selected varieties by Taylor Wine Company

The law of supply and demand—together with nature and intelligent management—ultimately determines the financial success of a given grape variety. Tons per acre and price per ton determine the bottom line because many expenses remain constant from year to year. Regrettably, growers are rarely compensated for superior quality fruit. In the case of Vinifera wine grapes, the quality of wine attained from yields of greater than three to four tons per acre becomes questionable if premium wines are the goal. With many of the European-American varieties, a diminished wine quality is more likely to occur when crop levels exceed the four-to-six-ton range.

Prices paid for grapes by estate wineries are often higher per ton than those paid by large wineries. In 1984 small wineries paid about $400 to $650 for popular non-Viniferas and $600 to $1,200 for Viniferas. At these rates, with consistent yields there is a profit to be made by growers after eight or more years. In order for prices to remain at a satisfactory level for growers, new winery construction and consumer consumption must keep pace with expanding acreage.

Significant variations in grape prices for the same variety occur from state to state as a result of different growing conditions and the current balance of supply and demand. Farm winery statutes provide incentives for using local grapes. Although the constitutionality of preferential taxation is being questioned, there is sound logic behind mandates that favor the use of local fruit. Wine derives its character from grapes, and the grapes derive their character from the place where they are grown. For a wine to have a regional identity, the grapes must come from that region: Tennessee wine can only come from Tennessee grapes; a wine made in Tennessee with out-of-state grapes is not Tennessee wine.

Juice from local grapes is very often, gallon for gallon, more costly than tank-car shipments from out-of-state. This economic reality creates a very real conflict of interest for the winemaker who wishes to develop a regional identity for a winery but must consider financial contingencies as well. Federal regulations dictate that any wine with a state or county appellation which is not made with at least 75 percent grapes from within the state or county must be labeled "American." Wines from a delimited viticultural area contain at least 85 percent grapes from that area.

Before Planting a Vineyard . . .

Before planting the first vine it is vital to determine in advance whether or not a site is suitable for grapes at all. Free advice can be obtained from a county extension agent, preferably a fruit specialist. Evaluations of air drainage and frost potential, soil tests, and nematode counts are all financed by our tax dollars. The soil conservation service should also be consulted about soil composition, depth, drainage, and erosion potential. If necessary, it is preferable to spend an extra year to prepare the land properly, especially when clearing trees is involved.

Buying used equipment or renting it is often advisable, especially for infrequently used items. Commercial acreage (more than two acres) will require a tractor, 25 to 45 horsepower; an air-blast sprayer, which will cost from $3,500 to $8,000; a mower; a disc; a grape hoe/cultivator or at least a weed boom. A plow, subsoiler, planter, post pounder, and post-hole digger may only be needed for planting and therefore should be rented unless plans for expansion dictate otherwise. Putting up a trellis and planting may be contracted out to an experienced crew on a per-vine or per-acre basis; this can be a time-saving and economical alternative to doing it oneself.

Materials for a one-acre trellis typically include 200 line posts (8' × 3"), 24 endposts (8' × 6"), 24 anchors, about 500 pounds of wire, wire holders and splicers, a wire dispenser, and staples. Miscellaneous reusable tools and supplies include tying implements, pruning shears (the $25 variety), and picking boxes (about $5 for a 40-pound lug). A brush rake or chopper, a fertilizer spreader, a farm fuel pump, a pickup truck, and a good set of tools are also desirable. A convenient water supply is essential both for filling the spray tank and for watering young vines if weather requires. Deer fencing is necessary in many remote sites.

Quantity prices for rooted cuttings in 1984 were approximately $0.80 per vine, and grafted vines were about $2.50 each. The number of vines per acre depends on vine spacing. Ten-foot aisles permit passage of pickups, the use of cross-arm trellises, and the accommodation of all conventional equipment. Nine-foot aisles are acceptable on low-vigor sites; narrower spacing requires special vineyard tractors. The distance between vines in the row generally varies from five to eight feet depending on variety and site: $10' \times 5' = 871$ vines per acre; $10' \times 6' = 726$; $10' \times 7' = 622$; $9' \times 5' = 966$; $9' \times 6' = 806$; $9' \times 7' = 691$; $9' \times 8' = 605$.

Given the amount of hand labor involved in raising grapes, there should be a residence on the site, along with a storage shed for equipment and spray materials. Depending on vineyard conditions and the degree of mechanization, a well-trained, full-time employee can manage anywhere from ten or more acres, with no extra help after planting and trellising, to thirty or more acres, given part-time help. In the absence of a mechanical harvester, more hands are always needed at harvest.

There is virtually no crop during the first two years. Some second-year vines are allowed to bear a few bunches in order to control excessive vigor. In the third year approximately one to two tons are harvested, and three to four tons in the fourth year. Consistent annual yields are the result of rigorous management and favorable weather.

Even if annual yields are good, there is the ever-present marketing dilemma. Will the price per ton cover the cost of production? As the history of grape growing tells us, the answer to that question is, *sometimes*. Cost studies of the New York industry illuminate the situation dramatically. In 1974 the average grape farmer with thirty-five acres of vines was able to realize $10.05 an hour from applied labor, in 1981, $0.09

an hour could be realized; and in 1982 applied labor realized a loss. A farmer needs an income to provide for future capital investment (for example, replanting to more profitable varieties), for amortizing indebtedness, and for personal living expenses.

Growers with below-average costs and above-average yields can make money even when the average grower loses. Given the often unfortunate vacillations in price from year to year and the perishable nature of fresh grapes, however, many wine-grape growers furnish themselves a market by establishing their own winery. This may be a wise investment or it may be jumping financially from the frying pan into the fire.

From Grapes to Wine

Those who intend to plant wine grapes should understand the grapes' role from a winery's point of view whether or not they intend to have a winery as well. It is all very well to say one must get X dollars per ton in order to stay in business, but one must also understand the impact that that price per ton has on the cost of a bottle of wine.

As a rough approximation, grapes account as a direct cost for $0.50 per bottle at $400 per ton, $1.00 a bottle at $800 per ton, and $1.50 at $1,200 per ton. Given the realities of the oft-used three-tier system—in which a producer sells to a wholesaler, who adds a percentage and sells to a retailer, who adds a percentage and sells to the consumer—all the costs, including the grapes, are magnified through the chain. Fifty cents ($400 per ton) is 16.7 percent of a $3.00 price per bottle, whereas $1.50 ($1,200 per ton) is 50 percent of that $3.00 and 16.7 percent of a $9.00 price.

How much wine can be made from a ton of grapes depends on several factors. Different varieties vary in their juice yields, and the same variety can vary from season to season. Winemakers adjust the pressure of the press according to the quality and quantity of juice they want to work with. Solids settling out of the juice result

in approximately a 10 percent reduction in volume from juice to wine. One can reasonably expect about 160 gallons of premium quality wine per ton of grapes. Juice volume can be increased at any of several stages: by rain during harvest, with water used to wash grapes before processing, and by adding water during amelioration.

A four-ton-per-acre crop will produce 600 gallons of wine (160 gallons × 4 tons) or 3,000 bottles per acre. An amateur wine grower with an eighth-acre vineyard (about 80 vines) can produce enough wine for a small family to enjoy a bottle each day of the year. For every ten acres of vines, a grape farmer can produce in the neighborhood of 6,000 gallons or more of wine.

Although small is not necessarily better where winemaking is concerned, it usually means a high degree of owner pride and direct involvement with the product. Winemakers indeed regard their wines as extensions of their own persona. At times this can lead to a lack of objectivity but rarely a lack of enthusiasm.

To make the leap from amateur to professional winemaker requires a substantial amount of capital. A very small commercial winery can limp along with some amateur-size equipment as long as there is sufficient labor to accomplish the work in a reasonable amount of time. There is no question, however, that technology is the winemaker's and wine consumer's friend. Contrary to popular belief, the more "high tech" the winery, the more likely it is that wines of reliable quality can be produced, because of better control over temperature and sterility.

The zeal that accompanies the dream of owning a vineyard and winery has been known to cloud the business sense of many otherwise intelligent individuals. To provide the neophyte with a more realistic perspective enologist Bruce Zoecklein compiled the following list of preliminary questions.

Required Information for Winery Planning

Site Selection:
Are wine grapes available?
Are they the right cultivars [varieties]?

How many grapes are in a bottle of wine? These calculations are based on Seyval blanc grapes grown in Tidewater Virginia in 1981. Figures will vary with variety, vintage, and vineyard.

Annual consumption by one moderate consumer = 1/2 bottle per day = 121,910 grapes = 182.5 bottles = 821 clusters = 1/16 acre per year.

What is the political atmosphere toward wineries in your area?

What are the waste water disposal requirements?

Does the site have good drainage?

What is the accessibility to public utilities?

Is there accessibility to public roads, public scales, etc.?

Are visitors included in your plan?

Is there a sufficient water supply?

Is the water quality adequate?

Equipment Selection:

All equipment should be selected prior to winery construction with full knowledge of electrical, water, and air requirements.

What is your initial daily tonnage capacity?

What is your ultimate tonnage capacity?

Which wines will be bottled as varietals and which ones will be blended to non-varietal labels?

What is the percentage of reds to whites, sweet to dry, still to sparkling, table to dessert?

What is your expansion schedule?

Will your processing equipment handle your proposed expansion?

How will grapes be transported to the winery?

How do you intend to empty grapes into the crusher?

What is your means of testing grape quality?

Will you pay incentive for quality?

What will be the time between harvest and crush?

Where do you intend to dispose of the stems?

What size lots do you intend to crush?

What size crusher and must pump are required?

What size lines are required?

Will you be crushing for other people?

How do you intend to ferment—in wood or stainless steel?

Do you want tanks on stands or pads?

What specific valves, vents, refrigeration hook-up, manways, designs, etc. do you require on your tanks?

What are the desired fermentation temperatures?

What is your present calculated refrigeration load? Future?

Will your refrigeration system lend itself to expansion?

How is the pomace to be removed from the tanks?

How do you intend to dejuice?

How do you intend to dispose of your pomace?

What are your hot and cold water requirements?

Is a centrifuge necessary?

How do you intend to remove CO_2 from the fermenting area?

What sort of small barrel program do you plan—which type of wood and for how long? For which cultivars?

Winery startup cost estimates are almost infinitely variable but range from about $5 to $25 per gallon depending on building and equipment costs. After the preliminary questions have been answered and costs researched and tallied, it is vital to determine how many years one can survive with a negative cash flow. Some very fine young vineyards and wineries have had to change hands at distressed prices because the original owner was not able to survive the early years of very high expenses with very low return. There is relatively more profit to be made in the winery than in the vineyard, but both require expert management, personal dedication, and the irrepressible passion for wine which led one into the vineyard in the first place.

APPENDIX I

ANTIQUE GRAPE GUIDE

Many of the old grape varieties mentioned by growers in the 1880 USDA survey are no longer grown commercially. Some may still be found in research collections, while others, especially those with good disease resistance and cold hardiness, undoubtedly exist in backyard arbors across America.

All of the historic books listed in Suggested Further Reading describe the popular grapes of the nineteenth century. The best antique ampelography is the *Illustrated Descriptive Catalogue of American Grape Vines* by St. Louis nurseryman Isidor Bush, his son, and his partner Meissner. The first edition was published in 1869. I have used the fourth edition, published in 1894, for reference. In the preface to the fourth edition, the authors sum up the situation of the past quarter century:

> Rot and mildew became so destructive and discouraging that grape-growing, to a large extent, east of the Rocky Mountains, was considered a failure until some preventive or remedy for those diseases might be discovered. At the same time the finest European grapes were grown so successfully and abundantly in California that the price of wine and table-grapes was reduced below the cost of their production in this part of the United States.

> But owing to the fact that some exceptionally favored regions were exempt from cryptogamic maladies, and to the love and enthusiasm entertained for the grape by some of its old cultivators, its culture was still maintained.

> Now, however, with the discovery of a remedy for grape diseases, renewed confidence to successful grape-growing has been inspired and, encouraged by many of our veteran viticulturists, we yielded to the flattering demand for a new edition.

Alexander. We described this, the nation's first commercial grape variety, in Chapter 1. There is no doubt that it has Labrusca heritage. New York horticulturist U. P. Hedrick was convinced it was a cross with Vinifera, whereas Montpellier viticulturist Louis Ravaz felt the specimen in his collection surely had Riparia genes. Its very late ripening suggests Vinifera rather than Riparia genes. Other names: Cape, Black Cape, Schuylkill Muscadell, Constantia, Spring-Mill-Constantia, Clifton's Constantia, Tasker's Grape, Vevay, Winne, Rothrock of Prince, York Lisbon.

177

Alvey. Introduced about 1860 by Dr. Harvey of Hagerstown, Maryland, the quality of its fruit and growth habit suggest that this is a cross between Aestivalis and Vinifera. Alvey has female flowers and therefore will not set fruit well on its own. Not a popular variety, it was said to prefer northern slopes and climates; on southern slopes it dropped its leaves prematurely.

Amber. Named for the color of its oblong, thin-skinned berries, Amber is a sister seedling—Labrusca × Riparia—of Elvira raised by Jacob Rommel of Morrison, Missouri.

Beauty. Another Rommel hybrid, this is an Aestivalis × Labrusca cross between Delaware (or possibly Catawba) and Maxatawney. Although the wine was supposed to be very agreeably and highly flavored, the vine was so subject to fungus infection in wet seasons that Rommel took it off the market. The Bushberg catalogue says it is worthy of trial now that growers have fungicides to protect the fruit.

Black Taylor. See Taylor.

Brighton. A Labrusca-Vinifera seedling of Diana Hamburg pollinated by Concord, Brighton was raised by Jacob Moore in Brighton, New York. The positive traits that made this a prominent commercial grape in the past are early ripening, good productivity and disease resistance, adaptability to different soils, and juicy, aromatic red fruit. The two major drawbacks are female flowers and the poor keeping quality of the fruit, which limit its usefulness for the fresh market.

Bullitt. See Taylor.

Cherokee. This Aestivalis seedling of unknown origin, raised by Dr. J. Stayman of Leavenworth, Kansas, was said to be productive and mildew-free, similar in appearance to Cynthiana. It has black grapes that ripen late.

Clinton. First called Worthington and later renamed, the origins of this Riparia-Labrusca variety go back to circa 1820 in Hamilton College, New York. Ravaz indicates that the Riparia genes are dominant. Bush's description of this hardy, disease-resistant vine as "exceedingly rank, straggling grower, and one of the hardest vines to keep under control" make it sound like an antique Baco noir. This vine found a home in some parts of France, first as a rootstock and then as a direct producer (and parent of other direct producers) yielding early-ripening fruit that attained high sugar and dark color. Most authors indicate that Clinton, made as a varietal, has a disagreeable taste.

Cottage. A seedling of Concord raised by Ephraim Bull, originator of Concord, Cottage was introduced in 1869. It is earlier ripening than Concord and the fruit is of better quality—less foxy and more delicate. However, it is not as productive and is more subject to uneven ripening.

Cunningham. Also known as Long, this Aestivalis variety was found in the garden of Jacob Cunningham, Prince Edward County, Virginia. Similar to Herbemont, its purplish black grapes made a deep yellow wine praised for its high quality both in the United States and France, where it was used as a rootstock and a direct producer.

Eumelan. A chance Aestivalis seedling found in Fishkill Landing, New York, Eumelan made rich red wine with must which had high sugar and low acid. The limiting factors of Eumelan were its female flowers, poor rooting ability, and susceptibility to disease.

Flowers. Found in a swamp near Lamberton, North Carolina, in the early 1800s by William Flowers, this Rotundifolia vine was also known as Black Muscadine. The vine had excellent disease resistance, and the very late-ripening fruit made a red wine that was much appreciated throughout the South.

Goethe. First appearing in 1858 as Roger's No. 1, this Vinifera-Labrusca cross was said to be both hardy and disease resistant with red fruit that had fine Vinifera character. Because of its late maturity, it was best adapted to the mid-Atlantic and the Ohio and lower Missouri valleys. As with many European-American crosses today, Goethe required cluster-thinning to prevent overbearing. This grape should perhaps be reintroduced into home vineyards in middle America.

Hamburg. Black Hamburg was a popular hot-house Vinifera table grape in England, Europe, and America. It grew well outdoors in California but was not a commercial variety in the East.

Hartford or Hartford Prolific. Raised from seed by Paphro Steele in West Hartford, Connecticut, in the late 1840s, this was a healthy, hardy vine noted for its very early ripening and very poor quality fruit. The Bushberg Catalogue exhorts growers: "Let us discard the Hartford, which only destroys the appetite for grapes, and injures the sale and price of all sorts: while a *really good* very early market grape would increase the demand for all later varieties."

Hermann. F. Langendoerfer of Hermann, Missouri, planted this Norton seedling in 1863, and some thought the hardy Aestivalis grape had great potential for producing a superior American sherry because of its brownish-yellow juice and strong fragrance. Although it never did achieve commercial success, a Hermann vine survives today on an arbor at West Seventh and Washington streets in Hermann.

Jefferson. A seedling of Concord and Iona raised about 1870 by James Ricketts in Newburgh, New York, Jefferson was said to have the best traits of both parents: a healthy vine and superior red grapes with delicate flavor and excellent keeping ability. Because it ripened two weeks after Concord and was not as hardy, it was not widely planted.

Lady. A pure Concord seedling, Lady was sold to nurseryman George Campbell of Delaware, Ohio, by Mr. Imlay of Muskingum, Ohio, about 1870. By all reports this very early (two weeks before Concord) white was an extremely hardy, disease-resistant vine with superior white fruit. It was recommended as far north as Ontario for home use or local markets; its only drawback commercially was poor shipping ability.

Lady Washington. J. H. Ricketts fertilized a Concord with Allen's Hybrid (Golden Chasselas × Isabella) to produce this white (pale amber) grape. The juicy and aromatic fruit had good keeping and shipping ability. The vine was said to be quite healthy and hardy and was well regarded in Illinois and Missouri, but it never achieved commercial importance.

Martha. Introduced by Samuel Miller of Calmdale, Pennsylvania, in 1868, Martha is a green-berried seedling of Concord. At one time among the most popular white varieties, it attained higher sugar levels than Concord and had a more delicate, less foxy flavor. The grapes did not ship well and superior varieties reduced commercial interest in Martha.

Mish. Found near Washington, North Carolina, by W. M. Mish about 1846, this was considered by many to be one of the most versatile Rotundifolia varieties—good for wine, juice, and table. Mish had perfect flowers and deep reddish-black fruit.

Perkins. An accidental seedling found about 1830 in the garden of Jacob Perkins in Bridgewater, Massachusetts, this was considered one of the hardiest, most disease-resistant Labrusca grapes available. The greenish-white fruit was strongly foxy and pulpy, but according to the Bushberg catalogue this reliable grape "is not without value as a wine grape: its foxy taste and odor grow less the older the wine becomes, and can be improved by gallisizing, or, better still, by blending with other white wines."

Prentiss. A seedling of Isabella raised about 1870 by J. W. Prentiss of Pultney, New

York, this attractive green grape was once recommended as a table grape. It was not sufficiently disease resistant or winter hardy to have lasting popularity.

Rebecca. Found about 1850 as a seedling in the garden of E. M. Peake in Hudson, New York, this Labrusca (× Vinifera?) variety produced exceptionally fine white grapes that were very juicy, sweet, slightly foxy, and reportedly delicious. Although it was recommended for amateur growers, the vine was far too tender and susceptible to disease to succeed commercially.

Ricketts. J. H. Ricketts of Newburgh, New York, produced hundreds of seedlings and received many awards from the American Pomological Society in the late 1800s. Some of his better-known varieties were Lady Washington, El Dorado, and Jefferson—all Concord seedlings. Well-known Clinton seedlings raised by Ricketts were Bacchus and Empire State. Although universally praised for their fruit quality, the Ricketts varieties lacked the hardiness and rusticity necessary for commercial acceptance.

Rogers 3, 4, 9, & 15. These numbered varieties were named: Massasoit, Wilder, Lindley, and Agawam respectively. They are among the fifteen or so seedlings (out of a total of forty-five) produced by E. S. Rogers in his small garden in Salem, Massachusetts, beginning about 1850, which achieved some notoriety.

Agawam (No. 15) was a cross between Mammoth Sage (wild Labrusca) and Black Hamburg (Vinifera) introduced in 1861. The fruit, considered attractive in appearance, had a thick, tough skin, coarse pulp, foxy flavor, and brownish-red or maroon color.

Lindley (No. 9) was named for English botanist John Lindley in 1869. It was a cross between Mammoth (wild Labrusca) and Golden Chasselas. Its brick-red grapes were regarded as beautiful and delicious and possessing superior keeping qualities. A highly recommended table grape; pollination critical to this female variety.

Massasoit (No. 3) was a red-fruited Labrusca-Vinifera cross with female flowers recommended as hardy and of good quality for the home vineyard.

Wilder (No. 4) was highly recommended as a table grape in the Bushberg catalogue, being a reliable, hardy, and productive Labrusca-Vinifera variety with black fruit resembling Black Hamburg. It had female flowers.

Taylor. Also known as Bullitt or Taylor's Bullitt, this was a wild Riparia-Labrusca found in the Cumberland Mountains near the Kentucky-Tennessee border and introduced to notice by Judge Taylor of Jericho, Kentucky. It was a rampant grower best suited to southern regions with long warm summers. The parent of such successful varieties as Elvira, Noah, and Missouri Riesling, it also served as a rootstock in France. The white berries were small with thin yet tough skin. Some considered the wine to be similar to a German Riesling, but its female flowers and small clusters caused it to be insufficiently productive for commercial production.

Telegraph. Also known as Christine, this early Labrusca variety was raised by Mr. Christine near Westchester, Pennsylvania, and introduced about 1865 by the editor of the Germantown *Telegraph,* P. R. Freas. The spicy-flavored black grapes were very attractive to birds and suffered badly from rot in warm, humid climates.

Venango. A very early Labrusca variety, also known as Minor's Seedling, this red grape was said to have been cultivated by the French at Fort Venango on the Allegheny River. The vine was healthy and productive, but the fruit was pulpy and foxy.

Worden. A seed of Concord planted about 1863 by Schuyler Worden of Minetto, New York, Worden ripened at least a week before Concord and produced larger berries and bunches. Many regarded it as a better grape except for the fact that the fruit cracked easily, making it a poor shipper. It was not recommended for warm, southern regions.

Wyoming. S. J. Parker of Ithaca, New York, introduced this grape and stated that it came from Pennsylvania in 1861. By all reports it was little different from Labrusca grapes found in the forests. The red grapes were very foxy with a tough pulp, and the vine was hardy and disease resistant. Other names for this undistinguished variety are Wilmington Red, Hopkins Early Red, and Wyoming Red.

APPENDIX 2

 # VITICULTURAL AREAS EAST OF THE ROCKIES

An approved viticultural area is a delimited grape-growing region distinguishable by geographical features, the boundaries of which have been recognized by the Bureau of Alcohol, Tobacco, and Firearms, Washington, D.C. 20226.

ARKANSAS
    Altus
    Arkansas Mountain (proposed)
    Ozark Mountains (proposed)
CONNECTICUT
    Southeastern New England
INDIANA
    Ohio River Valley
KENTUCKY
    Ohio River Valley
MARYLAND
    Catoctin
    Cumberland Valley (proposed)
    Linganore
MASSACHUSETTS
    Martha's Vineyard
    Southeastern New England
MICHIGAN
    Fennville
    Lake Michigan Shore
    Leelanau Peninsula

MISSISSIPPI
    Mississippi Delta
MISSOURI
    Augusta
    Hermann
NEW JERSEY
    Central Delaware Valley
NEW YORK
    Finger Lakes
    The Hamptons, Long Island (proposed)
    Hudson River Region
    Lake Erie
    North Fork, Long Island (proposed)
OHIO
    Grand River Valley
    Isle of St. George
    Lake Erie
    Loramie Creek
    Ohio River Valley
PENNSYLVANIA
    Central Delaware Valley

Cumberland Valley (proposed)
Lake Erie
Lancaster Valley
RHODE ISLAND
Southeastern New England
VIRGINIA
George Washington's Birthplace
(proposed)

Monticello
North Fork of the Roanoke River
Rocky Knob
Shenandoah Valley
WEST VIRGINIA
Kanawha River Valley (proposed)
Ohio River Valley
Shenandoah Valley

APPENDIX 3

SELECTED EASTERN WINERIES

Following is a selected list of eastern American wineries that have their own vineyards or use local grapes. Each entry includes founding date and total storage capacity. Information is drawn from 1984 data and from the author's knowledge of wineries planning to open in 1985. Directories with complete, up-to-date listings are available from *Eastern Grape Grower*, Box 329, Watkins Glen, NY 14891, and *Wines & Vines*, 1800 Lincoln Avenue, San Rafael, CA 94901 (the latter also includes California and Mexico).

ALABAMA

Braswell's Winery
1984/? gallons
Route 3, Box 295
Dora, AL 35062
(205) 648-8335
Ruth and Wayne Braswell

Chateau La Caia
1985/9,000 gallons
725 Greenville Pike
Hazel Green, AL 35750
(205) 828-6110
Aleksei and Sally Gimbolo
Frank and Caia Parente

Perdido Vineyards
1979/62,000 gallons
Route 1, Box 20-A
Perdido, AL 36562
(205) 937-WINE
Marianne and Jim Eddins

ARKANSAS

Cowie Wine Cellars
1967/10,000 gallons
Route 2, P. O. Box 110A
Paris, AR 72855
(501) 963-3990
Robert G. Cowie

Heckmann's Winery
1895/20,000 gallons
Route 1, Box 148
Harrisburg, AR 72432
(501) 578-5541
Dewayne and Nancy Utley

Mount Bethel Winery
1956/30,000 gallons
P.O. Box 137, U.S. Highway 64
Altus, AR 72821
(501) 468-2444
Eugene J. Post

Post Winery
1880/500,000 gallons
Route 1, Box 1
Altus, AR 72821
(501) 468-2741
Matthew J. Post and family

Wiederkehr Wine Cellars
1880/1,750,000 gallons
Route 1, Box 14
Altus, AR 72821
(501) 468-2611
Wiederkehr family

CONNECTICUT

Clarke Vineyard
1983/8,500 gallons
Taugwonk Road, RD 2, Box 151C
Stonington, CT 06378
(203) 535-0235
Barbara and Thomas Clarke

Crosswoods Vineyards
1984/25,000 gallons
75 Chester Maine Road
North Stonington, CT 06359
(203) 535-2205
Susan H. and Hugh P. Connell

DiGrazia Vineyards & Winery
1984/6,000 gallons
131 Tower Road
Brookfield Center, CT 06805
(203) 775-1616
Barbara A. and Paul V. DiGrazia, M.D.

Haight Vineyard
1975/16,000 gallons
Chestnut Hill
Litchfield, CT 06759
(203) 567-4045
Sherman P. Haight (owner)

Hamlet Hill Vineyards
1980/22,000 gallons
Route 101
Pomfret, CT 06258
(203) 928-5550
A. W. Loos

Hopkins Vineyard
1981/10,000 gallons
Hopkins Road
New Preston, CT 06777
(203) 868-7954
Judith and William Hopkins

Nutmeg Vineyard
1982/3,000 gallons
(Bunkerhill Road, Coventry, CT)
P.O. Box 146
Andover, CT 06232
(203) 742-8402
Anthony Maulucci

St. Hilary's Vineyard
1977/500 gallons
RFD 1
North Grosvenordale, CT 06255
(203) 935-5377
Mary Kerensky

Stonecrop Vineyards
1979/3,500 gallons
RD 2, Box 151A
Stonington, CT 06378
(203) 535-2497

DELAWARE

None using local grapes

FLORIDA

Alaqua Vineyard
1981/10,000 gallons
Route 1, Box 97-C4
Freeport, FL 32439
(904) 835-2644
Foster and Rebecca Burgess

Florida Heritage Winery
1981/20,000 gallons
Box 116
Anthony, FL 32617
Mr. and Mrs. Robert C. Price, Jr.

Fruit Wines of Florida
1972/180,000 gallons (a small
portion is table wine made with local
grapes)
513 South Florida Avenue
Tampa, FL 33602
(813) 223-1222
Joseph D. Midulla

Lafayette Vineyards
1983/24,000 gallons
6505 Mahan Drive
Tallahassee, FL 32308
(904) 878-9041
C. Gary Cox and Gary Ketchum

GEORGIA

B & B Rosser Winery
1983/15,000 gallons
437 Ray's Church Road
High Shoals, GA 30645
(404) 353-2876
Bill and Barbara Rosser

Chateau Elan
1983/60,000 gallons
Route 1, Box 563-1
Hoschton, GA 30458
(404) 536-8745
Ed Friederich

Georgia Wines
1983/5,000 gallons
Route 3, Box 98P
Chickamauga, GA 30707
(404) 931-2851
Maurice S. Rawlings and family

Habersham Vineyards
1983/10,000 gallons
GA Highway 365, Route 1
Alto, GA 30510
(404) 355-5775
Tom Slick

Happy "B" Farm Winery
1981/? gallons
Route 4, Box 447, Forsyth, GA 31029
(912) 994-6549
T. A. Bunn

ILLINOIS

Gem City Vineland Company
1857/40,000 gallons
South Parley Street
Nauvoo, IL 62354
(217) 453-2218
Fred Baxter

Terra Vineyard & Wine Cellar
1984/5,000 gallons
27927 108th Avenue North
Port Byron, IL 61275
(309) 523-2670
Wilfred W. Enders and Dominic DiIulio

INDIANA

Easley Enterprises
1974/gallons unpublished
205 North College Avenue
Indianapolis, IN 46202

(317) 636-4516
John J. Easley

Huber Orchard Winery
1978/40,000 gallons
Route 1, Box 202
Borden, IN 47106
(812) 923-WINE
Huber family

Oliver Wine Company
1972/35,000 gallons
8024 N. Highway 37
Bloomington, IN 47401
(812) 876-5800
William and Mary Oliver

Possum Trot Vineyards
1978/3,000 gallons
8310 North Possum Trot Road
Unionville, IN 47468
(812) 988-2694
Ben and Lee Sparks

St. Wendel Cellars
1975/50,000 gallons
10501 Winery Road
Wadesville (at St. Wendel), IN 47638
(812) 963-6441
Murli Dharmadhikari

Villa Milan Vineyard
1984/2,500 gallons
P. O. Box 248, Milan, IN 47031
(812) 654-3419
John A. and Dorothy M. Garrett

IOWA

Local wine grapes are hard to find in Iowa.
There are approximately fifteen wineries that
purchase grapes, ten of which are located in
the Amana area. All Iowa wineries make fruit
wines in addition to grape wines.

Private Stock Winery
1977/9,000 gallons
706 Allen, Boone, IA 50036
(515) 432-8348
Thomas H. Larson

KENTUCKY

None open for business in 1984

LOUISIANA

None

MAINE

Local wineries in Gouldsboro and Pembroke make wine from local fruit, not grapes.

MARYLAND

Berrywine Plantations Winery
1976/40,000 gallons
13601 Glisans Mill Road
Mt. Airy, MD 21771
(301) 662-8687
Aellen family

Boordy Vineyards
1942/28,000 gallons
12820 Long Green Pike
Hydes, MD 21082
(301) 592-5015
Robert B. Deford, III

Byrd Vineyards
1976/19,000 gallons
Church Hill Road
Myersville, MD 21773
(301) 293-1110
Bret and Sharon Byrd

Catoctin Vineyards
1983/17,500 gallons
805 Green Bridge Road
Brookeville, MD 20729
Robert Lyon, M. J. and Ann Milne,
Roger and Judy Wolf

Elk Run Vineyards
1983/2,000 gallons
15113 Liberty Road
Mt. Airy, MD 21771
(301) 755-2513
Fred and Carol Wilson

Montbray Wine Cellars
1966/7,000 gallons
818 Silver Run Valley Road
Westminster, MD 21157
(301) 346-7878
Hamilton Mowbray and family

Whitemarsh Cellars
1982/2,000 gallons
2810 Hoffman Mill Road
Hampstead, MD 21074
(301) 848-4488
DeWitt F. Truitt

Woodhall Cellars
1983/5,000 gallons
15115 Wheeler Lane
Sparks, MD 21152

(301) 467-8430
Al Copp, Michael DeSimone,
Herbert Davis, Kent Muhly

Ziem Vineyards
1977/5,000 gallons
Route 1
Fairplay, MD 21733
(301) 223-8352
Robert and Ruth Ziem

MASSACHUSETTS

Chicama Vineyards
1971/20,000 gallons
Stoney Hill Road
West Tisbury, MA 02575
(617) 693-0309
George and Catherine Mathiesen and family

Commonwealth Winery
1978/40,000 gallons
22 Lothrop Street
Plymouth, MA 02360
(617) 746-4138
David Tower

Huntington Cellars
1983/? gallons
Route 1, Box 204, Route 66
Huntington, MA 01050
(413) 667-5561
Marie B. and Chester S. Wilusz, Jr.

Inn Wines
1984/740 gallons
P. O. Box 464, 4 Elm Street
Hatfield, MA 01038
(413) 247-5175
Richard A. Phaneuf

Narragansett-Hillview Winery
1983/12,000 gallons
Pinewood Road
Plymouth, MA 02360
(617) 747-3334
Charles Caranci, Jr.

MICHIGAN

Boskydel Vineyard
1976/8,000 gallons
Route 1, Box 552
Lake Leelanau, MI 49653
(616) 256-7272
Bernard C. Rink and family

Fenn Valley Vineyards
1973/200,000 gallons
Route 4, 6130-122nd Avenue
Fennville, MI 49408
(616) 561-2396
William Welsch and family

Frontenac Vineyards
1933/500,000 gallons
39149 West Michigan Avenue
Paw Paw, MI 49079
(616) 657-5531
Edward and E. John Wieferman

Good Harbor Vineyards
1980/17,400 gallons
Route 1, Box 891
Lake Leelanau, MI 49653
(616) 256-9165
Bruce Simpson

Grand Traverse Vineyards
1974/50,000 gallons
12239 Center Road
Traverse City, MI 49684
(616) 223-7355
Edward O'Keefe

Lakeside Vineyard
1934/540,000 gallons
13581 Red Arrow Highway
Harbert, MI 49115
(616) 469-0700
Leonard R. Olson

Leelanau Wine Cellars
1975/85,000 gallons
Box 68
Omena, MI 49674
(616) 386-5201
Michael Jacobson

L. Mawby Vineyards / Winery
1977/2,500 gallons
P.O. Box 237, 4519 Elm Valley Road
Suttons Bay, MI 49682
(616) 271-3522
Lawrence Mawby

St. Julian Wine Company
1921/1,500,000 gallons
P.O. Box 127
Paw Paw, MI 49079
(616) 657-5568
David Braganini

Seven Lakes Vineyards
1982/10,000 gallons
1111 Tinsman Road
Fenton, MI 48430

(313) 629-5686
Harry and Christian Guest

Tabor Hill Vineyard
1970/90,000 gallons
Route 2, Box 720
Buchanan, MI 49107
(616) 422-1161
David Upton

Warner Vineyards
1939/3,000,000 gallons
706 South Kalamazoo Street
Paw Paw, MI 49079
(616) 657-3165
James J. Warner

MINNESOTA

Alexis Bailly Vineyard
1976/12,000 gallons
18200 Kirby Avenue
Hastings, MN 55033
(612) 437-1413
David and Nan Bailly

Lake Sylvia Vineyard
1976/5,000 gallons
Route 1, Box 149
South Haven, MN 55382
(612) 236-7743
David W. MacGregor

Northern Vineyards Winery
1983/4,500 gallons
Old Staples Mill Complex
402 Main Street
Stillwater, MN 55082
(612) 430-1032
The Minnesota Winegrowers
Cooperative

MISSISSIPPI

Almarla Vineyards
1979/50,000 gallons
Mississippi Highway 510
Matherville, MS 39360
(601) 687-5548
Alex and Margaret Mathers

Claiborne Vineyards
1984/2,500 gallons
302 North Highway 49W
Indiana, MS 38751
(601) 887-2327
E. Claiborne Barnwell

Old South Winery
1979/17,000 gallons
507 Concord Street
Natchez, MS 39120
(601) 445-9924
Scott Galbreath, Jr.

Thousand Oaks Vineyard & Winery
1978/30,000 gallons
Route 4, Box 293
Starkville, MS 39759
(601) 323-6657
Robert Burgin and family

The Winery Rushing
1977/29,500 gallons
Merigold, MS 38759
(601) 748-2731
Sam and Di Rushing

MISSOURI

Bardenheier's Wine Cellars
1873/950,000 gallons
1019 Skinker Parkway
St. Louis, MO 63112
(314) 862-1400
E. Dean Jarboe

Bias Vineyards & Winery
1980/3,000 gallons
Route 1
Berger, MO 63014
(314) 834-5475
James Bias

Bristle Ridge Vineyard & Winery
1979/7,000 gallons
Box 95
Knob Noster, MO 65336
(816) 229-0961

Carver Wine Cellars
1979/5,000 gallons
Box 1316
Rolla, MO 65401
(314) 364-4335
Laurence and Mary Carver

Eckert's Sunny Slope Winery & Vineyards
1984/3,500 gallons
Route 2, Box 817
Washington, MO 63090
(314) 532-3680
John and Sandra Eckert

Edelweiss Winery & Stone Church Vineyards
1979/5,000 gallons
Highway E and Stone Church Road

Route 4, Box 172
New Haven, MO 63068
(314) 237-2841
Gunther and Janet Heeb

Ferringo Vineyards & Winery
1981/9,600 gallons
Highway B, Route 2, Box 227
St. James, MO 65559
(314) 265-7742
Richard and Susan Ferringo

Green Valley Vineyards
1973/25,000 gallons
Highway D, RR
Portland, MO 65067
(314) 676-5771
Nicholas A. Lamb

Heinrichshaus
1978/5,500 gallons
Route 2, Box 139
St. James, MO 65559
(314) 265-5000
Heinrich and Lois Grohe

Hermannhof Winery
1852/50,000 gallons
330 East First Street
Hermann, MO 65041
(314) 486-5959
James Dierberg

Kruger Winery & Vineyard
1977/7,500 gallons
Route 1
Nelson, MO 65347
(816) 837-3217
Lawrence and Harold Kruger

Midi Vineyards
1977/7,000 gallons
Route 1
Lone Jack, MO 64070
(816) 566-2119
Dutton Briggs and George Gale

Montelle Vineyards
1969/8,000 gallons
Route 1, Box 94
Augusta, MO 63332
(314) 228-4464
Clayton Byers

Moore-Dupont Winery
1982/40,000 gallons
Box 211
Benton, MO 63736
(314) 545-4141
Jean-René Dupont and James Handy Moore

Mount Pleasant Vineyards
1881/60,000 gallons
101 Webster Street
Augusta, MO 63332
(314) 228-4419
Lucian and Eva Dressel

Osage Ridge Winery
1984/1,000 gallons
Missouri Highway 94
Box 147
Augusta, MO 63332
(314) 228-4505
Horace Peek and Paul Levine

Ozark Vineyard Winery
1976/20,000 gallons
Chestnut Ridge, MO 65630
(417) 587-3555
Hershel Gray

Peaceful Bend Vineyard
1972/3,000 gallons
Route 2, Box 131
Steelville, MO 65565
(314) 775-2578
Axel and N. A. Arneson

Pirtles Weston Vineyards
1978/5,000 gallons
502 Spring
Weston, MO 64098
(816) 386-5588
Dr. Elbert and Patricia Pirtle

Reis Winery
1978/6,500 gallons
Route 4, Box 133
Licking, MO 65542
(314) 674-3763
Val Reis

Rosati Winery
1934/75,580 gallons
Route 1, Box 55
St. James, MO 65559
(314) 265-8629, 265-3559
Robert H. Ashby

St. James Winery
1970/56,000 gallons
Route 2, Box 98A
St. James, MO 65559
(314) 265-7912
Patricia and Jim Hofherr

Stone Hill Wine Company
1847/126,000 gallons
Route 1, Box 26
Hermann, MO 65041

(314) 486-2221
James and Betty Ann Held and family

Winery of the Little Hills
1982/5,500 gallons
1219 South Main Street
St. Charles, MO 63301
(314) 723-7313
Anthony and Martha Kooyumjian

New Hampshire

Lakes Region Winery
1969/85,000 gallons
RFD 6, Box 218
Laconia, NH 03246
(603) 524-0174
John and Lucille Canepa

New Jersey

Alba Vineyard
1983/25,000 gallons
RD 1, Finesville
Milford, NJ 08848
(201) 995-7800, 843-2341
Rudolf Marchesi

Amalthea Cellars
1984/5,000 gallons
267-A Hayes Mill Road
Atco, NJ 08004
(609) 767-1402
Louis D. Caracciolo, Jr.

Amwell Valley Vineyard
1982/4,000 gallons
RD 1, Old York Road
Box 302
Ringoes, NJ 08551
(201) 788-5852
Elsa and Michael Fisher

Antuzzi's Winery
1974/25,000 gallons
Bridgeboro-Moorestown Road
Delran, NJ 08075
(609) 764-1075
Matthew J. Antuzzi

DelVista Vineyards
1982/9,000 gallons
RD 1, Box 84
Frenchtown-Everittstown Road, Route 513
Frenchtown, NJ 08825
(201) 996-2849
James and Jonetta Williams

Four Sisters Winery
1984/9,000 gallons
RD 2, Box 258, Route 519
Belvidere, NJ 07823
(201) 475-3671
Robert J. Matarazzo

Gross' Highland Winery
1934/185,000 gallons
306 East Jim Leads Road
Absecon, NJ 08201
(609) 652-1187
Bernard F. D'Arcy

Renault Winery
1864/500,000 gallons
Bremen Avenue
Egg Harbor City, NJ 08215
(609) 965-2111
Joseph P. Milza

Tewksbury Wine Cellars
1979/15,000 gallons
Burrell Road, RD 2
Lebanon, NJ 08833
(201) 832-2400
Daniel Vernon, Jr.

Tomasello Winery
1933/70,000 gallons
225 White Horse Pike
Hammonton, NJ 08037
(609) 561-0567
Charles and Jane Tomasello

NEW YORK

Ambrosia Farms Corp.
1983/100,000 gallons
1183 E. Keuka Lake Road, Route 54
Dundee, NY 14837
(607) 292-3678
Nicholas Papadakos

Americana Vineyards
1981/2,500 gallons
4367 East Covert Road
RD 1, Box 58A
Interlaken, NY 14847
(607) 387-6801
James and Mary Anne Treble

Baldwin Vineyards
1982/8,000 gallons
Hardenburgh Road
Pine Bush, NY 12566
(914) 744-2226
Jack and Patricia Baldwin

Barry Wine Company/Eagle Crest Vineyards
1872/160,000 gallons
7107 Vineyard Road
Conesus-on-Hemlock Lake, NY 14435
(716) 346-2321
Michael Secretan and Austen Wood

Benmarl Wine Company
1971/50,000 gallons
Highland Avenue
Marlboro, NY 12542
(914) 236-7271
Mark and Dene Miller

The Bridgehampton Winery
1982/10,000 gallons
P.O. Box 979
Bridgehampton–Sag Harbor Turnpike
Bridgehampton, NY 11932
(516) 537-3155
Lyle Greenfield

Brimstone Hill Vineyard
1980/1,500 gallons
Box 142, RD 2, Brimstone Hill Road
Pine Bush, NY 12566
(914) 744-2231
Richard and Valerie Eldridge

Brotherhood Corporation
1839/500,000 gallons
35 North Street
Washingtonville, NY 10992
(914) 496-3661
E. D. Farrell

Bully Hill Vineyards
1970/209,000 gallons
Greyton H. Taylor Memorial Drive
Hammondsport, NY 14840
(607) 868-3610
Walter S. Taylor

Cagnasso Winery
1977/32,000 gallons
Route 9W
Marlboro, NY 12542
(914) 236-4630
Joseph Cagnasso

Canandaigua Wine Company
1945/12,000,000 gallons (some of
which is made with Eastern grapes)
116 Buffalo Street
Canandaigua, NY 14424
(716) 394-3630
Marvin Sands

Casa Larga Vineyards
1978/11,000 gallons

2287 Turk Hill Road
Fairport, NY 14450
(716) 223-4210
Ann and Andrew Colaruotolo and family

Cascade Mountain Vineyards
1973/15,000 gallons
Flint Hill Road
Amenia, NY 12501
(914) 373-9021
William and Margaret Wetmore

Chadwick Bay Wine Company
1980/32,000 gallons
10001 Route 60
Fredonia, NY 14063
(716) 672-5000
George Borzilleri, Jr.

Chateau Esperanza
1979/32,000 gallons
Route 54A, P.O. Box 76
Bluff Point, NY 14417
(315) 536-7481
Angela Lombardi

Clinton Vineyards
1977/10,000 gallons
Schultzville Road
Clinton Corners, NY 12514
(914) 266-5372, (212) 582-5816
Ben and Kathy Feder

Cottage Vineyards
1981/1,500 gallons
Box 608, Old Post Road
Marlboro-on-the-Hudson, NY 12542
(914) 236-4870
Allan MacKinnon

De May Wine Cellars
1977/15,000 gallons
Route 88
Hammondsport, NY 14840
(607) 569-2040
Serge and Catherine De May and family

Eaton Vineyards
1981/5,000 gallons
Rural Route 1, Box 370
Pine Plains, NY 12567
(518) 398-7791
Jerome and Shirley Eaton

Fair Haven Winery
1981/3,000 gallons
4001 Searsburg Road
Valois, NY 14888
(607) 546-9861
John Peter Marmora

Finger Lakes Wine Cellars
1981/12,000 gallons
4021 Italy Hill Road
Branchport, NY 14418
(315) 595-2812
Arthur C. and Joyce H. Hunt

Four Chimneys Farm Winery
1980/10,000 gallons
RD 1, Hall Road
Himrod, NY 14842
(607) 243-7502
Walter Pedersen and Scott Smith

Frontenac Point Vineyard
1982/3,500 gallons
Route 89
Trumansburg, NY 14886
(607) 387-9619
Jim and Carol Doolittle

Gardiner Vineyard & Farms
1976/15,000 gallons
714 Albany Post Road
Gardiner, NY 12525
(914) 255-0892
George Nutman and Family

Giasi Winery
1981/5,000 gallons
Box 87G, Route 14
Rock Streams, NY 14878
(607) 535-7785
Mike Giasi

Glenora Wine Cellars
1977/45,000 gallons
Route 14 Glenora-on-Seneca
Dundee, NY 14837
(607) 243-5511
E. Eastman Beers

Hazlitt's 1852 Vineyard
1984/? gallons
Box 53
Hector, NY 14841
(607) 546-5812
Jerome Hazlitt

Heron Hill Vineyards
1977/43,000 gallons
Middle Road
Hammondsport, NY 14840
(607) 868-4241
Peter Johnstone

High Tor Vineyards
1951/10,000 gallons
High Tor Road
New City, NY 10956
(914) 634-7960
Christopher Wells

Hudson Valley Wine Company
1907/100,000 gallons
Blue Point Road
Highland, NY 12528
(914) 691-7296
Herbert Feinberg

Island Vineyards
1984/? gallons
P. O. Box 552
Laurel, NY 11948
(516) 298-5335
Daniel Kleck

Frederick S. Johnson Vineyards
1961/75,000 gallons
West Main Road, Box 52
Westfield, NY 14787
(716) 326-2191
Frederick S. Johnson

Knapp Farms
1982/7,000 gallons
2770 County Road 128
Romulus, NY 14541
(315) 549-8865, (607) 869-9271
Doug Knapp

Lakeshore Winery
1983/3,000 gallons
5132 Route 89
Romulus, NY 14541
(315) 549-8461
Bill and Doris Brown

Lake View Vineyards
1984/1,200 gallons
R.D. 1, Box 199
Himrod, NY 14842
(607) 243-7568
Juergen and Christa Loenholdt

J. Le Beck Cellars
1983/3,000 gallons
RD 1, Goodwin Hill Road
Dundee, NY 14837
(607) 292-6471
John Le Beck

Lenz Vineyards
1983/18,000 gallons
Box 28, Main Road
Peconic, NY 11958
(516) 734-6010
Patricia and Peter Lenz

Long Island Vineyards
1973/33,000 gallons
Alvah's Lane, Box 927
Cutchogue, NY 11935
(516) 734-5158
Alec and Louisa Hargrave

Lucas Vineyards
1980/10,000 gallons
RD 2, County Road 150
Interlaken, NY 14847
(607) 532-4825
William and Ruth Lucas

McGregor Vineyard
1980/7,000 gallons
5503 Dutch Street, Box 213, RD 1
Dundee, NY 14837
(607) 292-3999, (716) 924-7397
Bob and Margie McGregor

Magnanini Farm Winery
1983/? gallons
Strawridge Road
Wallkill, NY 12589
(914) 895-2767

Merritt Estate Winery
1976/40,000 gallons
2264 King Road
Forestville, NY 14062
(716) 965-4800
Marguerite Sample
William and Christi Merritt

Northeast Vineyard
1975/750 gallons
Silver Mountain Road
Millerton, NY 12546
(518) 789-3645
George Green

North Fork Winery
1984/? gallons
Main Road, Box 213
Jamesport, NY 11947
(516) 722-3034
Bob Granger

North Salem Vineyard
1979/7,500 gallons
RR 2
North Salem, NY 10560
(914) 669-5518, (212) 534-7222
George and Michelle Naumberg

Pindar Vineyards
1983/12,000 gallons
Main Road
Peconic, NY 11958
(516) 734-6200
Herodotus Damianos

Planes' Cayuga Vineyard
1980/17,500 gallons
RD 2, Route 89
Ovid, NY 14521
(607) 869-5158
Mary and Bob Plane

Poplar Ridge Vineyards
1981/20,000 gallons
RD 1, Route 414
Valois, NY 14888
(607) 582-6421
Dave Bagley

Rolling Vineyards Farm Winery
1981/8,000 gallons
5055 Route 414, P.O. Box 37
Hector, NY 14841
(607) 546-9302
Ed and JoAnne Grow

Royal Wine Corporation
1949/2,000,000 gallons
Dock Road
Milton, NY 12547
(914) 795-2240
Ernest Herzog

Schloss Doepken Winery
1980/6,000 gallons
East Main Road, RD 2
Ripley, NY 14775
(716) 326-3636, 326-2552
John S. Watso

Serenity Vineyards
1983/? gallons
West Seneca, Route 14
Dresden, NY 14527
(315) 536-6813, 536-6701
Barbara P. and Jeffery A. Smith

Straubing Vineyard, Inc.
1984/500 gallons
8150 Chimney Heights Blvd.
Wolcott, NY 14590
(315) 331-3520
C. R. (Bob) Straubing

The Taylor Wine Company
owned by Seagrams Wine Company
Great Western = 1860/5,399,000 gallons
Taylor Wine Co. = 1880/23,862,000 gallons
Gold Seal Vineyards = 1865/3,000,000
gallons/closed 1984
Hammondsport, NY 14840
(607) 569-2111
Michael J. Doyle, pres.

Vinifera Wine Cellars
1962/100,000 gallons
RD 2
Hammondsport, NY 14840
(607) 868-4884
Konstantin Frank, Willy Frank and family

Wagner Vineyards
1978/130,000 gallons

Route 414
Lodi, NY 14860
(607) 582-6450
Stanley (Bill) Wagner

Walker Valley Vineyards
1978/6,000 gallons
Box 24, Oregon Trail Road
Walker Valley, NY 12588
(914) 744-3449
Gary Dross

West Park Vineyards
1983/5,000 gallons
Route 9W
West Park, NY 12493
(914) 384-6709
Louis Fiore and Kevin Zraly

Wickham Vineyards
1981/43,000 gallons
1 Wine Place, Box 62
Hector, NY 14841
(607) 546-8415
Wickham Family

Widmer's Wine Cellars
1888/3,000,000 gallons
West Avenue & Tobey Street
Naples, NY 14512
(716) 374-6311
Charles E. Hetterich

Hermann J. Wiemer Vineyard
1979/18,000 gallons
Route 14, Box 4
Dundee, NY 14837
(607) 243-7971
Hermann Wiemer

Woodbury Vineyards
1979/32,000 gallons
Route 1, South Roberts Road
Dunkirk, NY 14048
(716) 679-WINE
Gary and M. Page Woodbury

Woodstock Winery
1983/5,000 gallons
62-1 Brodhead Road
W. Shokan, NY 12494
(914) 657-2018
George and Judy Boston

NORTH CAROLINA

Biltmore Estate Wine Company
1977/80,000 gallons
P.O. Box 5375, Biltmore Estate
Asheville, NC 28803

(704) 274-1776
W.A.V. Cecil

Duplin Wine Cellars
1975/250,000 gallons
Box 756 Highway 117 North
Rose Hill, NC 28458
(919) 289-3888
David Fussell

Germanton Vineyard & Winery
1981/10,000 gallons
Route 1, Box 1-G
Germanton, NC 27019
(919) 969-5745
William H. McGee

OHIO

Breitenbach Wine Cellars
1980/10,000 gallons
RR 1
Dover, OH 44622
(216) 343-3603
Floyd Jones

Brushcreek Vineyards
1977/4,000 gallons
RR 4, 12351 Newkirk Lane
Peebles, OH 45660
(513) 588-2618
Ralph and Laura Wise

Buccia Vineyards
1978/3,000 gallons
518 Gore Road
Conneaut, OH 44030
Fred and Joanna Bucci

Cedar Hill Wine Company
1974/7,000 gallons
2195 Lee Road
Cleveland Heights, OH 44118
(216) 321-9511
Thomas Wykoff

Chalet Debonne Vineyards
1971/80,000 gallons
7743 Doty Road
Madison, OH 44057
(216) 466-3485
Anthony P. and Tony J. Debevc

John Christ Winery
1946/4,000 gallons
32421 Walker Road
Avon Lake, OH 44012
(216) 933-3046
Alex Christ

Colonial Vineyards
1978/8,000 gallons
6222 North State Route 48
Lebanon, OH 45036
(513) 932-3842
Norman and Marion Greene

Daughters Wine Cellars
1981/5,000 gallons
5585 North Ridge Road
Madison, OH 44057
(216) 428-7545
Charles Jr., Charles Sr.,
and Dana Daughters

Ferrante Wine Farm
1982/? gallons
5585 Route 307 West
Geneva, OH 44041
(216) 466-6046
Tony and Peter Ferrante

Grand River Wine Company
1971/25,000 gallons
5750 Madison Road
Madison, OH 44057
(216) 298-9838
Willett Worthy

Granville Vineyard
1981/3,000 gallons
P.O. Box 497, 1037 Newark Road
Granville, OH 43023
(614) 587-0312
Stanley J. Brockman

Anthony M. Greco
1983/5,000 gallons
6266 Hamilton Lebanon Road
Middletown, OH 45044
(513) 539-8768
Anthony M. Greco

Hafle Vineyards
1974/15,000 gallons
2369 Upper Valley Pike
Springfield, OH 45502
(513) 399-2334
Dan Hafle

Heineman Winery
1888/50,000 gallons
Put-in-Bay, OH 43456
(419) 285-2811
Louis Heineman

Heritage Vineyards
1978/30,000 gallons
6020 South Wheelock Road
West Milton, OH 45383

(513) 698-5369
Edward Stefanko and John Feltz

Louis Jindra Winery
1980/7,000 gallons
2701 Camba Road
Jackson, OH 45640
(614) 286-6578
Louis J. and Louis V. Jindra

Klingshirn Winery
1935/30,000 gallons
33050 Webber Road
Avon Lake, OH 44012
(216) 933-6666
Allan and Barbara Kingshirn

Lonz Winery
Part of *Meiers*
Middle Bass Island
Middle Bass, OH 43446
(419) 285-5411
Robert Gottesman

McIntosh's Ohio Valley Wines
1972/30,000 gallons
2033 Bethel New Hope Road
Bethel, OH 45106
(513) 379-1159
Charles McIntosh

Mantey Vineyards
1880/100,000 gallons
917 Bardshar Road
Sandusky, OH 44870
(419) 625-5474
Robert Gottesman

Markko Vineyard
1968/10,000 gallons
RD 2, South Ridge Road
Conneaut, OH 44030
(216) 593-3197
Arnulf Esterer and Thomas H. Hubbard

Marlo Winery
1978/3,000 gallons
3660 State Route 47
Fort Loramie, OH 45845
(513) 295-3232
Milo Strozensky

Meier's Wine Cellars
1895/2,850,000 gallons
6955 Plainfield Pike
Silverton, Cincinnati, OH 45236
(513) 891-2900
Robert Gottesman

Mon Ami Champagne Company
1934/100,000 gallons

3845 East Wine Cellars Road
Catawba Island, Port Clinton, OH 43452
(419) 797-4482
Robert Gottesman

Moyer Vineyards
1973/18,000 gallons
U.S. Highway 52
Manchester, OH 45144
(513) 549-2957
Kenneth L. Moyer

Shamrock Vineyard
1984/1,500 gallons
Box 111, C.H. 25
Waldo, OH 43356
(614) 726-2883
Tom and Mary Quilter

Steuk Wine Company
1855/10,000 gallons
1001 Fremont Avenue
Sandusky, OH 44870
(419) 625-0803
William Charles Steuk

Still Water Wineries
1981/70,000 gallons
2311 State Route 55 West
Troy, OH 45373
(513) 339-8346
H. A. Jones II and III, J. R. Pour

Stone Quarry Vineyards Winery
1979/850 gallons
Box 142
Waterford, OH 45786
(614) 984-4423
Thomas and Timothy Simpson

Tarula Farms
1965/5,000 gallons
1786 Creek Road
Clarksville, OH 45113
(513) 289-2181
Gregory Haywood

Valley Vineyards Farm
1969/50,000 gallons
2041 East U.S. 22-3
Morrow, OH 45152
(513) 899-2485
Ken and James Schuchter

Vinterra Farms
1976/8,000 gallons
6505 Stoker Road
Houston, OH 45333
(513) 492-2071
Phyllis and Homer K. Monroe

Wolf Creek Vineyards
1984/3,400 gallons
2637 South Cleveland-Massillon Road
Barberton, OH 44203
(216) 666-9285
Andrew M. Wineberg

OKLAHOMA

Cimmarron Cellars
1983/10,000 gallons
Route 1, Box 79
Caney, OK 74533
(405) 889-6312
Dwayne and Linda S. Pool

NOVA SCOTIA

Grand Pré Wines Company
1981/20,000 gallons
Box 18
Grand Pré, NS BOP 1MO
(902) 542-7511
Roger Dial

Jost Wines and Vineyards
1984/10,000 gallons
RR1
Malagash, NS BOK 1EO
(902) 257-2248
Hans W. Jost

ONTARIO

Andrés Wines
1961/3,100,000 gallons
P.O. Box 550
Winona, Ontario LOR 2LO
(416) 643-4131
Joseph Peller

Barnes Wines
1873/1,500,000 gallons
P.O. Box 248, Martindale Road
St. Catherines, Ontario L2R 6S4
(416) 682-6631
J. K. Ward, pres.

T. G. Bright & Company
1874/over 10,000,000 gallons
4887 Dorchester Road
Niagara Falls, Ontario L2E 6V4
(416) 358-7141
Edward Arnold

Charal Winery & Vineyards
1975/100,000 gallons
RR 1

Blenheim, Ontario NOP 1AO
(519) 676-8008
Allan and Charlotte Eastman

Chateau des Charmes Wines
1978/125,000 gallons
P.O. Box 280
St. Davids, Ontario LOS 1JO
(416) 262-5202
Paul Bosc

Chateau-Gai Wines
1890/4,500,000 gallons
2625 Stanley Avenue, P.O. Box 360
Niagara Falls, Ontario L2E 6T8
(416) 354-1631
Michael Conde

Hillebrand Estates Winery
1979/190,000 gallons
RR 2, Highway 55
Niagara-on-the-Lake, Ontario LOS 1JO
(416) 468-7123
Joseph and Betty Pohorly

Inniskillin Wines
1974/180,000 gallons
RR 1, Niagara Parkway
Niagara-on-the-Lake, Ontario LOS 1JO
(416) 468-2187
Don Ziraldo and Karl Kaiser

Jordan & St. Michelle Cellars
1921/10,000,000 gallons
120 Ridley Road
St. Catherines, Ontario L2R 7E3
(416) 688-2140
owned by Carling O'Keefe
Richard Mitchell

Pelee Island Vineyards
1982/25,000 gallons
455 Highway #18 East
Kingsville, Ontario N9Y 2K5
(519) 733-5334
Walter Strehn

Reif Winery
1982/35,000 gallons
RR 1, Niagara Parkway
Niagara-on-the-Lake, Ontario LOS 1JO
(416) 468-7738
Ewald Reif

Vineland Estates Wines
1983/? gallons
Moyer Road
Vineland, Ontario LOR 2CO
(416) 562-7088
Dieter Guttler

Adams County Winery
1975/10,000 gallons
Peach Tree Road, RD 1
Ortanna, PA 17353
(717) 334-4631
Ronald and Ruth Cooper

Allegro Vineyards
1980/5,000 gallons
RD 2, Box 64, Chanceford Turnpike
Brogue, PA 17039
(717) 927-9148
John and Timothy Crouch

Stephen Bahn Winery
1981/2,600 gallons
RD 1, Box 758, Goram Road
Brogue, PA 17309
(717) 927-9051
Stephen and Anne Bahn

Blue Ridge Winery
1982/5,000 gallons
1101 Pine Road
Carlisle, PA 17013
(717) 486-5030
Peter A. Capossi

Brandywine Vineyards
1982/15,000 gallons
P.O. Box A
Kemblesville, PA 19347
(215) 255-4171
Tom McKeon and family

Brookmere Vineyards
1984/11,000 gallons
RD 1, Box 53
Belleville, PA 17004
(717) 935-5380
Don and Susan Chapman

Buckingham Valley Vineyard
1966/35,000 gallons
Route 413, Box 371
Buckingham, PA 18912
(215) 794-7188
Gerald and Kathleen Forest

Bucks Country Vineyards
1973/75,000 gallons
Route 202
New Hope, PA 18938
(215) 794-7449
Arthur Gerold

Buffalo Valley Winery
1978/7,000 gallons
RD 2, Buffalo Road
Lewisburg, PA 17837
(717) 524-2143
Charles W. Pursel

Chaddsford Winery
1981/20,000 gallons
U.S. Route 1, P.O. Box 229
Chadds Ford, PA 19317
(215) 388-6221
Eric and Lee Miller

Clover Hill Vineyards & Winery
1984/8,000 gallons
RD 2, Old Route 222, Box 340
Breinigsville, PA 18031
(215) 398-2798
Pat and John Skrip, Jr.

Conestoga Vineyards
1963/29,000 gallons
415 South Queen Street
Lancaster, PA 17603
(717) 393-0141
R. Martin Keen and Arthur H. Keen

Conneaut Cellars
1982/12,000 gallons
Route 322, P.O. Box 5075
Conneaut Lake, PA 16316
(814) 382-3999
Alan and Phyllis Wolf

Country Creek Vineyard & Winery
1978/15,000 gallons
133 Cressman Road
Telford, PA 18969
(215) 723-6516
Bill Scheidell

Doerflinger Wine Cellars
1975/4,000 gallons
3248 Old Berwick Road
Bloomsburg, PA 17815
(717) 784-2112
Ludwig and Virginia Doerflinger

Dutch Country Wine Cellar
1976/5,000 gallons
RD 1, Route 143 North
Lenhartsville, PA 19534
(215) 756-6061
Helen and Gabriel Tenaglia

Fox Meadow Farm
1983/3,000 gallons
RD 2, Box 59
Chester Springs, PA 19425
(215) 827-9731
Alice H. and Harry C. Mandell, Jr.

Franklin Hill Vineyards
1982/10,000 gallons
RD 3, Franklin Hill Road
Bangor, PA 18013
(215) 588-8708
Charles and Elaine Flatt

Heritage Wine Cellars
1977/30,000 gallons
12162 East Main Street
North East, PA 16428
(814) 725-8015
Robert, Kenneth, and Beverly Bostwick

Hillcrest Winery
1982/? gallons
Humphrey Road, RD 5, Box 301
Greensburg, PA 15601
(412) 832-5720
Joseph and Pamela Policastro

Kolln Vineyards & Winery
1978/6,000 gallons
RD 1, Box 439
Bellefonte, PA 16823
(814) 355-4666
John and Martha Kolln

Lancaster County Winery
1979/50,000 gallons
RD 1, Box 329
Willow Street, PA 17584
(717) 464-3555
Todd and Suzanne Dickel

Lapic Winery
1977/10,000 gallons
682 Tulip Drive
New Brighton, PA 15066
(412) 846-2031
Paul and Josephine Lapic

Lembo's Vineyards
1977/14,000 gallons
34 Valley Street
Lewistown, PA 17044
(717) 248-4078
Joseph and Antoinette Lembo

The Little Vineyard
1982/5,000 gallons
951 East Cherry Road
Quakertown, PA 18951
(215) 536-8709
Charles and Barbara Stackhouse

Robert Mazza
1972/25,000 gallons
11815 East Lake Road
North East, PA 16428

(814) 725-8695
Robert Mazza

Mt. Hope Estate & Winery
1980/50,000 gallons
P. O. Box 685
Cornwall, PA 17016
(717) 665-7021
Charles Romito

Naylor Wine Cellars
1978/35,000 gallons
RD 3
Stewartstown, PA 17363
(717) 993-2431
Richard and Audrey Naylor

Neri Wine Cellar
1980/5,000 gallons
373 Bridgetown Pike
Langhorne, PA 19047
(215) 355-9567
Thomas Broccardi

Nissley Vineyards
1976/40,000 gallons
RD 1
Bainbridge, PA 17502
(717) 426-3514
Nissley Family

Nittany Valley Winery
1980/10,000 gallons
724 South Atherton Street
State College, PA 16801
(814) 238-7562
Tom and Marina Mebane

Peace Valley Winery
1984/? gallons
P. O. Box 94
Chalfont, PA 18914
(215) 249-9058
Susan Marlene Gross

Penn-Shore Vineyards
1969/175,000 gallons
10225 East Lake Road
North East, PA 16428
(814) 725-8688
Blair McCord

Presque Isle Wine Cellars
1964/10,000 gallons
9440 Buffalo Road
North East, PA 16428
(814) 725-1314
Douglas and Marlene Moorhead

Quarry Hill Winery
1982/3,500 gallons

RD 2, Box 168
Shippensburg, PA 17257
(717) 776-3411
Eugene and Nedra Cromer

Shuster Cellars, Inc.
1984/50,000 gallons
2900 Turkey Farm Road
Irwin (North Huntington), PA 15642
(412) 864-4691, 351-0979
Anthony (Tony) J. and Clara Shuster

Tucquan Vineyard & Winery
1978/5,000 gallons
RD 2, Box 1830
Holtwood, PA 17532
(717) 284-2221
Tom and Cindy Hampton

Victorian Wine Cellars
1982/2,000 gallons
2225 Marietta Avenue
Rohrerstown, PA 17603
(717) 295-WINE
Richard J. Tobias

Whispering Valley Wine Cellars
1983/2,000 gallons
1267 Old Pittsburgh Road, RD 1
Wampum, PA 16157
(412) 758-4206
Ford family

Wilmont Wines
1976/5,000 gallons
200 Mill Road
Schwenksville, PA 19473
(215) 287-6342
Frank Wilmer

York Springs Winery
1979/12,000 gallons
RD 1, Box 194
York Springs, PA 17372
(717) 528-8490
Andrew and Betty Campbell

RHODE ISLAND

Philip R. DeSano Vineyards
1980/1,000 gallons
Stony Lane
Exeter, RI 02822
(401) 272-2900
Philip R. DeSano

Diamond Hill Vineyard
1979/1,500 gallons
3145 Diamond Hill Road

Cumberland, RI 02864
(401) 333-2751
Peter, Clara, Andrew, and Jean Berntson

Prudence Island Vineyards
1973/4,500 gallons
Sunset Hill Farm
Prudence Island, RI 02872
(401) 683-2452
Bacon family

Sakonnet Vineyards
1975/40,000 gallons
West Main Road
Little Compton, RI 02837
(401) 635-4356
James A. and Lloyd A. Mitchell

SOUTH CAROLINA

Truluck Vineyards Winery
1976/29,000 gallons
Drawer 1265
Lake City, SC 29560
(803) 389-3400
Jim and Jay Truluck

TENNESSEE

Doc's Berry Farm
1982/1,800 gallons
Box 160
Loretto, TN 38469
Ray Methvin

Highland Manor Winery
1980/5,000 gallons
Box 203, Highway 127 South
Jamestown, TN 38556
(615) 879-9519
Fay Wheeler

Laurel Hill Vineyards
1984/5,000 gallons
1370 Madison Avenue
Memphis, TN 38104
(901) 725-9128
Ray Skinner and family

Smokey Mountain Winery
1981/15,000 gallons
Highway 73 East
Gatlinburg, TN 37738
(615) 436-7551
Everette and Miriam Brock

Tiegs Vineyards
1980/2,400 gallons

Route 3, Jackson Bend Road
Lenoir City, TN 37771
(615) 986-9949
Terry and Peter Tiegs

TEXAS

Chateau Montgolfier Vineyards
1982/10,000 gallons
Aledo, TX 76008
(817) 448-8479
Henry McDonald and family

Cypress Valley Winery
1982/12,000 gallons
Goeth Ranch
P. O. Box 128
Cypress Mill, TX 78654
(512) 825-3333
Dale and Penny Bettis

Fall Creek Vineyards
1979/33,000 gallons
Tow, TX 78672
(512) 476-3783
Ed Auler

La Buena Vida Vineyards
1978/40,000 gallons
Springtown, TX 76082
(817) 523-4366
Bobby G. Smith and family

Llano Estacado Winery
1976/88,000 gallons
P.O. Box 3487
3 mi. east of U.S. 87 on F.M. 1585
Lubbock, TX 79452
(806) 745-2258
Kim McPherson

Messina Hof Wine Cellars
1983/15,000 gallons
Route 7, Box 905
Bryan, TX 77802
(409) 779-2411
Paul and Merrill Bonarrigo

Oberhelman Vineyards
1981/35,000 gallons
Llano Route, Box 22
Fredericksburg, TX 78624
(512) 685-3297
Robert and Evelyn Oberhelman

Pheasant Ridge Winery
1982/7,000 gallons
Route 3, Box 191
Lubbock, TX 79401

(806) 746-6603
Robert Cox, Jr. and C. Robert Cox, III

Ste. Genevieve Vineyards
1984/150,000 gallons (rapidly expanding)
(1,000-acre vineyard at Ft. Stockton, TX
79735)
7312 South I-35
Austin, TX 78745
(512) 447-9555
Paul Merrigan

Sanchez Creek Vineyards
1980/6,000 gallons
DSR Box 30-4
Weatherford, TX 76086
(817) 594-6884
Ron Wetherington

Sanuvas Vineyards
1984/4,000 gallons
P. O. Box 599, Clint, TX 79836
(915) 851-3539
Jim and Cathy Conway

Texas Vineyards
1983/6,000 gallons
P. O. Box 33
Ivanhoe, TX 75447
(214) 583-4047
James Bledsoe

Val Verde Winery
1883/10,000 gallons
139 Hudson Drive
Del Rio, TX 78840
(512) 775-9714
Thomas M. Qualia

Wimberly Valley Winery
1983/30,000 gallons
Route 1, Box 65
Driftwood, TX 78619
(512) 847-2592
Lee Hereford and Dean Valentine

VIRGINIA

Bacchanal Vineyards
1982/10,000 gallons
Route 2, Box 860
Afton, VA 22920
(804) 272-6937
David and Betty Mefford

Barboursville Winery
1979/36,350 gallons
RD 1, P.O. Box F
Barboursville, VA 22923

(703) 832-3824
Gianni Zonin

Blenheim Vineyards
1982/1,000 gallons
Route 6, Box 75
Charlottesville, VA 22901
(804) 295-7666
John Marquis

Burnley Vineyards
1984/1,500 gallons
Route 1, Box 122
Barboursville, VA 22923
(703) 382-3874
Clare and Pat Reeder and family

Chateau Morrisette Winery
1980/9,000 gallons
Box 766
Meadows of Dan, VA 24120
(703) 593-2865
William and David Morrisette

Chateau Naturel Vineyard
1982/? gallons
RFD 4, Box 314
Rocky Mount, VA 24151
(703) 483-0758
Arthur and Ercelle Hodges

Chermont Winery
1981/6,000 gallons
Route 1, Box 59
Esmont, VA 22937
(804) 286-2639
Josh Sherman

Farfelu Vineyard
1974/4,000 gallons
Flint Hill, VA 22627
(703) 364-2930
Charles Raney

Guilford Ridge Vineyard
1983/? gallons
Route 2, Box 117
Luray, VA 22835
(703) 778-3853

Ingleside Plantation Winery
1980/30,000 gallons
P. O. Box 1038
Oak Grove, VA 22443
(804) 224-7111
Carl and Doug Flemer

La Abra Farm & Winery
1973/10,000 gallons
Route 1, Box 139

Lovingston, VA 22949
(804) 263-5392
A. C. Weed, II

Locust Hill Vineyard
1983/1,000 gallons
Route 624, Lost Corner Road
Rectortown, VA 22140
(703) 364-1138
John M. and Phyllis McCreary

Meredyth Vineyard
1975/30,000 gallons
Box 347
Middleburg, VA 22117
(703) 471-4399, 687-6277
Archie Smith, Jr. and family

Misty Mountain Vineyard
1984/? gallons
State Route 2, Box 458
Madison, VA 22727
(703) 923-4532
Dr. and Mrs. J. M. Cerceo

MJC Vineyard
1981/12,000 gallons
Route 1, Box 293
Blacksburg, VA 24060
(703) 552-9083
Karl and Myra Hereford

Montdomaine Cellars
1980/20,000 gallons
Route 6, Box 168A
Charlottesville, VA 22901
(804) 977-6120
Waldemar Dahl

Naked Mountain Vineyard
1981/5,100 gallons
off County Route 688
P.O. Box 131
Markham, VA 22643
(703) 364-1609
Robert and Phoebe Harper

Oakencroft Vineyard & Winery
1983/5,000 gallons
Route 5
Charlottesville, VA 22901
(804) 295-8175
Felicia Rogan

Oasis Vineyards
1980/100,000 gallons
Route 1
Hume, VA 22639
(703) 635-7627, 549-9181
Dirgham Salahi

Piedmont Vineyards & Winery
1973/12,000 gallons
Box 286
Middleburg, VA 22117
(703) 687-5134
Mrs. Thomas Furness
Mrs. William Worrall

Prince Michel Vineyards
1984/100,000 gallons
200 Lovers Lane
Culpeper, VA 22701
(703) 547-3707
Joachim Hollerith

Rapidan River Vineyards
1981/42,000 gallons
Route 4, Box 199
Culpeper, VA 22701
(703) 399-1855

Rose Bower Vineyard & Winery
1979/5,000 gallons
P.O. Box 126
Hampden Sydney, VA 23934
(804) 223-8209
Tom O'Grady

Shenandoah Vineyards
1977/35,000 gallons
Route 2, Box 323
Edinburg, VA 22824
(703) 984-8699
James, Jr., and Emma Randel

Stonewall Vineyards
1983/5,000 gallons
Route 2, Box 107A
Concord, VA 24538
(804) 993-2185
Howard and Betty Bryan

Tri-Mountain Winery
1981/15,000 gallons
Route 1, Box 1844
Middletown, VA 22645
(703) 869-3030
Joseph C. Geraci

Willowcroft Farm Vineyards
1984/2,000 gallons
Route 2, Box 174A
Leesburg, VA 22075
(703) 777-8161
Lewis Parker and family

Winchester Winery
1984/2,000 gallons
Box 188, Mt. Falls Route
Winchester, VA 22601

(703) 877-1275
Raymond F. Scott and Stephen R. Smith

West Virginia

Fisher Ridge Wine Company
1977/5,000 gallons
Fisher Ridge Road
Liberty, WV 25124
(304) 342-8701
Wilson E. Ward

Robert F. Pliska & Company Winery
1982/1,000 gallons
101 Piterra Place
Purgitsville, WV 26852
(304) 289-3493, 289-3900
Pliska family

Vandalia Wines & Tentchurch Vineyard
1983/? gallons
RD 1, Box 218
Colliers, WV 26035
(304) 527-3916
Robert and Rita Thomas

West-Whitehill Winery
1981/3,700 gallons
Route 1, Box 247A
Keyser, WV 26726
(304) 788-3066
Stephen and Lucy West,
Charles and Rebecca Whitehill

Wisconsin

Christina Wine Cellars
1979/22,000 gallons
109 Vine Street
Lacrosse, WI 54601
(608) 785-2210
Lawlor family

Spurgeon Vineyards & Winery
1981/9,000 gallons
RR 1, Box 201
Highland, WI 53543
(608) 929-7692
Glen and Mary Spurgeon

The Wollersheim Winery
1857/30,000 gallons
Highway 188
Prairie Du Sac, WI 53578
(608) 643-6515
Robert and JoAnn Wollersheim

SUGGESTED FURTHER READING

Note: The USDA National Agricultural Library in Beltsville, Maryland, has an excellent collection of both rare and current books, pamphlets, and magazines about grapes and wine from around the world.

Historic Books

Adlum, John. *A Memoir on the Cultivation of the Vine in America, and the Best Mode of Making Wine.* 1823. Second ed., 1828. Reprint. Hopewell, N.J.: Booknoll Reprints, 1971.

Buchanan, Robert. *The Culture of the Grape and Wine-Making.* Cincinnati: Moore, Wilstach, Keys, 1850.

Bush, Isidor, & Son, and Meissner. *Illustrated Descriptive Catalogue of American Grape Vines. A Grape Growers' Manual.* 4th ed. St. Louis: R. P. Studley, 1895.

Fuller, Andrew. *The Grape Culturist: A Treatise on the Cultivation of the Native Grape.* New York: Orange Judd, 1866.

Hedrick, U. P. *Manual of American Grape-Growing.* 2d ed., revised. New York: Macmillan, 1924.

———, ed. *The Grapes of New York.* State of New York Department of Agriculture Fifteenth Annual Report. Vol. 3, part 2. Albany: J. B. Lyon, 1908.

Husmann, George. *American Grape Growing and Wine Making.* New York: Orange Judd, 1885.

Muench, Frederick. *School for American Grape Culture.* Trans. Elizabeth H. Cutter. St. Louis: Conrad Witter, 1865. (Reprint available from Mount Pleasant Vineyards, 101 Webster Street, Augusta, MO 63332.)

Munson, T. V. *Foundations of American Grape Culture.* 1909. Reprint. Denison, Tex: Denison Public Library, 1975. (Available from the library, at 300 West Gandy Street, Denison, TX 75020.)

Ravaz, Louis. *Les Vignes américaines: Porte-greffe et producteurs-directs.* Montpellier: Coulet, 1902.

United States Department of Agriculture. *Report upon Statistics of Grape Culture and Wine Production in the United States for 1880.* Washington, D.C.: Government Printing Office, 1881.

Books

Adams, Leon D. *The Wines of America.* Boston: Houghton Mifflin, 1973.

———. *The Wines of America.* 2d ed., revised. New York: McGraw-Hill, 1978.

———. *The Wines of America.* 3d ed., revised. New York: McGraw-Hill, 1985.

Amerine, Maynard A., ed. *Wine Production Technology in the United States.* Washington, D.C.: American Chemical Society, 1981.

Cattell, H., and L. Miller. *Wine East of the Rockies*. Lancaster, Pa.: L & H Photojournalism, 1982.

Church, Ruth Ellen. *The Wines of the Midwest*. Athens, Ohio: Swallow Press, 1980.

Crosby, Everett. *The Vintage Years: The Story of High Tor Vineyards*. New York: Harper & Row, 1973.

De Blij, Harm Jan. *Wine: A Geographic Appreciation*. Totowa, N. J.: Rowman & Allanheld, 1983.

Galet, Pierre. *A Practical Ampelography*. Trans. Lucie T. Morton. Ithaca, N.Y.: Cornell University Press, 1979.

Gohdes, Clarence. *Scuppernong: North Carolina's Grape and Its Wines*. Durham, N.C.: Duke University Press, 1982.

Jackisch, Philip. *Modern Winemaking*. Ithaca, N.Y.: Cornell University Press, 1985.

Jackson, D., and D. Schuster. *Grape-Growing and Winemaking: A Handbook for Cool Climates*. Orinda, Calif.: Altarinda Books, 1981.

Johnson, Hugh. *The World Atlas of Wine*. New York, N.Y.: Simon and Schuster, 1978.

Kraus, George. *The Story of An Amana Winemaker*. Iowa City: Penfield Press, 1984.

Lichine, Alexis, et al. *New Encyclopedia of Wines and Spirits*. 3d ed., revised. New York: Knopf, 1984.

Miller, Mark. *Wine: A Gentleman's Game*. New York: Harper & Row, 1984.

Pongracz, D. P. *Practical Viticulture*. Cape Town, South Africa: David Phillip, 1978.

Schoonmaker, Frank. *Encyclopedia of Wine*. New York: Hastings, 1973.

Vine, Richard P. *Commercial Winemaking*. Westport, Conn.: AVI, 1981.

Wagner, Philip M. *Grapes into Wine: The Art of Winemaking in America*. New York: Knopf, 1976.

————. *A Wine-Grower's Guide*. 3d ed., revised. New York: Knopf, 1984.

Weaver, Robert J. *Grape Growing*. New York: John Wiley, 1976.

Webb, A. Dinsmoor, ed. *Chemistry of Winemaking*. Washington, D.C.: American Chemical Society, 1974.

Webb, Marilyn, ed. *Oregon Winegrape Grower's Guide*. 3d ed. revised, 1983. (Available from Viticulture Committee, North Willamette Chapter, Oregon Winegrowers Association, 4640 S.W. Macadam, Suite 150, Portland, OR 97201.)

Winkler, A. J. *General Viticulture*. 2d ed., revised. Berkeley: University of California Press, 1974.

Pamphlets

Ace, D. L., and J. H. Eakin, Jr. *Winemaking as a Hobby*. State College, Pa.: Pennsylvania State University, 1977.

Cattell, H., and H. L. Stauffer. *The Wines of the East: The Hybrids*. Lancaster, Pa.: L & H Photojournalism, 1978.

Cattell, H., and L. S. Miller. *The Wines of the East: Native American Grapes*. Lancaster, Pa.: L & H Photojournalism, 1980.

————. *The Wines of the East: The Vinifera*. Lancaster, Pa.: L & H Photojournalism, 1979.

Jordan, T. D., R. M. Pool, J. P. Tomkins, and T. J. Zabadal. *Cultural Practices for Commercial Vineyards*. New York State College of Agriculture and Life Sciences, Cornell University, Ithaca, N.Y., Miscellaneous Bulletin 111. 1981.

Scoville, G. P., *An Economic Study of Grape Farms in the Eastern United States, Part 1: Production*. Cornell University Agricultural Experiment Station, Ithaca, N.Y., Bulletin 605. May 1934.

Zabadal, Thomas. *Grape Pest Control Guide*. (Available annually from Finger Lakes Grape Coop, 110 Court Street, Penn Yan, NY 14527.)

Publications Available from the American Wine Society

The following publications may be ordered directly from the American Wine Society, 3006 Latta Road, Rochester, NY 14612 (Tel. 716/225-7613).

Applegate, H. E. *Wine Analysis*. ($1.25)

Grape disease slides (on loan). A five-page syllabus and thirty-four 35mm slides. ($20.00 deposit; $3.00 service charge plus postage deducted from deposit when refunded.)

Jackisch, P. F. *Wine Blending*. ($3.00)

Leonholdt, J. *Planting and Care of Grafted Vines*. ($1.50)

McGrew, J. R. *Basic Guide to Pruning*. ($4.50)

————. *Guide to Winegrape Growing*. ($3.00)

————. *A Review of the Origin of Interspecific Hybrid Grape Varieties*. ($1.50)

Mowbray, G. H. *Elements of Wine Tasting*. ($3.00)

Nardone, Angel. *Home Wine and Beer Makers' Information*. ($1.25)

Nelson, R. *PEQ Pleasure, Enjoyment, and Quality of Wine*. ($1.50)

Peynaud, Emile. *Use of Sulfur in the Preservation of Wines*. Trans. G. H. Mowbray. ($2.00)

Phillips, E. S. *Still Wines from Grapes.* ($4.00)

Plane, Robert, and Leonard Mattick. *Wine Acidity: Taste, Management, and Control.* ($2.00)

Scheer, R. *Vintage Chart Update.* ($2.00)

Schuster, C. *A New Method of Making Sparkling Wine at Home.* ($1.25)

Selected Periodicals

American Society of Enology & Viticulture Journal, P.O. Box 1855, Davis, CA 95617. Very technical scientific research results, reviews, and abstracts of international scope. Four issues per year.

American Wine Society Journal, 3006 Latta Road, Rochester, NY 14612. Entertaining and educational. Four issues plus additional special publications included with annual membership.

California and Western States Grape Grower, 4974 East Clinton Way, Suite 212, Fresno, CA 93727. Many articles of interest to eastern growers in this monthly magazine.

Eastern Grapegrower & Winery News, P.O. Box 329, Watkins Glen, NY 14891. The East's leading magazine, with indispensable annual directory. Bimonthly plus one extra issue.

Friends of WINE, P.O. Box 627, Holmes, PA 19043. A connoisseur's view of the world's wines, including those from the East. Bimonthly.

Practical Winery, 15 Grande Paseo, San Rafael, CA 94903. Must reading for those concerned with the fate of their grapes after harvest. Bimonthly.

Wine East, 620 North Pine Street, Lancaster, PA 17603. Up-to-date coverage of the eastern grape and wine scene. Bimonthly.

Wines & Vines, 1800 Lincoln Avenue, San Rafael, CA 94901. The leading monthly trade magazine in the United States, with important annual directory.

Wine Spectator, Opera Plaza, Suite 2040, 601 Van Ness Avenue, San Francisco, CA 94102. Twice-monthly newspaper for the wine world.

SOURCES

For complete bibliographical information, if not given here, see Suggested Further Reading.

Chapter 1. Colonial Times

Page 23. Washington's letter to de Malesherbes is from vol. 27 of *The Writings of George Washington from the Original Manuscript Sources, 1745–1799*, ed. John C. Fitzpatrick (Washington, D.C.: Government Printing Office, 1976), p. 55.

Pages 23–24. Jefferson's letter to Adlum is from John Adlum, *A Memoir on the Cultivation of the Vine in America*, p. 149.

Chapter 2. The Birth of American Viniculture

Pages 31, 33. The passage is from Leon Adams, *The Wines of America*, 2d ed., revised, p. 23.

Pages 28–29. The maps are from *Agriculture Yearbook: 1925* (Washington, D.C.: U.S. Department of Agriculture, 1926), pp. 277–281.

Chapter 3. Prohibition

Pages 39–40. The first quote is from Jefferson's letter of March 21, 1819, from Monticello, to Dr. Vine Utley; the second is from his letter of May 3, 1823, from Monticello, to Gen. Samuel Smith. Both appear in *The Life and Selected Writings of Thomas Jefferson*, Modern Library edition (New York: Random House, 1944), pp. 690–692, 707.

Chapter 4. Out of the Ashes

Page 43. Frank Schoonmaker's comments appear in his *Encyclopedia of Wine*, p. 91.

Pages 44–45. Philip Wagner is quoted from his article "The East's New Wine Industry," *Wines & Vines*, March 1979, p. 24.

Page 49. Leon Adams is quoted from *The Wines of America*, 3d ed., revised, p. 125.

Chapter 5. Climate Separates East from West

Pages 57–58. The guidelines appear in Jordan et al., *Cultural Practices for Commercial Vineyards*, pp. 3–4.

Pages 55, 59. Data for the charts was drawn from *Scientific American*, June 1974, p. 112.

Pages 56, 57. Charts from *Climatic Atlas of the United States* (Washington, D.C.: U.S. Department of Commerce, 1968), pp. 27, 25.

Chapter 6. Grape Families

Page 61. Terry Acree's remarks were made during a conversation with me in September 1984 at the Geneva station, New York.

Page 68. Genealogy from J. A. Mortenson, "Suwannee: An Early Bunch Grape," University of Florida Circular S-301, Gainesville, March 1983.

Chapter 8. Wine Regions and State Politics

Page 92. Chart from Chauncey D. Leake and Milton Silverman, *Alcoholic Beverages in Clinical Medicine* (Chicago: Year Book Medical Publ., 1966).

Chapter 9. North and Mid-Atlantic States and Provinces

Page 97. Shorn Mills, "The Wine Industry Potential in Northeastern Connecticut: A Feasibility Study," report to the Economic Development Administration (Washington, D.C.: U.S. Department of Commerce, 1979), p. 7.

Page 108. Chart from J. Wiebe and E. T. Andersen, "Site Selection for Grapes in the Niagara Peninsula," Horticultural Research Institute of Ontario circular (Vineland Station: Ontario Ministry of Agriculture and Food, 1976).

Chapter 11. Central States

Page 130. Justin Morris's comments were made in a letter to me of December 2, 1980.

Chapter 13. Inside the Winery

Page 160. Bruce Zoecklein, "White Wine Production Techniques," lecture delivered to the Missouri State Horticultural Society, January 26, 1981.

Pages 167, 168. Charts developed by the Rochester, N.Y., chapter of the American Wine Society.

Chapter 14. Vinicultural Economics Past and Present

Page 171. Charts from the Missouri Agricultural Experiment Station Bulletin 273, 1928.

Pages 170–171. The passage is taken from G. P. Scoville, *An Economic Study of Grape Farms in the Eastern United States, Part 1: Production*, Bulletin 605, Cornell University Agricultural Experiment Station, Ithaca, N.Y., May 1934, pp. 46–48.

Pages 174, 176. Bruce Zoecklein's list is from *Winery Cost and Planning Review*, 1982, for the Missouri Department of Agriculture, table 6.

 # PHOTO CREDITS

We gratefully acknowledge the contribution of photographs from the following individuals and wineries.

Amana Society/Joan Liffring-Zug: 132

Brotherhood Winery: 34, 164

Canandaigua Wine Company: 35

Kenneth Garrett: frontispiece, 38 (bottom left), 43, 44 (top right), 111, 128, 138 (top)

Philip Hiaring/*Wines & Vines:* 134

Philip Jackisch: 93 (bottom)

Henry C. McDonald: 126

Meier's Wine Cellars: 60

Dick Sherer: 34 (bottom), 40

Stone Hill Wine Company: 138 (bottom), 166

Taylor Wine Company: 33, 46

Texas A & M University: 115 (top)

Tim Thielke: 122 (label, top)

Paris Trail: 69, 70, 147

Philip Wagner: 45

Wiederkehr Wine Cellars: 129

Willard Volz/*Washington Star:* 159

INDEX

Page numbers in italics denote illustrations. For information about individual wineries, consult Appendix 3, listed by state.

Library of Congress Cataloging in Publication Data

Morton, Lucie T.
  Winegrowing in eastern America.

  Bibliography: p.
  Includes index.
      1. Viticulture—Northeastern States.   2. Viticulture—
Southern States.   3. Viticulture—Middle West.
  I. Title.
  SB387.76.N93M67   1985   634′.8′0974   85-47696
  ISBN 0-8014-1290-0   (alk. paper)